NEW SITES FOR SHAKESPEARE

New Sites for Shakespeare argues that our understanding and enjoyment of Shakespeare is limited by the kinds of theatre we have seen. On repeated visits to Asia, John Russell Brown sought out forms of performances which were new to him, and found that he had gained a fresh and exciting view of the theatre for which Shakespeare wrote. *New Sites for Shakespeare* shares these extraordinary journeys of discovery.

This fascinating study pays close attention to particular theatre productions and performances in Japan, Korea, China, Bali, and especially India. The book is divided into separate chapters which consider staging, acting, improvisation, ceremonies, and ritual. The reaction of audiences and their interaction with actors are shown to be crucial factors in these theatrical experiences.

Bringing to bear his background as theatre director, critic, and scholar, the author considers current productions in Europe and North America, in the light of his insights into Asian theatre. Ultimately this book calls for radical change in how we stage, study, and read Shakespeare's plays today.

Theatre writer and director, **John Russell Brown** was an Associate Director of the National Theatre, London for fifteen years and has taught at various universities in the UK and US. He is currently Consultant to the School of Drama at Middlesex University.

NEW SITES FOR SHAKESPEARE

Theatre, the audience and Asia

John Russell Brown

London and New York

First published 1999
by Routledge
11 New Fetter Lane, London EC4P 4EE

Simultaneously published in the USA and Canada
by Routledge
29 West 35th Street, New York, NY 10001

Typeset in Perpetua by Routledge
Printed and bound in Great Britain by Biddles Ltd, Guildford and King's Lynn

British Library Cataloguing in Publication Data
A catalogue record for this book is available from the British Library

Library of Congress Cataloging in Publication Data
A catalogue record for this book has been requested

ISBN 0–415–19450–4 (pbk)
ISBN 0–415–19449–0 (hbk)

CONTENTS

v

PLATES

ACKNOWLEGEMENTS

My debts to others while writing this book are huge and numerous; I could have done very little alone. At the University of Michigan, Ann Arbor, I enjoyed the help of students, friends, and colleagues, especially Erik Fredricksen, the Chairman of the Theatre Department, P.A. Skantze, who commented on a first version, and all those students who enabled me to put what I was learning into practice in a series of productions that included plays by Chekhov, Farquhar, Goldoni, Mamet, Racine, and Shakespeare, and the première of *Blue*, by Surrena Goldsmith. The University's various grant-giving committees in the Theatre Department, the School of Music, the School of Graduate Studies, and the Office of the Vice-Provost for Research contributed generously to my expenses. At Middlesex University, I am indebted to Leon Rubin who showed me how to use the opportunities of travel and with whom I could talk through my adventures.

Away from home, I owe a very special debt to Ram Gopal Bajaj who invited me to teach and direct at the National School of Drama, New Delhi. I am most grateful for his generous help, and that of his colleagues, students, and many friends, during those months. My thanks are also due to Vicki Ooi for inviting me to contribute to a Conference on Asian Performing Arts, to King-fai Chung and Fredric Mao for two invitations to work with actors at the Academy of Performing Arts in Hong Kong, and to the Japan Foundation in Tokyo and London for generous assistance at all times.

Several critics and friends have encouraged and helped me as the book was being written: Robert Weimann by his careful response to early versions of several key chapters; Dennis Kennedy by reading and commenting on an early draft and inviting me to Trinity College, Dublin; A.K. Thorlby by meticulously annotating the same draft and helping me to consider the wider implications of my theme; and Talia Rodgers whose work as editor at Routledge has not only guided and supported this publication but provided inspiration to many besides myself who try to write about theatre and performance. I am deeply grateful for all this help.

To numerous editors, I am indebted for publishing several articles which were, in effect, preparations for writing this book: 'Acting Shakespeare', *Shakespeare from Text to Stage* (Bologna: Cooperativa Libraria Universitaria Editrice Bologna, 1993), 'Jatra Theatre and Elizabethan Dramaturgy', 'Representing Sexuality in Shakespeare's Plays', and 'Theatrical Pillage in Asia', *New Theatre Quarterly* (1994, 1997, 1998), 'Shakespeare, Theatre Production, and Cultural Politics', *Shakespeare Survey* (Cambridge: Cambridge University Press, 1995) and 'Theatrical Tourism' in *Journal of Literature & Aesthetics* (Kollam, Kerala; 1997). I am grateful for permission to use later developments of material from these publications. I have also drawn upon passages in 'Back to Bali', originally published in *The Critical Gamut: Notes for a Post-Beckettian Stage*, ed. Enoch Brater (Ann Arbor, MI: University of Michigan Press, 1995).

On my travels I found help and friendship on all hands: more especially, in Japan, from Takahashi Yasunari, Suzuki Tadashi, Ninagawa Yukio, Wayne Silka, and Kondo Hiro, together with the helpful officers of the Japan Foundation; in Korea, from O Tae-suk and Kim Su-gi; in China, from Luo Jian Fan, Rong Guang Run, and Chang Shu; in Bali, from A. Badra and I.B. Alit. My indebtedness in India is particularly extensive: in Calcutta, to Pratibha Agrawal, Samik Bandyopadhyay, and Usha Ganguli; in Orissa, to Byomakesh, Biswakesh, and Byotakesh Tripathy; in Kerala, to K.N. Panikkar and K.A. Paniker; in Bangalore, to Arundhati Raja, Girish Karnad, B. Jayashree, B.V. Karanth, and Sunder Raj; in Bombay, to Feroz Khan, Rajeev Naik, and Shata Gokhle; and during an early visit to New Delhi, to Smita Nirula and Balwart Gargi.

In these many ways, my book has had many contributors and its merits will be in large part due to them; its faults and failures, likely to be numerous when working with such a wide perspective, are very much my own.

While preparing this book for the printer, I have been greatly helped by Tom Keever at Columbia University, New York, and by Jason Arthur and Ian Critchley at Routledge; I am most grateful.

Quotations from Shakespeare's plays are from Peter Alexander's edition of 1951, unless otherwise noted.

John Russell Brown,
Court Lodge, Hooe.

INTRODUCTION

Over the course of more than six years I have been able to visit theatres in Asia that were almost entirely new to me. Previously, I had seen productions which had toured Europe or North America, but I had seen none playing in their own theatres and to their own audiences. What had started almost by chance continued as a determined quest, for I not only enjoyed many of the plays I saw in Japan, Korea, China, and various states of India, but I found that my view of what theatre was capable of being in our present age was changing with each successive visit. In particular – and this is the main focus of this book – my understanding of Shakespeare's plays and how best they can be studied and staged was also changing. Some previous ideas were strengthened or modified, but I was seeing other elements in the texts as if for the first time and making better sense of what is generally known about the theatre of Shakespeare's day. I was also developing plans for productions I could never have imagined until I had visited Asia.

At the start of my explorations, I went to Japan more often than any other country. Traditional forms of theatre are honoured and protected there and many entirely new plays are written and produced for crowded young audiences. Besides, other critics and scholars had already made similar journeys and written about relationships between Shakespeare's theatre and the traditions of Nō, Kabuki, and Bunraku so that help was at hand wherever I travelled. Latterly, however, I have visited India more often than anywhere else. Its traditional theatres are not run in such authoritarian ways as the Japanese, and many of them play to much wider audiences than the retirees, schoolchildren, sponsored parties, and tourists I have sat amongst in Tokyo and Kyoto. Theatre in parts of India can still be genuinely popular, with audiences drawn from almost all sections of a community. Traditions are varied and contemporary plays, while lacking the evident success of the Japanese, show a determination to experiment and pursue forms suitable for the present time. To visit India in search of new theatre experiences is to enter a world with a great inheritance and where the future is being confronted with open minds as well as respect for the past.

I travelled elsewhere, too, throughout the 1990s, to China, Korea, Thailand, Indonesia, Bali, and numerous parts of Europe and North America. All these journeys have helped me to write this book but they have not turned me into an authority on any of the theatres I have visited away from home. I hope to raise interest in those I write about, but I have not attempted, after less than ten years of travel, to write a scholarly introduction to any one of them. Still less have I attempted to make a comparative study of various cultures: I do not possess the languages or life-experiences that would permit a first footing into that difficult and most interesting field of study. It will also be evident very quickly that I do not presume to be a theatre anthropologist and am not, in this book, concerned with systematic descriptions of performance. What is on offer is an attempt to share my own experiences in the theatres I visited for the first time using the terms I am accustomed to at home, and to show how this has influenced my thinking and practice with regard to theatre in general and to Shakespeare's plays in particular.

By centring this study on my own experiences I have forfeited a great deal of the support that most writers about theatre and Shakespeare derive from working within a reassuring network of other people's scholarship and theorising. I have, of course, read all that I could find in English about the theatres I have seen and wearied the experts I met with my questions, but comparatively little of this will be seen in this book. My subject leads me to deal with imprecise and personal impressions as much as facts, and the facts that I do relate are more important here for how they were perceived than for themselves as observed objectively and scientifically. I have willingly, and not ignorantly, worked in this way because theatre's essential life lies in the imaginations of audiences, not in playscripts or what happens on stage. If we are to rate its successes and try to understand its processes, we must deal in terms of an audience's experience and, in this case, my own response must stand in for those of many others.

This book will not, therefore, be rigorous and thorough in the customary ways of scholarship. It will convince only by its own story and the telling of it. Writing about theatre calls for such risks. As Marvin Carlson has warned: 'Performance by its nature…resists the sort of definitions, boundaries, and limits so useful to traditional academic writing and academic structures.'[1] I am here trying to bring to Shakespeare studies the same experiential understanding that others have begun to use when writing about theatre.

I have chosen to focus on Shakespeare because that is where my thoughts repeatedly led me. His plays are at the centre of most of the European and North American theatres that I know and in which I have worked. As they attract each new generation of actors, directors, writers, and audiences, they have remained a constant touchstone for innovation and have sometimes provided a model. I have found that they have the same value when trying to understand theatre history and observing how any theatre functions. Indeed, wherever I travelled, Shakespeare seemed to have been there before me. Much that was new to me I found out subsequently was already implicit in the ways he had written. Indeed, knowledge of his plays helped me to grasp the fleeting impressions that were exciting my imagination.

Today most theatres in Europe and North America occupy only a part of the spectrum of what theatre can be and we have become so used to accepting this that, without thinking about the process, we view Shakespeare's plays through this distorting filter. If we are to understand Shakespeare more fully and develop a theatre to meet the unfamiliar challenges of a very new age, we need to gain knowledge of those parts of the spectrum of theatre that have been forgotten or ignored in practice and in criticism.

Part I

VISITING

1

OPEN STAGES

Presence and occasion

Thinking of Shakespeare's plays in performance in his own times, we tend to visualise the Globe Theatre with its massy wooden and encircling walls, a storeyed background for a platform stage set against one side of its interior. All too often, for lack of the real thing, this theatre is, in our mind's eye, an empty model, a toy-like replica rather than the full-sized version with an actual audience. We have an even less distinct notion of the smaller Blackfriars Theatre which had come into use around 1610 when Shakespeare began to withdraw from London and the writing of plays. A visit to the full-sized Globe replica in London will not completely correct these mental images because Shakespeare's plays were not always performed in the London theatres. They were also to be seen at court, fitting as best they could into a banqueting hall, and were performed up and down the country in guildhalls, market-places, inns, and the comparatively small halls of colleges, schools, or country houses, almost anywhere that could hold an audience and provide an acting-space. The Chamberlain's Men and later the King's were often travelling, carrying along a few of their most popular plays and using the minimum number of larger stage properties.

London theatres were outstanding and upstanding buildings (to judge from perspective drawings made of London at that time) and were said to be 'of notable beauty': not seen as the hand-crafted, eloquently simple structure that has risen on the South Bank in London but, to Elizabethan eyes, magnificent, sumptuous, and gorgeous playhouses painted to catch the eye with simulated splendour. The plays were very much at home there, since the senior actor-sharers of the King's Men were part-owners of the theatre as well as the acting company, but in performance they often had to survive in very different circumstances, on makeshift stages and often at short notice, before crowds who were witnessing an exceptional occurrence, as part of a small repertoire of well-tested plays which could draw their properties and costumes out of the same portable kit. These were not cut-down versions of the plays, as used to be thought: a full company would travel and the playing-time seems to have been as lengthy as it was in London.[1]

Plate 1.1   Jatra actors prepare backstage; for a performance by Orissa Opera at Puri, Orissa
Photograph: Biswakesh Tripathy

Plate 1.2 Jatra actors ready for cross-gender roles; for a performance by Orissa Opera at Puri, Orissa
Photograph: Biswakesh Tripathy

With these thoughts in mind, I was quick to take the opportunity to see Orissa Opera, a Jatra (or 'touring') theatre, when it was performing at Puri, a place of pilgrimage near the coast, south-west of Calcutta and north of Madras.[2] The company was in town for a little over a week and its members had spent the first day setting up their gear on a raised stage under a great temporary awning supported on long bamboos lashed together. The site was just off the broad main street, at once an approach to the Juggernauts' temple and a busy concourse and market-place. That night I was amongst an audience of three or four thousand to watch a performance which started about 11.30 p.m. and finished around 6.30 in the morning, after the sun had risen. Spectators were mostly male and mostly under the age of thirty or so, although there were some groups of women and mixed company. Just in front of me sat a three-generation family, grandmother and mother taking turns to hold the youngest child and deal with a son of about seven who would fall asleep and then wake and struggle to follow the play. Tea, coffee, breads, nuts, and other refreshments were brought round for purchase from time to time. Here was a well-run and commercially successful theatre company with a 'popular' audience, as at the Globe, and an auditorium as temporary as those of an Elizabethan touring circuit. I had found a new setting in which to imagine Shakespeare's plays in performance and since that time it comes to my mind whenever I re-read the texts.

* * *

I had seen Jatra performances before on video,[3] but that was no preparation for the actual experience of sitting amongst the crowd surrounding this open stage. The entertainment started with songs and dances and a short play with a good deal of music, singing, and elaborate costumes. The long rows of chairs filled gradually, and yet still more people were moving around or standing in the aisles. After about an hour and a half, the main offering of the night began. It was a new play about contemporary life and was received warily at first, as if it were on trial, but by three o'clock in the morning the audience began to join in, not so much with applause as with encouragement: jeers and occasional laughter – never very prolonged – and sometimes intense silence. Individuals would shout out their advice or warnings about impending danger.

One feature of the play which was being performed was quickly apparent. Although I knew no word of the language, I could hear that its text was very repetitive. The same things were said again and again, three or even four times, until the audience would know what was coming. This knowledge encouraged some of the spectators to shout out to hurry on the characters in the play; others began to say key words, joining in with the actors. A more general response was a kind of indulgence: satisfied that it knew what was happening, the audience was

9

happy to watch and observe *how* everything happened, how each character in turn was affected, how some new incident modified what had already been said and done. Seldom was anything rushed and so the audience had time to exchange opinions without fearing that the play would leave them too far behind. The actors, having to hold or regain attention, were always finding new resources or new tricks whenever the text of the play was not doing this work for them: repetition both enlarged and clarified performance.

I do not mean that the four-hour play engrossed the audience all the time. Around four-thirty in the morning, the episodes of its story seemed to follow each other with determination rather than sprightly invention. Yet this phase passed and, towards the end with the coming of dawn, the audience was roused anew to greet large scenes of reconciliation and celebration with satisfied applause; the play was moving now at a slower pace as each resolution of the plot was clearly marked. The conclusion was received as if everyone had completed a physically taxing job together and in good form. By this time, the actors might be said to be sharing the play with the audience, and the other way about: both actors and audience had made it all happen. No great applause greeted the actual conclusion; it was taken as if for granted with a somewhat tired satisfaction. The crowd then relaxed, packed up their belongings, stretched their legs, and prepared unhurriedly to leave and rejoin their daily lives.

Handling the large audience was a crucial part of the whole enterprise. The dramatist had had to judge when it would be ready for a new initiative or for a resolution of conflict. The actors, surrounded on three sides of the stage, had to be constantly aware of their supporters and their critics, so that they responded to the crowd's silences as well as its impatience or its hectorings and encouragements. The audience's response is so important to this company that the next day's play is not chosen until the one being played has almost reached its end and the mood of the crowd has been judged; then an announcement is made saying what will be on offer if they come back tomorrow. A couple of songs from this new attraction are played on the sound system, as if trailers for a forthcoming film.

This performance in Puri both unsettled some of my assumptions about English theatre at the end of the sixteenth century and seemed to explain some anomalies. For example, the way in which the play was written to encourage this audience's active participation in the unfolding of events could explain why an Elizabethan theatre, in contrast to those of our own day, always took more money when it offered an entirely new and unknown play, whoever had written it. On those days, it now seems to me, the audience would have been happy to enjoy a more active role, the actors being more open to its encouragement or censure; there would have been more enjoyable risk on both sides. Another example of the rethinking which followed this performance at Puri concerns the Elizabethan practice of concluding performances in public theatres with a grotesque dance,

Plate 1.3 The stage crowded for a dance by Jatra actors at the beginning of an evening's entertainment; performed by the Orissa Opera at Puri, Orissa
Photograph: Biswakesh Tripathy

called a jig. The custom makes more sense having seen how long it took for this auditorium to empty, everyone filing out through the single narrow gateway which had controlled entry more than six hours earlier. As this was happening, some songs and dances were performed to amuse those who could not make a swift departure. However much the play had pleased, this audience still had to be watched and provided for.

Dramaturgically, the performance also made good Elizabethan sense. Repetition of certain phrases in Shakespeare's early history plays could work on an audience in the same way as the Jatra repetitions. In the first scene of *Henry the Sixth, Part Three*, 'resign', 'crown', 'throne', 'come,...away!' sound repeatedly, bell-strokes that the audience comes to expect. What I had not realised before was that this would alter the audience's relationship to the play's characters: no longer surprising spectators, or keeping them waiting, or intriguing them, but laying the characters wide open for the audience to urge them on. Repetition I now saw as a means of drawing the audience in so that it would participate in the play's action.

Richard the Third is particularly full of repetition, between the women, for example:

— ...Thou hadst an Edward, till a Richard kill'd him;
Thou hadst a Richard, till a Richard kill'd him.

> —— I had a Richard too, and thou didst kill him;
>   I had a Rutland too, thou holp'st to kill him.
> —— Thou hadst a Clarence too, and Richard killed him.
>
> (IV.iv.40ff.)

Later, the Ghosts who appear before the Battle of Bosworth conclude their curses on Richard with 'Despair and die!' and most of their blessings on Richmond with 'Live and flourish!' (V.iii.120–64). Often the audience will know what to expect and, at Puri, they would have joined in, as a free and willing chorus in support. The effect of all these repetitions on a Jatra audience might well include that impression of formal ordering which strikes a reader of the text today, but it would also alter the relationship between stage and auditorium. Free to share in the making of the performance, audience members might join together in competitive outcry, or register the absurdity, as well as the force, of the play's dynastic power struggles, or share with the persons in the play a sense of inevitability and so watch more helplessly.

Once I had seen that repetition gives scope for audiences to respond as they see fit and so their take part in the making of a play, I found that Shakespeare had used it in many different ways. In *Romeo and Juliet*, for example, Capulet, Paris, Lady Capulet, and the Nurse repeat their various cries several times: 'O woe…O day…O love…O child…' (IV.v.50–62) and Friar Laurence, in the last scene, tells his part the story which the theatre audience knows very well by this time. The repetitions in both these incidents are often reduced in number for modern productions and sometimes whole speeches are cut; the audience knows that the cries of grief are unnecessary and it hears nothing new from the Friar. But in Puri they would have served an essential purpose in helping the audience to stay ahead of the fateful story and, in these instances perhaps, encourage them to feel superior to the persons in the play, to stand back from the characters' responses and view them more adversely than they would otherwise. In this way, repetition can alter the effect of what the actors do by empowering the audience to believe it might have done better and allowing the expression of that judgement. In response, the actors would have to fight against this disapproval and possible rejection.

In *King John*, the Bastard's comic reiteration of Constance's mockery of Austria for wearing a lion's hide on his back, would have had the Puri audience joining in with the mockery, taunting him with each repetition: 'And hang a calf-skin on those recreant limbs' (III.i.129–34, 220, 298–9). But later in the same play, Shakespeare used a simpler, far less confident repetition to show a depth of feeling which the speaker cannot adequately express. The King repeats the Messenger's news in the fewest words sometime after he has heard it: 'What! mother dead!' (IV.ii.127) and then, fifty lines later, 'My mother dead!' (IV.ii.180).

These repetitions may well, like others, draw the audience into the character's thought and feelings but, because they are unexpected and seemingly unwilled, they will draw attention to what lies hidden, rather than making the audience feel superior to the character or confident in knowledge of what is happening. Here repetition at first sets a challenge for the audience's understanding and then offers opportunity to confirm what has been sensed.

Some scenes whose effectiveness has seldom been questioned may be revalued if repetition is considered in the light of Jatra techniques. Young Arthur's repetitive ingenuity when he pleads for Hubert's pity in *King John* (IV.i.9–121) or Bassanio's when he chooses the correct casket in *The Merchant of Venice* (III.ii.73–107 and 114–29) may be designed as much to encourage audience-participation as to reveal the speaker's state of mind and the dynamics of the dramatic situation. In *Hamlet* at the close of the Closet scene (III.iv), the five repetitions of 'Good night, mother', with only slight variations, are usually taken as indicating an intellectually or passionately tormented mind, as if a deeply insecure Hamlet were reaching for the security of an earlier relationship or stumbling in what most deeply concerns him, and perhaps recognising this progressively with each repetition. I now think these repetitions were Shakespeare's way of encouraging the audience to feel fully at one with the hero at this crucial moment by giving them opportunities to share in a certainty which is new to him and to realise, unmistakably, that he now feels free to leave his mother and devote himself to further action against the king. The same technique may be at work in the repeated 'To a nunnery' in the crucial scene with Ophelia (III.i). Wherever repetition is found in Shakespeare's plays, an experience of the Jatra audience has led me to look for the way in which the author wished to affect the audience–stage relationship, either to draw spectators in to take part in the speaker's thoughts and feelings or to encourage their critical judgement about them.

The slow ending of a Jatra play, in which each element of the story comes to its almost expected conclusion and the audience has ample time to take notice and respond, is very unlike the way we expect plays to conclude in our theatres and here, too, this Indian practice may be closer to Shakespeare's. The Friar's summary of past events in *Romeo and Juliet* has already been mentioned: Burgundy's account of the despoiled land of France in the last scene of *Henry the Fifth* (V.ii.23–67); the speeches and song at Hero's monument in *Much Ado About Nothing* (the whole of V.iii); Touchstone's disquisitions on lies and quarrels at the end of *As You Like It* (V.iv.62–101); the entry of the Ambassadors with Fortinbras at the end of *Hamlet* – and even the entry of Fortinbras himself – all these are parts of Shakespeare's conclusions which are not necessary to give plot-information or mark character-development and, not surprisingly, they have frequently been cut in the productions of post-Shakespearian theatres. In the original performances, however, they may all have helped to give the audience a sense that they had thoroughly

13

assimilated the stories' endings and that there was time to look around and stretch themselves, mentally and physically, free from a climactic excitement.

By slowing up the conclusions and so preventing the most intense reactions to it, Shakespeare was inviting the audience to enter into its multifaceted events. With repetition and the introduction of unnecessary business – the bringing on stage of the bodies of Goneril and Regan – the last scene of *King Lear* has been considered too slow-moving for twentieth-century audiences and it is always cut to some extent for performance, sometimes by more than a hundred lines.[4] The differences between the Quarto and Folio texts show that Shakespeare's handling of the conclusion was questionable from the very start of the play's history.

The end of *Othello* has many different devices to draw an audience into the action and encourage a quite unusual intimacy. The repetitions of Desdemona's reveries and singing in IV.iii give access, in the stillness, to the mood in which she prepares for bed at Othello's request. Repetitions occur several times in his opening soliloquy of the last scene: 'It is the cause....Put out the light....One more...' – each said three times. They hold him still, as it were, for the audience's comprehension and invite empathy or judgement. In the subsequent duologue, repetition occurs still more rapidly, as in Othello's 'take heed, take heed...' or Desdemona's 'I never did...never loved...never gave...never gave...'; and also in Desdemona's:

> And yet I fear you:...
> Why I should fear I know not,
> Since guiltiness I know not; but yet I feel I fear.
>   (II. 40–2)

If the play were performed on an open stage, the audience sharing much the same light as the actors, a bewildering, appalling, and yet delicate ending would have to take its own time, moving in accord with the audience's reactions on that particular occasion. The effect would be protected and shepherded by the actors by the simplest of means compatible with the highly charged situation.

In Puri, the forward pull of the performance was often allowed to go slack, so that the audience could take its own time and make its own decisions. Jatra's customary pace and style allow spectators that freedom and so, as Dhiren Hash says in *Jatra, The People's Theatre of Orissa* (Bhubaneswar, 1981), 'Spectator's participation is an every-day affair' (p. 8). The Jatra audience is encouraged by playtexts and performances to give themselves wholly to the experience and sometimes seem about to take possession of the occasion. Sitting in that audience, I came to feel that the audiences for Shakespeare in our theatres are kept too much in thrall to the excitement of moments and encouraged too consistently to wait for some conclusive revelation or stage effect. When reading Shakespeare's texts and recalling

14

Jatra performances, I wonder whether I allow sufficient scope to my own personal responses and reflections upon the action that is unfolding in my mind's eye. If the plays were written to make room for the entry and expression of our own convictions, then we should consider them as a site for collusion and remaking, rather than for meaningful shows, political statements, or the development and exposure of particular feelings. These playtexts do not exist entirely in their own right. We have more than a right to reinterpret: this is an invitation to take part in performance, with the possibility of taking it over and changing what is received. I take this to be a momentous distinction, that I may have sensed previously but without realising its far-reaching consequences.

Although used to performer–audience interplay in public political meetings, gospel services and sermons, stand-up comedy, communal music-making, and some party games, possessive intervention and mutual collusion during performance of a scripted play are not familiar in Europe and North America. Recognising the validity of this degree of interaction will entail a shift in our understanding of the ways in which Shakespeare's plays were expected to function.

* * *

Second to the audience, the actors were the most striking feature of the night's entertainment. The play was Ramesh Panigrahi's *Majhi Naire Ghorea*, or *The House in Mid-river*, a contemporary work about contemporary people and events. What happened on stage was immediately recognisable by the audience: what was spoken echoed their own talk and concerns; the clothes worn by the characters were the same as they wore. But the play was not altogether life-like: the people on stage were grander; not pompous or remote, but remarkable, resourceful, dynamic. The clothes they wore were new and bright; their actions and speech decisive. Whatever these characters did, they did fearlessly and completely. Not all the actors were equally skilled, but that was not hidden; it was all part of the variegated liveliness of performance. On the square platform set up in the middle of the audience, the actors were on display on all sides and, in order to present their characters, they had to exert and, even, flaunt themselves.

The long speeches and the occasionally protracted stage-business of the plays I have seen could only be played by actors able to hold attention and this, according to published accounts, is true of all good Jatra performers. According to Balwant Gargi's *Folk Theater of India* (second edition; Calcutta, 1991):

A Jatra actor can be recognized by the way he stands – a tilted tower. He does not hold himself back but throws his weight forward. Passionate, charged with energy, he explodes into fiery dialogue. He moves like a

tornado in the small arena. In spite of continuous action, he has a firm
grip on the ground.

(p. 11)

The Jatra actor has a sense of composition and speech delivery. He is
superbly aware of the four-sided audience and is sturdily graceful from
all angles. There is speed, action, flamboyance. Sharp turns in mood,
abrupt flares and sudden drops in pathos are underlined by orchestra.
Drums clatter and thump and rumble.

(p. 20)

Dhiren Hash is unequivocally partisan and takes the power of Jatra for granted.
He stresses simplicity and popular brashness in performance, while at the same
time claiming an educational importance:

The production style of the Jatra of Orissa is absolutely simple with the
acting area (stage) in the centre with spectators all around it....With
stylised gaits, ornate costumes, tuneful traditional music, plenty of
dances, songs, conflicts and humour, Jatra of Orissa has remained not
only a mere place of entertainment but also an essential institution for
learning for the people in general.

(Op. cit., pp. 8–9)

Jatra dramaturgy has been developed to draw upon and encourage this strong
style of performance. The play I saw at Puri presented a narrative with several
strands competing for attention, with each of the leading characters given a series
of scenes in which to shine and hold attention. In brief, the story told about a
family and, more especially, its younger generation. Ambition, greed, love, and
pleasure were the motives in incidents involving danger, deceit, drugs, drink,
sharp business practice, and gangster violence. Halfway through, when everyone
came on stage dressed for a grand wedding, it seemed that the play was about to
conclude, but the father, who had got into debt, was now in prison and another
two hours were used to bring him back to the family. Time was also needed for
another wedding to be prepared and for his daughter to become a police officer.
The story was handled so that it provided a series of conflicts which pitted the
characters against one another in vigorous argument or in more physical combat
using a wide variety of weapons, from fists to revolvers and whips. The scenes
seldom presented large-scale engagements, but usually set one character against
another, or one against two or three. While the lengthy narrative had similarities
with soap-opera television, the stand-offs, the constant testing of strength, and
the exposure of everyone on stage to unrestricted scrutiny, gave rise to a very

different experience for the audience. The stage looked like a boxing-ring and very often it was used like one to present a series of bouts which tested the mettle of all the characters in turn and the skill of all the actors.

Soliloquies are common in Jatra. They bring no lessening of dramatic interest but, rather, a heightening as if the audience knew that a secret was about to be shared. The active attention of three or four thousand people would be concentrated on the single actor, seen without visual distraction: in rare silence, he will hold attention by what his character says and, through the eye of that needle, draw the thread of the dramatic action carefully and cleanly. Everything in these moments is dependent on dramatist, actor, and audience working together. By their means, each character at Puri had the chance to establish an independent point of view as every member of the cast had a solo-spot. On video, I have seen how a Jatra drunkard, after being reviled by everyone he had encountered, was given a soliloquy in which he has the pleasure of explaining why he drinks and will not stop doing so. I was reminded of Falstaff holding forth about Honour.

In comparison with its frequency in Jatra, soliloquy is a rare feature in the texts of Shakespeare's plays, but not the concentrated focus on single characters on which the device depends. Their common reliance on strong and assertive acting can be seen in the treatment of entries and exits. No matter what is going forward on the Jatra stage, attention is drawn to whichever character is arriving or departing. Access to a Jatra stage is by means of two long gangways leading at either side from the actors' dressing-room. In between these, a large area is occupied by a band of some fifteen players and a smaller one, closer to the stage, by the stage manager and technicians. On the way to the stage and dividing these two lower positions, the gangways are joined to form a small secondary stage on which short scenes can be acted by characters in the process of making their entries or exits (see p. 18). For smaller Jatra companies, a single Puspa Patha, or entrance passage, runs at ground level until it approaches the stage by a number of steps. Whichever configuration is used, these pathways ensure that each character has to make a lengthy entry or departure and so can hold focus for a considerable time on his or her own terms and can be appreciated independently of whoever occupies the main stage.

On video I have seen a Jatra actor playing a queen and mother take about five minutes to make her way to the dressing-room while her children remain on the main stage. About to move down the Puspa Patha, she stood still and alone, weeping with heaving breast, her gestures alternately expressing encouragement for her children and grief for herself. She stopped again a little further down the pathway, out of communication with the main stage, to soliloquise with tears flowing in unreal quantities. I had thought this must be part of some ceremonial of departure appropriate for the ancient setting of this drama or that the actor was milking the moment or teasing the audience, but exits and entries were just

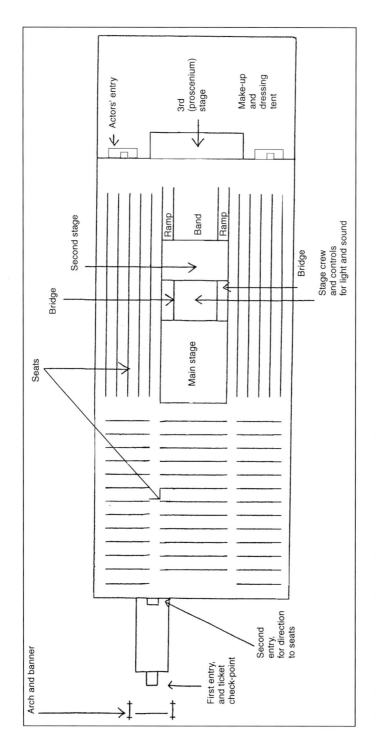

Plan of a Jatra stage, as used at Puri by Orissa Opera, November 1992

as prolonged in the contemporary play at Puri and were supported by music and special lighting effects. Here I was also aware of the active attention of the audience which explained for me how pausing while making an entry had the effect of a camera close-up and was an opportunity especially created for a display of feelings or an explanation of an individual point of view before the character joined those already in the action on the main stage. On leaving the stage, the actor had a similar opportunity to assert disapproval, indifference, reluctance, or terror, as appropriate to the character and story.

The dramatic effect of these prolonged entries and exits can be complicated, creating a double focus or double time-scheme. The audience pays attention to a new initiative without losing sight of the ongoing situation. The after-effects of a conflict are seen from both the victor's and victim's point of view, as first one and then the other takes time to make an exit. Individual and personal issues are given prominence because each character is assured of independent stage-life.

This close-focus device is heightened by the use of many costumes. On entry, a new costume is able to register a turn of the story instantaneously, even if the character appearing in the new guise does not acknowledge this or is unable to speak of it. Many entries are devised to take advantage of this and Jatra companies

Plate 1.4 A Jatra actor makes an exit; from *Khona*, performed by Satyamber Opera at
       Perulia, West Bengal
Photograph: Sangeet Natak Akademi, New Delhi, India

will go to great expense to build and maintain a large wardrobe of well-made and well-laundered costumes, which is what their Elizabethan counterparts also did. Out of the Vesha Ghara – a tent with uneven earth floor, crowded with clothes-racks, make-up tables, and very busy people – the play's characters appear in a succession of new clothes, whether it is a contemporary or historical drama. Careful choice was evident in each garment at Puri and every opportunity was taken to make a change. Reappearance in a new outfit was sometimes greeted with loud approval by the audience because it said so much and spoke so clearly of the latest change in the character's fortunes.

While the cost of staging an Elizabethan play today has led our theatre companies to use the smallest practicable number of costumes, it would better suit Shakespeare's plays to imitate Jatra practice and use them in the greatest possible number and variety; the texts were written for entries to be exploited in this way. On the open stages of Elizabethan theatres, the distance to centre stage was not so long as in the Jatra but was quite enough for each new entrant to make a distinct impression, clothes as well as deportment signalling a development in story and character. Shakespeare sometimes underlined this effect by insisting on sufficient time for entries with comments such as: 'Look where he, or she, comes.' Some entries in *Hamlet* are accompanied with descriptions of a new appearance or stage-properties:

> QUEEN: But look where sadly the poor wretch comes reading.
> POLONIUS: Away, I do beseech you, both away:
> I'll board him presently. O, give me leave.
>
> (II.ii.167–9)

Or, more elaborately:

> HAMLET: But soft! but soft! awhile. Here comes the King,
> The Queen, the courtiers. Who is this they follow?
> And with such maimed rites? This doth betoken
> The corse they follow did with desperate hand
> Fordo its own life. 'Twas of some estate.
> Couch we awhile and mark.
>
> (V.i.211–6)

Occasionally Shakespeare's dialogue registers the effect of a new costume after the audience has seen and enjoyed the transformation, so that the manner in which the clothes are worn can become the cause of renewed laughter. Such are the comments on the love-struck Benedick in *Much Ado About Nothing* (III.ii) or the fortunate shepherds in their new finery at the end of *The Winter's Tale* (V.ii).

20

Jatra practices suggest that many entrances and costume changes in Elizabethan plays should be given greater prominence than the words of their texts explicitly suggest. For example, in the Council-chamber scene of Act I of *Othello*, after the cry '*within*' of 'What, ho! what, ho! what, ho!' and with the Officer's brief identification of 'A messenger from the galleys', the Sailor's entry would have had prolonged impact so that the audience could take note of his haste, his work-clothes, and the urgency of all his actions. The second Messenger, whose entry is marked some twenty lines later, may well have started to come on stage some time before this to establish his presence and urgent business; this man is ready to give his news before being asked a question. Alternatively, the half-line of the Officer's 'Here is more news' might indicate a pause while the entire company as well as the audience has to wait for this anonymous character to reach centre stage and then speak. The combined effect of these urgent and anonymous messengers, spot-lit by the use of prolonged entries, contrasts with the Venetian splendour of the council meeting and suggests the danger underlying all its wealth and superiority, as well as the need for Othello's military acumen and authority.

If Elizabethan performances used something like the Jatra method with entries and exits, Shakespeare exploited this in many different ways. In the same scene of *Othello*, the next entry of Othello, Brabantio, Iago, Roderigo, and various Officers, has six lines (47–52) to accompany it and these imply complicated movements on stage. A nameless Senator reacts first, speaking as if he sees Brabantio and Othello together. However, the Duke's words then imply that he sees only Othello; then, having talked with him, he adds to Brabantio, 'I did not see you; welcome, gentle signior,….' Rehearsal could find many different ways of accounting for this discrepancy, but what seems certain is that Brabantio and Othello are intended to be two independent and mutually exclusive centres of attention on the stage and that the audience would be encouraged to see both. Desdemona's entry at line 170 is identified as a particularly long entry by Othello's 'Here comes the lady: let her witness it.' It could be staged, however, in several different ways. She might begin to come into view with Othello's earlier line, 'This only is the witchcraft I have us'd', so that she enters on this mysterious cue either in conscious response or by some fateful instinct. Alternatively, Othello could see her at the first possible moment and speak of her at once; she then would continue to make her entry and hold the audience's attention during the next ten lines, establishing a silent but sensational visual counterpoint to the words of her father and the Duke. How Othello responds to her presence in continued silence still further complicates this entry, the first appearance on stage of the play's heroine of whom the audience has already heard a great deal from conflicting viewpoints.

Shakespeare used similar devices even in his earliest plays. In III.i of *Titus Andronicus*, at the very moment when Aaron cuts off Titus' hand, Lucius and Marcus re-enter still at 'strife' as to which of them shall offer his hand, so that the audience is made acutely aware of how far the story has already leapt ahead. Exactly when they enter is left, however, for the actors to decide: they may be too late to stop what is happening or they may enter earlier but be so involved with each other that they cannot see anything until too late; or they may see all that is happening on stage but become so moved that they cannot speak or do anything. Either way the entry will mark the horror and cunning of what Aaron has done and also carry the story forward. On his subsequent exit, Aaron must pause to speak an aside (ll. 203–6) and so will draw attention to the contrasting pleasure that he takes in his villainy. At the end of the scene, a slow and painful movement off stage draws all the Andronici together, except Lucius who is about to go into exile: some of his words accompany the silent procession and express for the audience its speechless horror. Lucius then draws attention to his own purposeful exit in a soliloquy which defines his own purposes.

A strong and prolonged shift of focus on entry and exit is a Jatra device that on many occasions would strengthen a performance of Shakespeare's text. This is not simply a 'montage' effect, marking contrasts and the progression of narrative, although that is part of what is achieved. Irony, subversion, heightened expectation, tension, laughter can also be introduced as the new entrants establish their different sense of the dramatic moment. But the main effect is to enhance the presence and power of individual characters; it is a primary resource for plays which are grounded in narrative and personal conflict. When we read the plays, we are apt to sense only the sequence of speeches and their combined effect; seeing a play in Jatra-like performance, we would repeatedly be impressed by the separate point of view and the power of each character, the irreconcilable aspects of his or her involvement in the action that tend to pull the play apart rather than maintain progress in a story or establish a single argument.

Many of the dramatic devices of the Jatra stage – strong entries and exits, frequent costume changes, soliloquies, plot development through a series of conflicts or bouts, repetitions which serve to put the audience ahead of the characters in understanding of the drama – all serve to focus attention on individual characters. Scenically, too, everything works in much the same way. The main stage, some fourteen or sixteen feet square, is bare except for a small rostrum with three steps which is set to one side between the two entrances. On this characters sit to rest or reconsider, or to make love or share confidences; or they stand on it to dominate proceedings. In some companies, the rostrum is replaced by a single chair which, as Mr Hash remarks, can be used as: 'a king's throne, a poor man's hut, a bed cot, a lover's bench, a tree, a hiding place, even a weapon to fight with, as the story demands in different scenes' (pp. 8–9). The stage does have ornate decorations hanging around and above it but these do not change during the play and therefore do not compete with the dynamic of figures moving within its small compass.

Plate 1.5   The stage-manager's and control position behind a Jatra stage; for a
            performance by Orissa Opera at Puri, Orissa
Photograph: Biswakesh Tripathy

The play's characters in action and interaction on the open stage were the source
of dramatic energy and the means for arousing expectation and defining the
progress of its story. Even those with minor parts to play are written so that they
are able, at certain moments, to attract the same uninterrupted attention. Here was
the heart of the performance throughout the night at Puri and here, too, may be the
heart of Shakespeare's plays as he imagined them in performance – not only what
their characters say, but what happens to them as complete, independent, and
active beings, alive in physical actions and reactions, as well as in thoughts, feelings,
and imaginations. When we read the texts and try to understand them, we need
special prompting to reach a similarly multi-focused, physical, interactive, space-
enclosed, time-locked realisation of what is afoot, moment by moment, in the play's
action. When staging the plays, all the characters should be given opportunities to
shine individually, as they are in Jatra performances.

* * *

When a Jatra company comes to town for a week or more bringing a dozen or so
plays in its repertoire, three or four being new that season,[5] an audience member
can see a different play every night, some of them set in the present, some in the
past. Attention is bound to be gained, under these conditions, not only by the
characters but also by members of the company, the actors who are the constant

elements from night to night. Behind a succession of varied characters the audience will get to know the actor who plays them and becomes increasingly more recognisable no matter what disguise is being worn.

Before long I could see that the Puri audience knew individual actors very well and even intimately, as football supporters know the players of their own team. But here the game was being played much closer to the spectators, in an arena so small that all of it could be seen at any one time; and it was played nightly in varying forms for a short season, always on the same ground and with the same players. The game was usually played between no more than two, three, or four individuals; at times a single player would hold attention with no one in opposition. The audience assumed a role in the game by vocal appreciation of the finest moments of play and by encouragement and admonishment of the players. Sometimes an actor would respond to this audience or might egg it on by seeming to pay no attention. When an especially acute comment came from one of the spectators, an actor would find some way of acknowledging it. Towards the end, a few in the audience moved up to the stage to offer flowers and other tributes to the player they particularly admired as he made an exit; some would tuck rupee banknotes into his clothing. Occasionally an actor would drop out of character to receive a gift and then resume the exit in character. I could not distinguish, during the closing hour or so, whether this audience was responding to the characters of the play or to its players.

From this distance in time, we cannot tell how similar the Elizabethan audiences were in this respect, but we do know that actors were recognised off stage. In *Hamlet* (II.ii), the prince makes the players welcome as people known to him personally, calling them 'Masters…good friends…my old friend…my good friends…'. In an Induction for a revival of Marston's *Malcontent* at the Globe Theatre in 1604, John Webster brought two audience members to life on the stage, one of them boasting; 'I am one that hath seen this play often, and can give them intelligence for their action: I have most of the jests here in my table-book' (ll.14–16). He has personal acquaintance with three actors, Henry Condell, Richard Burbage, and William Sly – Sly was, in fact, the actor who was playing this playgoer. In *The Duchess of Malfi* (1614), Webster implied that actor and role were often confused:

> we observe in tragedies
> That a good actor many times is curs'd
> For playing a villain's part.
> (IV.ii.288–90)

Thomas Nashe had asserted, more than twenty years earlier, that the 'very name…of Ned Alleyn on the common stage was able to make an ill matter good'.[6] As an actor was sometimes seen beneath the role, so, when the performer was good enough, the role was said to find its life in the living person of the actor. An elegy for Richard Burbage, chief actor of the Chamberlain's and King's Men, claimed that he had acted Shakespeare's Hamlet, Lear, and Othello so well that these fictional characters 'lived in him'.[7]

Modern critics often note the frequent references to the actor's art in Shakespeare's plays and those of his contemporaries, and have deduced that their audiences must have maintained a double and critical view of the stage, so that what was enacted was seen for what it was, simultaneously real and unreal, substantial and fictive. But in the Jatra performance I witnessed, a recognition of the actors in their roles seemed rather to make the fictive character more real, or at least more accessible, than they would be otherwise. As Hamlet was said to have 'lived *in*' Burbage, so the characters of this play *lived in* each actor's familiar features and, seemingly, in his real being and mentality. The actors were hailed as familiar and very special individuals who were going to entertain them. In consequence, all that happened on stage tended to be received as topical and of local importance: here were well-known people who were appearing as various other people for the pleasure of a conniving audience. Actors were not segregated from their public, but amongst them on an open stage, their favourite representatives: adventurers who vicariously acted for them; the play's characters lived in and through them. It was a theatre of engagement and trust, as well as of make-believe and entertainment; for the audience, an experience about lives like their own and, in that sense, it was political because, imaginatively, they were all in it together.

Even plays set in historical or mythological times could catch the conscience of this audience. Sometimes, I have been told, politically topical lines are added to an old playscript. So long as the story is strong enough, the actors will make it live in the present for the audience. Balwant Gargi tells of *Neel Kothi*, a popular Bengali play of the 1930s about a workers' revolt in the nineteenth century; the British banned it and confined its author to his own town because its performance spoke too clearly and directly of a contemporary and explosive political situation.[8] *Rhaumukta*, a tale of a peasants' revolt in ancient times, was first produced in 1954 and was given such topical meaning that it continued to be performed for many years, attracting huge crowds wherever it travelled; and it is still being staged today.[9]

The House in Mid-river was only one of the plays in Orissa Opera's repertoire dealing with contemporary life. Byomakesh Tripathy's *Baaje Nataka Banda Kara*, or *Stop This Vulgar Opera*, is also about corruption and social ills. The plot has many strands and involves two generations so that it repeatedly challenges established authority:

Subir, a high-caste boy, woos Bharati, a low-caste girl, gets her pregnant, and then deserts her: their child, Bijay, is adopted and at seven years old is orphaned.

Meanwhile, Guru, a journalist, is threatened for exposing political corruption and, when he does not listen, his wife and one of their two sons are killed; he turns terrorist in revenge, disguising himself as a beggar; he finds and adopts Bijay, the son of the other couple.

Time passes and Bharati becomes a politician and Chief Minister of Orissa; Subir becomes a multimillionaire industrialist: they are pitted against each other. Guru trains Bijay to be a terrorist like himself, while his son who had escaped the killings becomes a police officer and is given the task of arresting the beggar-terrorist who is his own father. Bijay, too, meets his parents. Ultimately the policeman gives up his job to join his father in fighting injustice.[10]

In such a play, the contemporary issues are self-evident, no matter what the characters say, because the action itself has political implications without recourse to political slogans or verbal allusions to real persons. Politically committed speeches would have obvious advantages, but a dramatist will often prefer to let the story speak for itself because words can easily be censored or cause the whole play to be banned. A strong story is able to speak for itself and when members of a Jatra audience become imaginatively engaged in it they can relied upon to shout out and say what must be done to remedy injustice and stop violence. The leisurely pace of performance, the open stage, and the audience's familiarity with the actors will together ensure that all is accessible and well understood. The size of the audience – for Jatra is hugely successful – encourages bold responses and invites a competition in making the most telling comment. The cries of the audience become more urgent when repetitions ensure that it understands what is happening better than the characters in the play.

Thinking of Elizabethan theatres, I began to wonder whether dialogue alone was a sufficient indication of the political power of their plays. Performed on open stages before popular and vocal audiences, the very story of Hamlet when he finds himself alone in a corrupt world would speak inescapably to those spectators without the help of words addressed specifically to them. So, too, would the stories of Macbeth, ambitious in violent and treacherously deceitful times, of Lear, unpredictable and old-fashioned in a divided and distrusting nation, and of Coriolanus, trusting his own courage and pride alone amongst a nation of cowards and then, at the cost of his own life, acting upon instinct for compassion and loyalty. These stories speak for themselves, arousing strong reactions because of what can be seen to be happening on the stage.

Shakespeare's history plays would have awoken political consciousness more strongly when the kings and politicians of former times were impersonated by

26

actors the audience knew very well as people from their own world. I have previously wondered why his *Richard the Second* was performed in 1601 in support of the Earl of Essex's rebellion which was due to start the following day when what is *said* in the play so often emphasises a monarch's sacred prerogative and the dangers of insurrection. But the Jatra performance at Puri suggested that words that brand Bolingbroke as a dangerous, self-serving adventurer may have mattered less than the action of a successful deposition staged in full view of a large and actively responding crowd: to this spectacle, the audience could have brought their own thoughts and used their own words. Their vocal reaction would displace the historical world of the play and substitute other players for its characters. In the ears of a popular audience, authority will always sound suspect and encourage some of its members to think and speak for themselves. Shakespeare, I suspect, must have known this and expected such a response.

Perhaps twentieth-century readers of Elizabethan plays should not only look for words to nail down the topical political references in the text, but also consider what enactment of a play's story might suggest to the minds of an Elizabethan popular audience. A dramatist of Shakespeare's generation could be imprisoned for what was said on the stage; he was more free to choose what was *done* because he could not be held responsible for what the audience said.

A critic trained in a textual tradition will not easily believe that story – action, bodily presence, interaction, change, and completion – is more powerful than speech. Shakespeare's dazzling and inexhaustible verbal invention makes this adjustment especially difficult but, for holding attention in Elizabethan public theatres, a dramatist's most important asset may well have been his ability to create strong stories that place characters in situations that arouse the audience's own thoughts and its verbal participation. To thrive in this theatre, Shakespeare would have needed a strong non-verbal or pre-verbal imagination. This would explain why John Manningham, having seen *Twelfth Night* in the winter of 1602–03, noted the 'good practice' of the counterfeit letter against Malvolio but recorded nothing in his diary about all that was said and done by Viola, Feste, Sir Toby, or Sir Andrew – their roles do not have such strong story-lines when judged by their implications for a lawyer. Dr Forman, seeing *Macbeth*, *Cymbeline*, and *The Winter's Tale*, in 1610–11, showed the same preference for story and action. While quoting some actual words from Macbeth's encounter with the witches which are crucial for understanding the plot, he was mainly concerned with what actually happened whether on stage or off; for example:

And Macbeth contrived to kill Duncan, and thoro' the persuasion of his wife did that night murder the king in his own castle, being his guest. And there were many prodigies seen that night and the day before. And when Macbeth had murdered the king, the blood on his hands could not

27

be washed off by any means, nor from his wife's hands, which handled the bloody daggers in hiding them, by which means they became both much amazed and affronted.[11]

At some plays a few audience members would have had their 'table-books' to note down verbal jokes and wise sayings, but the 'action' of a play was what lodged in their memories effortlessly. As we read Shakespeare's texts we should try to stage them in our minds as if in performance before such an audience.

* * *

In several ways a Jatra audience is unlike that for which Shakespeare's plays were written. Almost all the members of the one I had joined were seated throughout the evening. Only those near the stage were in approximately the same light as the actors. Their ears were sometimes filled with amplified popular music. They watched throughout the night and not in the middle of a working day. Before the performance began, some of them might have noticed an actor breaking a coconut, lighting incense, and saying prayers on the stage. The play they watched would not be published as some of the most popular of Shakespeare's were in his own day. But despite all this, similarities were plentiful, far more numerous than when we compare the Elizabethan audience with those of European and North American theatres today.

Seeing a Jatra performance was for me the start of a determined search for the most suitable context in which to imagine Shakespeare's plays. I had been given a whole night's entertainment and was left with vivid impressions as clues to be followed. Of these, the most hopeful seemed to be that the nature of an audience is one of the most necessary parts of the puzzle to try to get right.

2

AUDIENCES

On stage and off stage

I travelled to Bali in the hope of seeing one of the dance dramas for which the island is famous. Years after witnessing a staged version at a Colonial Exhibition in 1931, Antonin Artaud remembered them as 'the most beautiful manifestation of pure theater it has been our privilege to see',[1] and as more people followed him to Bali to see the plays in their proper form and setting, their reputation grew. I had hoped to see an Odalan, or temple feast, where the ancient dramas still fulfil their original purposes for people who gather on special days, but my timing was wrong or my information misleading. I could see only the demonstrations which are staged routinely and almost nightly for tourists. Crudely lit so that cameras and video recorders can capture evidence to be carried back home as trophies and subjects for study, these performances showed little competence, except in the leading drummers and two or three of the dancers. But Bali did provide one extraordinary experience when I attended a cremation ceremony in a small village deep in the jungle. Reacting to this pre-arranged and public event, I found that my views of what an audience might contribute to a theatrical performance had to change yet again.

* * *

The cremation was on a working day, a Friday, but five or six hundred people had taken time off from ordinary business to attend. I arrived a good hour before it was due to start and already the lane outside the house of the deceased was crowded, and also the courtyard and the home itself. Further down a forest track, its earth levelled and tidied for the occasion, two gaudily decorated structures of bamboo, cloth, and tinsel stood waiting. One was the bier surmounted by a structure of many small storeys, the other a large black animal, with a parasol poised above it. Both towered above their attendants. The ritual started when the body was brought out of the house and placed on the bier. Various offerings and gifts were brought with it, tokens of the deceased's life to accompany his soul as it

29

passed out of the body: a small, framed photograph, a coconut filled with rice, a small eggshell lamp to represent the soul itself. Then the bier and effigy were lifted onto many shoulders and a procession gathered to make its way for some half-mile through the jungle to an open space near the largest of the village temples. Here the beast was placed under an awning that had been prepared to receive it. Then its stomach was cut open and the corpse moved from the bier and placed inside. More offerings, including food and coins, were brought and prayers were said. The deceased had been a policeman and so ten of his colleagues in uniform formed themselves into a squad and made their own presentation. Everything was unhurried so that those who did not know what to do could be given instructions or led through the appropriate part of the ritual. At length all was ready for fire to be applied to the beast-effigy with the corpse inside and to the offerings piled-up around it. Flames rose into the sky and the last stages of the spirit's journey were completed.

The crowd, as much as the rituals, held my attention. I could see none of the lonely grieving figures to be found at English-speaking funerals, standing apart and inconsolable. Nor was any one group of persons actively participating throughout, but individuals would fulfil some particular duty and then, with that completed, would be lost in the crowd again and, as it seemed, forgotten. The spectators were in small groups, which shifted in membership from time to time.

Plate 2.1 Preparations for a cremation on Bali
Photograph: John Russell Brown

Women and small children stood together, sometimes holding hands or with an arm around another's shoulders. Some young men walked or stood in couples, linked together by two little fingers. Others, in a tight knot and wearing Harley Davidson T-shirts, were more restless, engaging in sharp bouts of talk and laughter. Older people tended to keep somewhat apart. Everyone seemed to have their own thoughts and their own concerns, as important to them as the ritual or the deceased's life and death. On this Friday morning, however, they had all forgotten about earning their livings so that they could be present with the body and spirit of a deceased friend, family member, fellow villager, or fellow police officer. This also meant that they were present with each other and involved with each other in whatever groupings they chose or happened to join, according to the ongoing affairs of their daily lives.

Plate 2.2 A cremation procession on Bali
Photograph: John Russell Brown

31

Plate 2.3 The crowd around a pyre on Bali
Photograph: John Russell Brown

Everyone had made an effort to be there and everything took place in some previously determined way and sequence, but that is about all the organisation that could be observed. No one moment appeared to be more important than another, no place of vantage privileged, no one way everyone had to face; I could see no prescribed attitude or posture for prayer. No singing or chanting drew everyone into a single reaction and the music had ceased long before the flame was applied to the corpse. Various tourists, like myself, were also present, intermingling anywhere with no attention being paid to them. Whatever we saw and whatever we did was part of one essential action; whatever we thought was our own business.

Attendance at this cremation has proved a more lasting memory than being present at almost any other funeral. It is also clearer in my mind than visits to native North American rituals, where I have always been aware of my strangeness, or encounters with English Mummers' plays, where performers have seemed locked into a world of their own. From Bali I can still recall the non-exclusive, unprogrammed attentiveness which was both singular to each watcher and shared between us all. Many had travelled considerable distances to this remote village and everyone had broken ordinary routines to participate in the artificial, garish, lengthy, and significant happening as if it were a matter of course and an unquestioned part of their lives. The event was favoured by having a special day allotted to it, as decreed by the local temple's priest, but not so that other concerns and relationships had to be put aside. I did not see any one component of the ritual which transfixed or transformed the entire crowd of spectators, making them all react as one, as would happen at a public event in Europe or North America, such as a President's swearing-in, a state funeral, or a football game. Music never held everyone rapt; it kept the procession moving and filled in any gaps in the ritual, and that's about all. Individuals seemed to pay attention as they wished, from wherever they happened to be and at whatever time suited themselves. The mood was unforced and unprogrammed: alert and contagious at times, but often no more than watchful or, even, passive.

As a visitor with no understanding of the language and only book-knowledge about what I was watching, I cannot claim any authority for my description of this event beyond how it seemed to me and the effect it had on myself. Curiously, I had felt very much at home here and at first this struck me as absurdly presumptuous. Only afterwards did I begin to think that this was a consequence of the way the event had been managed. I also began to wonder whether I might have been one in a crowd of spectators that was more like an audience in an Elizabethan public theatre than any I had known before. For this reason, an event which was not theatrical finds its place in a book about Shakespeare and theatre.

Obviously it was not the same: no professional actors were involved and we did not applaud; we knew ahead of time exactly what was meant to be happening – a spirit travelling out of the body in which it had lived. The similarities were, however, self-evident and significant. We had all decided to give four or five hours of a working day to be in this company and watch a representation of a life and death. Most of us stood and could move around as and when we wished. We were in the same light as the spectacle we watched. That spectacle had many and varying parts as a whole lifetime was brought before us. What surprised me most and, on reflection, seems as though it also might have belonged to early audiences for Shakespeare, was the freedom we all enjoyed to interrupt any part of the show by paying attention to our own concerns and, consequently, to invest the occasion with whatever interests we happened to bring with us. Very obviously, these people continued to live their own lives and think their own thoughts, even as they also shared in the ritual.

* * *

Surviving evidence about audiences at Elizabethan theatres can be interpreted in many different ways, the more so in that scholars are writing about circumstances that have long since disappeared so that none of their conclusions can be brought to the test of experience. When they try to imagine what play-going was like, they tend to rely on the very different circumstances of European or North American theatres at the present time to guide their thoughts and lend them some substance. Stephen Greenblatt, for example, envisages a submissive audience for Shakespeare's plays:

> The triumphant cunning of the theater is to make its spectators forget that they are participating in a practical activity, to invent a sphere that seems far removed from the manipulations of the everyday. Shakespeare's theater is powerful and effective precisely to the extent that the audience believes it to be nonuseful and hence nonpractical.[2]

Although it held attention without fuss or strict control over the course of many hours, the event I witnessed in Bali provoked a very different reaction. The occasion was not 'triumphant' by means of some 'cunning' or because the audience had forgotten their daily concerns and private relationships. Its meaningful content seemed to have been taken for granted, without any recognition that it was 'far removed from the manipulations of the everyday'. Moreover the whole colourful and artificial ritual *was* 'practical', and in several different ways: we could see how everything was contrived and it was assumed that all this had to be enacted; besides, everyone wanted to take some kind of part in it.

If Shakespeare wrote for such a practical and independent audience, we would be wrong to look for any single 'meaning' in one of his plays or the resolution of any problematic issue. Rather we should expect conditions that encouraged a performance to be accessible to an audience and consider how its members might make the play their own according to individual and pre-existing interests.

The earliest plays, with the exception of *The Comedy of Errors* which is indebted to the tighter forms of Roman comedy, have an ample and unhurried variety of incident which would allow an audience to pick and choose, to give most attention to whatever caught its fancies, not bothering with episodes which did not. *The Two Gentlemen of Verona* is so written that its performance will give a great deal of pleasure with a number of its scenes missing: Speed can be treated as redundant; Julia talking with Lucetta in Act I, scene ii can make her mind clear enough in any twenty of the scene's hundred and forty lines; Panthio talking with Antonio (I.iii.1–87) is expendable; and so on. Launce with his dog in Act II, scene iii is an enlightening comic turn no one would want to miss but, should that happen, the play would be understood well enough without it; on the other hand, if this was where someone first gave attention to the play, the following scenes would be clear enough without any of those that came earlier.

The play's action proceeds with great variety of incident, but all its scenes, many of them very short, start by clearly defining what is afoot and much of the story so far:

SPEED: Launce! by mine honesty, welcome to [Milan]...
(II.v.1)

PROTEUS: To leave my Julia, shall I be forsworn;
To love fair Silvia, shall I be forsworn.
(II.vi.1–2)

JULIA: Counsel, Lucetta; gentle girl, assist me;...
How with my honour, I may undertake
A journey to my loving Proteus.
(II.vii.1–7)

DUKE: Sir Thurio, give us leave, I pray, awhile;
We have some secrets to confer about. (*Exit* Thurio.)
Now tell me, Proteus, what's your will with me?
(III.i.1–3)

DUKE: Sir Thurio, fear not but that she will love you
Now Valentine is banish'd from her sight.
(III.ii.1–2)

Critics have often remarked on the variety of incident in Shakespeare's earlier plays, but the instant credibility of each scene and the disposability of many of them are equally remarkable. The episode of Thurio's song, 'Who is Silvia?' (III.ii.16–80), exemplifies all three characteristics.

A member of the audience could take his or her own way through *The Two Gentlemen* and still have an enjoyable entertainment to go along with any more ordinary and personal thoughts as might continue at the same time: fantasy and reality could mingle to mutual benefit, even if they clashed or sometimes displaced each other. Perhaps this is why the most critical moment in the entire story is treated with utmost economy or, to put a different face on it, with a completely inadequate explanation of what is going on in the minds of its principals. Perhaps the author and actors were well aware that, by this last scene, the audience would still be sufficiently in charge of their own minds to put their own valuations on the shocking abruptness with which many things happen almost at once: Proteus asks for pardon; Valentine gives him 'All that was mine in Silvia' (V.iv.83); Silvia continues to say nothing; Julia swoons; the ring is recognised and all is revealed; and everyone accepts the outcome or, at least, no one protests. Independently minded members of an audience are likely to have many different opinions about what has happened and are liable to start arguing amongst themselves before the entry of the Outlaws together with the Duke and Thurio. Now moral judgements do start to be made on stage, as the hapless Thurio is condemned as 'degenerate and base' (l. 136) – words, it may be, that have been in some minds amongst the audience a few moments earlier, but with reference to one or both of the so-called gentlemen of Verona. In sharp contrast, a free pardon is pronounced for the Outlaws although they have been responsible for murder, theft, and other crimes committed in the 'fury of ungovern'd youth' (IV.i.44–52). Then, at this very latest possible moment, the audience's thoughts are sent back in an earlier direction as Valentine introduces Julia to the Duke, drawing attention to her blushes as she stands speechless in boy's clothing (V.iv.165). The conclusion of this comedy needs robust playing while the audience is repeatedly given opportunity to exercise its own sense of right and wrong, and of what is laughable.

In Shakespeare's early history plays, the march of events and consequences of actions are given much more weight, but here also the audience is encouraged to follow as it wishes and make its own judgements. The sheer accumulation of scenes in the three Parts of *Henry the Sixth* or in the long text of *Richard the Third* would make for bewilderment if all were given equal and adequate attention. In modern productions, these plays are cut, shaped, and interpreted, and then some precise issues are emphasised by means of careful rehearsals, strong lighting-changes, scenic and sound devices, and fine tuning of many kinds, all resources which were not available in Shakespeare's day. In the nineteenth and early twentieth centuries, the Henry the Sixth plays were not played at all and *Richard the Third* was very heavily cut both within scenes and by the excision of whole episodes. These texts came back into favour only when they had been doctored and rearranged to give a concerted, powerful, and meaningful experience to their audiences. However, between late twentieth-century control and nineteenth-century neglect another course may be possible.

If these plays were put back into something like the context of their original staging by performing them before audiences who were in the same light as the stage and free to follow their own individual thoughts and varying interests, then the curse of complexity and burden of length might both be lifted. Some scenes would hold attention while others would not, or only partly so, and the audience would find its own way through the play. Actors could shine in a variety of incidents and the audience might sense a lively competition between them. All of which could add to the efficacy of whatever parts proved able to draw the whole crowd together in its response. The audience would have the impression that *they* were the persons who had made sense or, possibly, nonsense of history; and that would give a pleasurable sensation of involvement and achievement.

All this supposes a very different audience from that which Stephen Greenblatt imagined to be wholly caught up in a 'nonuseful' and 'nonpractical' world of the play, as if living, for a time, in a 'sphere' far removed from ordinary life. These individuals would have to be held with a looser rein, as the Prologue to *Henry the Eighth* mockingly explains:

> Those that can pity here
> May, if they think it well, let fall a tear:
> The subject will deserve it. Such as give
> Their money out of hope they may believe
> May here find truth too. Those that come to see
> Only a show or two, and so agree
> The play may pass, if they be still and willing,
> I'll undertake may see away their shilling
> Richly in two short hours...
>
> (ll. 5–13)

The cunning of this kind of theatre lies in giving the audience its own head, and so allowing its own thoughts about everyday matters and longer-lasting social or personal problems to interact with the fantastic or 'truthful' happenings of the play, each with its own distinct demands for attention.

In *Richard the Second*, for instance, the pace of narrative is sometimes hurried, so that Bolingbroke seems to return to England before there has been time for his banishment to start, and yet the dialogue is often very slow, especially when ceremonies or arguments are elaborated. In telling this tale, Shakespeare has created a number of stopping-places where the situation is exposed and explored in varying ways and which, in consequence, can almost stand on their own. Some scenes could be dropped without confusing the narrative or main characterisations but with gain in forward energy. In modern productions, Act I, scene ii is sometimes cut so that the Duchess of Gloucester does not appear in the play. The Earl of Salisbury and Welsh Captain in II.iv are similarly removable. The Queen need not meet the Gardners (III.iv), Aumerle, Percy, and Fitzwater need not throw down their gages (IV.i) – this is a favourite cut because it can raise unwanted laughter – and the Duke of York need not call repeatedly for his boots and horse, his Duchess need not kneel before the new king (V.ii and iii). The entire abdication of King Richard was omitted in the first three printings of the text, almost certainly in accord with stage practice at the time. The end of this history is spread over two separate scenes – one of Richard's death and the other of Bolingbroke's reception of the news – so that the audience is left to relate one to the other, to think well or ill of the murdered king as he lies in his coffin, and also of the new king who is the cause of his death. Bolingbroke prompts such questions, without admitting guilt directly:

> ...my soul is full of woe
> That blood should sprinkle me to make me grow.
> (V.vi.45–6)

As Shakespeare developed ways to draw attention more intimately into the minds of his characters, from *Romeo and Juliet* onwards, the structure of the plays became less amenable to excision; dramatic focus was brought to bear upon a few principal characters with more sustained insistence. A comparison of, say, *Love's Labours Lost* and *Twelfth Night* illustrates these changes, although the plays follow-ed each other within only a few years. The same is true of *Richard the Third* in comparison with *Henry the Fifth*, and both of them compared with *Macbeth*. The dramatist was taking stronger charge, as if he wanted, now, to draw his audience closer into the heart of some mystery. But the development of Shakespeare's stagecraft was not all one way, which suggests that he knew his audience remained very ready to take matters into their own heads and would do so when that was what he wanted. For example, the scene in England in the fourth Act of *Macbeth* is often staged today in a shortened version, despite the overall shortness and concision of the playtext. Shakespeare relaxed tension here and took time for an account of the English king curing the sick and for Malcolm's detailed pretence that he is a more evil man than Macbeth as a way of testing Macduff's loyalty – a virtue which the audience could scarcely doubt without one word of interroga-tion to help.

Whatever control Shakespeare began to exercise over his audience, several of his old plays continued to be performed and they would keep alive its earlier freedom. Besides, he encouraged its independence in some of his latest works, especially in *Pericles* and parts of *The Winter's Tale*, and in a final history, *Henry the Eighth*. Even when most wishing to take charge, he may still have calculated on a spirited counter-pull from his audience, its members bringing a sturdy sense of common reality to engagement in his fictions and drawing independent strength from each other's responses. Such an audience is hard to visualise today when in our theatres only the stage is lit and members sit comfortably in their seats, seldom stirring or talking, or calling out in approval or disapproval. They expect rather to leave their own, more practical, everyday thoughts behind them.

Where a play has survived in more than one version we may deduce that atten-tion was paid to how the text was received. If Shakespeare expected his audience to exercise the freedom of response that the structure of many of his earlier plays invites, he would be unlikely to resist when asked to delete, add, or change to suit the reactions of audiences. Between the Quarto and Folio texts of *King Lear* various adjustments took place, allowing new episodes to be added and others dropped or adjusted. This play has a structure which allows two stories to inter-weave and offers a wide range of incidents and characters: if some had found favour and others had not, changes in the script could readily be made and its longer than usual playing time reduced. If these were the conditions in which these two versions came about, the Folio text should not be preferred over an earlier one simply because it came later from Shakespeare's hand. So far as struc-ture is concerned, the Quarto may well be the closer of the two to what Shakespeare wanted his play to be.

* * *

Structure and plotting vary markedly at different stages of Shakespeare's career, but at all times he wrote dialogue that calls upon audiences to bring their own concerns to the theatre in such a way that they become an inextricable part of their response to the plays in performance. As his story-telling was often calculated to allow this freedom of mind, so his choice of words, while giving expression to character, narrative, and the play's various themes, at the same time serves to awaken the audience's memories of ordinary living and individual experience. Alongside thoughts and feelings arising directly from the great or fantastic events of the drama, instinctive sensations are also provoked that belong to every mind's huge reservoir of memory filled with matters of everyday consequence. When Richard II is being most intellectual and his predicament most unlike that of his audience in the theatre, Shakespeare has made him touch on the simplest needs and feelings that belong to everyone:

> I live with bread like you, feel want,
> Taste grief, need friends.
> (III.ii.175–6)

The same appeal is made no less confidently in the most gripping and highly wrought of the later plays. When *Othello* drives towards its conclusion and the dramatic focus narrows to draw a very intense and exceptional attention, at that very time the words spoken evoke quite ordinary sense-experiences, both in Desdemona's frightened responses and in the impassioned utterances of Othello. Repetition, as we have seen, ensures that the audience is encouraged to take full possession of the hero's predicament in these accessible terms: 'My wife! my wife! what wife? I have no wife!' (V.ii.100). At other times actuality is evoked in a single but strongly placed image:

Methinks it should be now a huge eclipse
Of sun and moon, and that th'affrighted globe
Did *yawn* at alteration.

(V.ii.102–4)

Ordinary words and affective commonplace imagery go together with matters of great profundity:

Where should Othello *go?*
Now, how dost thou *look* now? O ill-starred *wench*
Pale as thy *smock!*

(V.ii.274–6)

In *Macbeth*, the appeal to mundane and individual experience is perhaps most arresting of all, not only drawing daily events and perceptions into its account of a metaphysical, political, and moral dilemma, but also the actual attendance of the audience at the current performance:

To-morrow, and to-morrow, and to-morrow,
Creeps in this petty pace from day to day
To the last syllable of recorded time,
And all our yesterdays have lighted fools
The way to dusty death. Out, out, brief candle!
Life's but a walking shadow, a poor player,
That struts and frets his hour upon the stage,
And then is heard no more; it is a tale
Told by an idiot, full of sound and fury,
Signifying nothing.

(V.v.19–28)

An active-minded and independent audience could find immediate echoes of their own everyday experiences at the conclusion of Shakespeare's most terrible tragedy and so, as individuals, become closely involved on their own accounts. The play supplies common 'bread' for the imaginations of its audience.

* * *

Accounts of play-going that have survived from Shakespeare's times back-up this hypothesis. Thomas Heywood's praise of 'our domestic histories' in his *Apology for Actors* (1612) has often been quoted in other contexts:

40

What English blood seeing the person of any bold English man presented and doth not hug his fame, and honey at his valor, pursuing him in his enterprize with his best wishes?

(Sig. B4)

Familiarity with these words should not allow us to miss how active the verbs are, speaking of *hugging* and *honeying* as if the audience were responding intimately and sexually (compare 'honeying and making love / Over the nasty sty!', *Hamlet*, III.iv.93–4), and of *pursuing* the play's characters as if, in imagination, it were clambering up onto the stage itself.

Thinking about the forthcoming theatricals, Duke Theseus in *A Midsummer Night's Dream* explains how much he is willing to give, as an audience, when over-anxious performers 'dumbly have broke off':

> Out of this silence yet I pick'd a welcome;
> And in the modesty of fearful duty
> I read as much as from the rattling tongue
> Of saucy and audacious eloquence.
>
> (V.i.100–3)

Thinking of the actors who were about to entertain his guests, he looks forward to a similarly active participation:

> Our sport shall be to take what they mistake;
> And what poor duty cannot do, noble respect
> Takes it in might, not merit.
>
> (V.i.90–2)

In the event, the responses of the on-stage audience to *Pyramus and Thisbe* reveals to the audience in the theatre the differing natures of its members. In much the same way Mrs Quickly in *Henry the Fourth, Part I*, Polonius, Hamlet, Ophelia, Gertrude, and Claudius in *Hamlet*, and the superior young courtiers in *Love's Labour's Lost* are all shown, as Puck says in the *Dream*, to be more than passive 'auditors' of what is performed for their pleasures and are all shown for what they are in their individual responses to a play in progress.[3]

In such a theatre, a playtext is agent for a multiple arousal. It inspires and activates the performers and, through their acting, awakens memory, expectation, argument, resentment, fear, pleasure in the minds of the audience, so that the performance is experienced with a sense of personal discovery and such intimate sensations as hugging, honeying, and pursuing. The performers learn how to play the text and to play with – and play off – their audience. Timing is a large part of the skill needed to handle such an event: phrasing, suggestive intonation, varying of pitch or volume are all as effective as they are for a stand-up comic playing with an audience, with no stooge or settled script in support, but relying on a skilled adaptation of prepared routines to the needs of each particular performance. In response, members of the audience soon learn how to play with the actors and text, and with all sorts of personal memories, fears, and desires. They can make the play their own, the 'shadows' on stage attaining their fullest life in their imaginations.

For these reasons, when critics try to understand and assess Shakespeare's texts, they should explore the dynamic relationship between actors and audience as the plays come to life between them both. Their task is not to decode a hieroglyph or provide specific meanings for a series of signs written on paper, but rather to discover what can happen, both on stage and in the minds of the audience, and to show how, between the actors and the audience, the play may please. Of these two elements, the second is the more difficult to trace and yet just as crucial to understanding as the first. A critic should understand how the audience's thoughts will 'deck' the kings and queens – as the Prologue to *Henry the Fifth* reminded his hearers – and all the other *dramatis personae* that are presented.

Knowledgeable about the life and times of Shakespeare's day and aware of many theories about how the world goes at present, a critic will be deeply immersed in the host of ideas which could be aroused by the enacting of a text. Which are the most significant? Which judgement should oversway others? This book will return to these questions. So far, the best answer would seem to be that those ideas that can be traced throughout the action of a play, being relevant in more than a single episode, are ones which should be given most attention. To this a proviso is necessary: any idea should be evaluated with regard to its power to entertain an audience – to awaken instinctive, sensuous, and individual responses, as well as intellectual certainty or debate about generally valid issues. We should value the plays' openness as much as their intellectual power and effectivness.

The effect of finding myself amongst a crowd of spectators on Bali, whose varied members were both attentive and independent, was an almost total surprise to me. As a member of that 'audience', I had rediscovered a sense of self-possession. The strange ritual aroused unexpected thoughts and sensations, all intimately connected with my own life, whereas when I see a Shakespeare production or read a book of criticism, I am usually expected to submit to what is placed before me.

3

RITUAL
Action and meaning

At one time, European theatre was thought to have derived from religious rituals, such as funerals, weddings, sacrifices, purifications, initiations, and other rites or 'mysteries'. In the late nineteenth and early twentieth centuries, this view of theatre's origins made the pursuit of realism, which was then the current fashion, seem staid and hidebound, a cul-de-sac from which escape should be attempted by retracing steps towards a more impressive and elevating past. As Gordon Craig wrote in 1905: 'The first sign we have of the art of the theatre is in the religious rites. All the arts which I wish to see back again in the theatre were brought together and focused in the religious rites.' T.S. Eliot was to echo him: 'drama springs from religious liturgy, and...cannot afford to depart far from religious liturgy'.[1]

A play is not, however, the same as a religious ritual. Seldom in Europe has attendance at a theatre involved worship of a supernatural power or promised either spiritual rebirth or human benefit. Seldom, since the late middle ages, has one play been like other plays in representing a significant event or action on which they have all been modelled. (The variety of the ancient Greek plays that have survived was not a feature to which the ritualistic critics paid much attention; like Aristotle, they were trying to define common factors, rather than account for individual examples.) In so far as a priest re-enacts a past action or kills a beast to represent the death of a hero, victim, or scapegoat, a ritual can be called a dramatic representation, but turning this statement around, to claim that theatre is like a religious ritual, is a confusing half-truth.

While recognising similarities between some plays and pre-existing religious rituals, the origins of European theatre may also be located elsewhere. Processions or parades, which celebrated and to some extent re-enacted an actual event to the greater glory of its human agents, contained some features of theatre which were not ritualistic in a religious sense, because their validity was temporary and unrepeatable: were it not for the human conqueror or human prisoner, they would not be taking place. Public debates, an essential part of ancient Greek democratic society and government, are now recognised as another source for a play's structure, theme, and diction, and, sometimes, for its characters and setting as well. Games and comp-etitions provided models for engagement and resolution. Still more influential was public story-telling, especially when supported by music, illustrated in dance, and supplied with dialogue using the different voices of various characters. In Christian times, sermons contrasting hell and heaven, good persons and bad, sometimes contained dramatised narrative or debate with each side given a voice. All these activities could bring the past to present life, dealing with far distant places, long periods of time, varied adventures of heroes or victims, and changes in families, societies, and nations. They provided models for plays on modern or ancient themes. Here, together with rituals that celebrated what was believed to be of constant significance in human existence, are sources for the great and various wealth of theatre. Beyond Europe and its colonial influence, theatre has still other origins such as trance, medicine, cultivation of the land and other forms of labour, propaganda, and education.

How Shakespeare created his distinctive plays out of theatre's many resources is a question that leads into the most hidden reaches of his art and can be approached only with greatest difficulty. In countries where religious observances are still a familiar part of contemporary life, as they were in Shakespeare's England, there is, however, an obvious and valuable opportunity to reassess the effect of rituals in the plays. Because other religions, histories, languages, and ways of life are involved, simple equations are not possible, but comparisons can help to identify those basic elements that are common to both heritages and observe their different applications.

* * *

The cremation ritual on Bali, which was described in the last chapter, held crowds for longer than most religious rituals that survive in European countries. Procession, offerings, and culminating fire were its distinguishing features during the four or five hours of its duration, but none of these provided one crucial action to which everyone paid attention; one phase eased, as it were, into another, and everything could be witnessed without rush or tension. I sensed, rather, that each of these elements was implicit in every moment and that this was largely due to the permanent presence of the two large and gaudy constructions which accompa-nied the corpse from the deceased's home to the burning ground. These provided a strong statement of the nature of the entire event. They dominated the field of vision throughout and together they spoke of a life that had been concluded and of the aspiration and journey of its soul.

Such over-sized visual constructions provide continuous points of focus in many Christian rituals. A cross or some holy image — a depiction of Christ in Glory or of Mary as Mother of God — is raised high above an altar so that it is visible to a large congregation, or the image of some local saint is carried on many shoulders in a commemorative procession. In Western Europe, such strong visual statements are also found in secular meetings where political protests tend to be dominated by words written large on banners and placards or by a simpli- fied logo often semi-abstract in design like the swastika. Occasionally religious practice is followed more closely when political rallies are dominated by giant figures; and sometimes the crowd is processional rather than static, following the image to one particular and meaningful landmark. This is more common in Asia and Africa than in European countries. A world-famous example was the assembly in Tiananmen Square, Beijing, on 30 May 1989, when an all-white figure of the Goddess of Democracy and Freedom, more than thirty feet tall with hands lifted high, was carried until it stood over against the enlarged portrait of Chairman Mao in its permanent place in front of government headquarters in the ancient palace, known as the Forbidden City; by its means a confrontation was marked for all to see and to acknowledge by being present in the procession.

In Shakespeare's day, dramatists would sometimes use similarly dominant visual devices that held attention over long periods and could impress an audience by more permanent means than ever-changing words or human actions. To mark the hero's passage through the two parts of *Tamburlaine* (1587), Christopher Marlowe brought on stage crates of captured treasure, a man-sized cage for Bajazeth, a chariot drawn by kings, and the embalmed body of Zenocrate covered in gold. Some of these striking visual images give significance to the action over the course of several scenes while, in the last moments of *Part Two*, both chariot and hearse, together with a map of the world, build up a comprehensive visual statement that contrasts with Tamburlaine's boastful and courageous words. Ben Jonson started *Volpone* (1605) with an impressive locker or 'shrine' for the hero's treasure and a bed for his supposedly infirm body, and both remained on stage for much of the play as powerful visual reminders of its basic situation and theme. John Webster used a strong ritual image for one short scene in *The Duchess of Malfi* (1614) located, in an unusual stage direction, at the 'Shrine of Our Lady of Loretto' (III.iv). This shrine was famous for its statue of the Virgin and two Pilgrims are brought on stage to wonder at its 'goodly' spectacle. Webster's heroine kneels in front of this visual manifestation of virtue, as she had knelt previously at her betrothal and as she will again in submission to her executioners.

In Shakespeare's plays, such visual statements of permanent value are less dominant. The most common ones are political rather than religious – throne, crown, and heraldic impresa – and seldom are they used straightforwardly. In *Henry the Fourth, Part I*, the king sits on his throne or chair of state and gives audience in three successive scenes (I.i, I.iii, and III.ii), but the centralised group- ings around this symbol of inherited power are contrasted with intervening scenes in which the king's restless son occupies no fixed point of focus and rebel leaders try to manage their business without any of the generally acknowledged signs of rule and dominion. In *King John*, the crown is at first given solemn significance, the smallness of the object offset by the respect paid to it, but later, at the start of Act V, the same crown is tendered to and fro, between John and Pandolph the Papal Legate, so quickly that as a sign of inherited power it is open to ridicule. In the deposition scene of *Richard the Second* (IV.i.155–320), the crown is a symbol of an 'anointed king' and 'God's deputy', but it is held in very human and unpriestly hands, and transferred in an improvised act of deposition. A formal coronation is announced 'solemnly', but this ritual takes place off-stage.

Shakespeare used other conventional stage properties as visual images of timeless and general significance: a coffin, tomb, monument, bed, the bar of a court of law, or the furnishings of a church or friar's cell will set a scene and give expression to generally accepted ideas of morality, mortality, religion, or politics. The use of these symbolic properties is, however, limited. The formal rituals involved with them take place off stage: kings enter *after* their coronations, the princess Elizabeth *after* her christening (*Henry VIII*, V.v.80); brides prepare for weddings and leave before they take place. The start of a marriage may be on stage, but both Martext and Friar Francis are interrupted and the ritual never resumed. Acts of mourning are shown on stage, but they have no presiding priest and follow no prescribed order. The operation of Justice in courtroom or by combat is an occasional exception to this refusal to stage formal rituals, but here the focus is on an uncertain outcome, not the ritual process itself.

Clothes appropriate to rituals are used more frequently, as part of the exploitation of entrances and exits that was noticed in Chapter 1. Hamlet's mourning clothes are a generally accepted sign which makes a silent statement as soon as he appears off-centre amongst members of Claudius' court who are standing submissively before their king and dressed richly for a celebration. Later his disordered clothes, with 'doublet all unbrac'd' (II.i.78), make a different counter statement by destroying the first well-ordered image that he had presented. In Act V, a 'sea-gown scarf'd' (V.ii.13) about him contrasts with the black mourning clothes of everyone else dressed for Ophelia's funeral. In the last scene, as Hamlet faces Laertes in the duel, he may be indistinguishable from his opponent who, like him, is stripped for action. Clothes have been used, as in a ritual, to mark distinct stages of the narrative by signs that are generally valid and commonly understood.

In most of the plays clothes make some strong contributions of this kind. Prospero's cloak and staff representing his power over nature are striking visual signs in *The Tempest* that are ritualistically meaningful, especially as they are being put on or laid aside. In *King Lear*, the visual trappings of power are potent at first, but a stripping-off takes place that associates the king with the nakedness of Poor Tom whom he takes to be a Bedlam beggar; then it is his unkingly appearance, together with his white hairs and enfeebled body, that has long-lasting impact on everything that happens in his presence. Whatever the audience thinks of what Lear does and what is done to him, as he struggles to keep his sanity and assert his will, his scant and soiled clothes have a general validity that mark him as suppliant or outcast. Probably Shakespeare's boldest single use of costume as a dominant visual sign is Shylock's 'Jewish gaberdine' (*The Merchant of Venice*, I.iii.107) together with other marks of his racial difference.

Such visual statements contribute to the plays from first to last, but come far short of establishing that religious ritual was an influence on their composition or that any action in the play has a general and timeless significance. The comedies, alluding to various folk rites that were still honoured in rural England of Shakespeare's day,[2] come closest to following a ritual form by reproducing festivities on stage. In *A Midsummer Night's Dream*, Duke Theseus hunts on May morning and in the last scene the fairies dance throughout the house in honour of the weddings. In *As You Like It*, the killing of a deer is celebrated in song, two pages sing of springtime, and the god Hymen makes an entry to choral singing to bless the conclusion. Shakespeare was well aware of the 'rites' that marked the progress of the year (see *Midsummer Night's Dream*, IV.i.130), but his use of them was incidental and allusive, rather than basic and structural as they were in the numerous 'Entertainments', celebratory welcomes, and court masques common at the time. Thomas Nashe's *Summer's Last Will and Testament* (c.1593) is a rare example of a thoroughly festive Elizabethan play.

The last comedies, or romances, contain stronger ritual elements. In *The Tempest*, Prospero has presiding power over spirits as well as other characters, all of whom, sooner or later, pay reverence to him. The arrival on stage of gods in *Pericles*, *Cymbeline*, and *The Winter's Tale* give shorter but strongly positioned moments when every element of the drama is given a more than human importance. These supernatural appearances are developed furthest in *Cymbeline*, where circling apparitions prepare for Jupiter who descends '*in thunder and lightning, sitting upon an eagle*'; he throws a thunderbolt and the Ghosts fall to their knees as he speaks. When he ascends and the ghosts vanish, the mortals who remain report that they have smelled the sulphur of his breath and seen the 'marble pavement' close as he entered 'his radiant roof' (V.iv.114–21). Yet even this awesome event provides no conclusion for the play: before that can come, all the characters must resolve their own problems and, at that time, Jupiter is remembered only when a Soothsayer is called upon to interpret the message he had left behind. Then the King instructs his people to leave the stage in order to visit his temple after the play has ended:

> And let our crooked smokes climb to their nostrils
> From our bless'd altars.

> (V.v.475–6)

47

That Shakespeare was well aware of the power of ritual is most evident in *Macbeth* with the dancing, chanting, oblations, and invocations of the witches as they worship the spirits whom they serve. The authenticity of the text is questionable in Act III, scene v, when Hecate descends to take command of her subjects, but that ritual appearance in some form would provide a climax after the two earlier scenes in which the witches do acts of reverence to their superiors and a fitting preparation for their last, most elaborate and definitive contribution to the play's action in Act IV, scene i. Shakespeare's use of ritual here, with its influence on language and events throughout the play, cannot be missed by any reader or spectator: it indicates the power that it might have had in other plays. Yet, even here, ritual is not central to his purpose. Without Macbeth's ambition, guilt, and courage, or without his awareness of the predicament to which his decisions and deeds have led him, the tragedy's conclusion would have been merely terrible and inevitable. Without Macbeth's changing relationship with Lady Macbeth, and with servants and soldiers, the last scenes would have much less power to catch and hold attention. As the tragedy draws to its close, the witches and their rituals have long since disappeared from the stage.

* * *

Compared with ancient Greek or medieval religious theatre in Europe, or with many theatres in non-European countries today, the theatre of Shakespeare's England was not only non-ritualistic in basic form but also in the expectations of actors and audience. A visit to Asian countries or to the remains of ancient theatres in Greece and its colonies will make this clear. Elizabethan theatres, unlike many in other countries, were not sited either within or near a temple; there was no altar on stage. Many of the England's priests or 'ministers of religion' were opposed to theatre of any kind. Treatment of religion and politics was forbidden on stage and these rules enforced by powerful censorship. More than all this, its theatre companies were commercial enterprises, not organisations responsible to Church or State. Their noble patrons were protectors against interference by persons or institutions, not masters to be served and very specifically honoured. Theatres and acting companies were run by their owners and for their own benefit.

The company with which Shakespeare was involved, the Chamberlain's (later, the King's) Men, was owned by its leading actor-sharers of which he was one. Each member's status was the result of individual initiative and achievement, not dependent on the gift or purchase of some official position. Influence and nepotism might sometimes be involved, but to join the company or enter the profession did not require membership of any family, guild, union, or incorporated institution. Everyone involved was a venturer, an individual rather than a functionary or servitor. Their plays, prepared for the general public, were also performed as entertainments at court and other occasional employment was found, but members of the company had no regular involvement with official occasions or public rituals. Such independence is comparatively rare in the history of theatre and sets the company to which Shakespeare belonged apart from very many others.

Almost all theatres in modern Europe and North America are run under more restrictive conditions. Most receive some form of annual subsidy from state, municipal, or private institutions, or from individual or commercial patrons, and are therefore responsible to a publicly constituted board or trust. Most 'commercial' theatres serve no masters except persons with management, financial, and other producing functions; to these proprietors, the actors are responsible and the success of their performances is measured by return on money that has been invested. In Asia, the contrast to Elizabethan practice is greater still: there many theatre companies have official status and responsibility for public or religious celebrations. Frequently they also have long-lasting family affiliations, three or even four generations being active together in a single company under the senior member. Without any of these stabilising arrangements and lacking the support of modern bureaucracy, the wonder is that Elizabethan theatre companies stayed together for so long and maintained such varied repertoires. The one to which Shakespeare belonged, and which he partly owned, was the most permanent of them all and the most favoured. Some of its members, and he chief amongst them, made private fortunes out of the enterprise.

In some countries, the very fact of making theatre is still considered a ritualist act that fulfils a public and permanent need, even when a company is clearly the product of individual enterprise. Suzuki Tadashi's theatre bears his own name – the Suzuki Company of Toga – but everyone involved is very conscious of a ritual attaching to performance. Its buildings in the Japanese mountain village of Toga are constructed out of simple and beautifully crafted local materials: they are kept at an extraordinary degree of cleanliness, floors polished and unobstructed; space is carefully and very obviously ordered; silence often seems obligatory; the journey to Toga is long and difficult, even with modern transport. The actors follow a demanding all-day regime which would be totally unacceptable to theatre unions elsewhere and an exclusive loyalty is assumed. Their performances are all in accord with strict and codified criteria and actors are instructed to perform, not to the audience or for the audience, but as if to an unseen presence above both stage and auditorium.[3] This theatre does not have the rich and abundant repertory of the Elizabethan and it does not work in the midst of a thriving city, yet its difference in practice goes deeper than that. Performance is ritualistic: ancient traditions are studied and copied; everything has a purpose beyond each moment, certain images being constant throughout the play; the action is both in the present and in the past; and the audience witnesses rather than interacts. Such a theatre marks how far away from ritual Shakespeare's theatre had placed itself.

Austerity and discipline are not the only signs that a theatre sees its performances as rites and seeks to represent more than the individual and temporal on stage. In India, the text of the *Natyasastra*, some two thousand years old, lays down rules for making theatre and explains its origin in the gods' desire to give pleasure to men and women and to show them the nature of life, especially of the eight basic *rasa* or sensations. Performing a play was a way to honour the gods:

> Of all duties of the king, this has been proclaimed as possessing the best result. Of all kinds of charities, allowing people to enjoy a dramatic show without payment has been praised most.
>
> Gods are never so pleased on being worshipped with scents and garlands as they are delighted with the performance of dramas.[4]

Influenced by these ideas, almost any theatre performance in India is implicated in ritual, because what happens on stage has its source and justification elsewhere.

In the popular Jatra theatre, as already mentioned, the breaking of a coconut on stage by a single member of the company before the play began, together with the burning of incense and saying of prayers, was a ritual act of dedication for the entire performance and this ritual was taken further behind the stage in the dressing room. As the whole company was getting ready, a conch shell was blown, its sound gaining immediate attention. Everyone stopped whatever he or she was doing and in silence turned towards a young man, dressed all in white, who made an offering at a small altar and said prayers. Then preparations for performance resumed with a new quietness and concentration while the chief actor, who was to play the father in the performance that night, moved around the tent offering to everyone a small piece of the coconut that had been broken on stage. As a visitor, I was included as a matter of course. No fuss attended this ritual; it was part of a daily routine and an accepted recognition of the significance of what they were doing.

When I had taken part in this ritual and was back in my seat in the auditorium, I wondered if anything had been done to effect a similar sense of shared purpose behind the tiring-house facade of an Elizabethan theatre. Some kind of discipline must have been needed to achieve good order in that confined and crowded space, where everyone was working on a multitude of very different tasks all of which had to be completed on time and where the actors had to make themselves ready with the necessary individual concentration for performance. Few records of difficulties or errors in all this back-stage business have survived, beyond some accounts of late or ill-prepared entries, and yet there is no record of a bell or other signal being used to mark the beginning of preparations or to summon attention. Perhaps the 'book-keeper', who seems to have been both prompter and stage manager, went around giving the final word, but that could not have been as effective for the company as a whole as some more general call for attention. All that is known to have signalled the start of a performance was the trumpet, drum, or flag whose chief purpose was to attract the public to the playhouse. In Shakespeare's theatre, it was perhaps those signals, augmented by the sounds of a gathering audience, that provided the final impetus to the company as a whole and gave the cue for concentration in preparation for performance. If this was the custom, they all made ready because they each, individually, knew that their audience was ready for them. Their chief playwright, when he was preparing to go on stage as an actor, would have had the same attitude to his work.

In India, theatre is treated as a god-given art and in consequence many theatres are situated within a temple precincts and gods are represented on stage with proper ritualistic respect. Even in theatres run as commercial businesses in large modern cities, some of the actors will kiss the stage before they tread on it, whether to rehearse or to perform. Many common practices are reminders of a world beyond that of either audience or stage. In a crowded market-place, I have seen a story-teller squatting down on a piece of carpet amongst the stalls, with a microphone and an open, red-bound book in front of him. He had created a separate space in which to exercise his art. His speech was half-intoned, his bearing relaxed and yet intent. An audience of about a dozen youths listened and sometimes talked amongst themselves. When he had finished, without marking any obvious climax, he bowed his head over closed hands, and prayed aloud, 'Shantih', three times; then he closed the book and bound it up in a red cloth along with two other volumes. The audience started to move away, throwing a few coins into a copper bowl set down on the mat in front of him. When they were gone, he collected the money and a few other belongings, and then, with the parcel of books under his arm, his small stooped figure was soon lost in the crowd. I suppose that he or another story-teller would soon reoccupy the place where he had left unattended the piece of carpet and sound-equipment.

Story-telling in many different forms, and often accompanied by music, is an entertainment throughout India and other Asian and African countries and is in effect a simplified form of theatre that can claim significance by being performed in the presence of the gods. Shakespeare's theatre, in contrast, based its validity and legal status on the service of some noble or royal patron who had little or nothing to do with the running of the company. However constrained by censorship and by social and political pressures, its actors and dramatists recognised, in their day-to-day business, no other authority than that of those colleagues who were personally responsible for the staging of plays so that they satisfied their audiences. This comparative freedom from ritual and public responsibilities brought its own difficulties, as independence is always open to disaster, but it also encouraged Shakespeare to write about life as it was actually lived and to show aspirations and fears as experienced within the wide range of the public that crowded the theatres up and down the land.

Shakespeare's plays may have timeless significance, but they were not written in order to celebrate any religious faith or public event, and attendance at them was not thought to have any specific effect. They cannot in such primary senses be considered as rituals. For other plays and at other times, these were important functions of theatre and in other countries they are so still. But, as readers, critics, theatre directors, or actors of Shakespeare, we will bring very different expectations than those of their author, actors, and audiences if we search the texts for overriding or timeless significances. We should look, first of all, for a representation of human behaviour that will hold the attention of audiences, and for the workings of an unusually independent mind.

4

CEREMONY

Behaviour and reception

In one respect, Shakespeare's England was very familiar with ritual and so was its theatre. In daily life, for all classes of people, the lesser rituals of ceremony were everywhere apparent. Personal interactions, in private as well as in public, were defined by ceremonies – that is, by the repetition of actions and forms of speech which have general rather than individual or personal meaning and acknowledge power or authority. To our eyes, it would have been a very formal age: even when at home, young people rose to their feet when a parent entered the room, and paid some form of respect; a teenager would kneel to receive his or her father's blessing. Age and class also had their privileges. Official regulations laid down the kind and quantity of ornamentation proper to the dress of persons in each walk in society and anyone would be expected to stand aside, to 'take the wall', when a superior was approaching.

Such formalities, ceremonies, or little rituals would be duly represented as part of the imitation of life on the stage and send their wordless messages as part of a play's meanings. At that time, these signs could be decoded by anyone and needed no reinforcement, but to recapture them today requires very special care. Readers of a Shakespeare text are given little or no notice of ceremonial activities and may leave them out of the performance that they visualise in their mind's eye. Theatre directors frequently omit them from performance as meaningless waste of time and effort. In at least two ways the plays suffer in consequence: first, because ceremony is a natural resource of theatre; and second, because it was part of social life as Shakespeare would have known and represented it.

How much is lost will be obvious to any traveller to countries that still use everyday ceremony. In Europe and North America, it governs very few relationships between people, either in public or private, and we commonly pride ourselves on that freedom. Some public occasions are conducted with time-honoured ceremonial, but we feel awkward when we try to adjust our ways and thoughts to such formality and predetermination. Normally we do not wish to waste time on mere ceremony. In these respects, a visitor to Asia senses a difference at once and, in my experience, this is most noticeable in Japan. Here ceremony is used constantly, in greetings and farewells, with hands placed together, heads and bodies bowed – how low they are bowed depends on the status of the person addressed. Television announcers bow to their unseen audiences and I have seen some viewers bowing back in return. Ceremony is used on entering a house, on being served a meal in a restaurant – even when one dines alone – and when taking a bath or going to bed in a traditional inn. In services at a shrine, worshippers may be seen standing in strict line and equidistant apart, their responses in staccato and brief unison, apparently allowing no scope for expression of individual piety or doubt. Ceremony is a part of business negotiations and the giving of gifts; it is involved in choice of dress and presentation of self. Looking into a Tokyo department store, early in the morning before it had opened for customers, I saw rows of uniformed assistants being drilled in the proper approach to a member of the public, how to bow and what to say. Ceremony will even enter the running of a theatre company; after a break in rehearsals I have seen a director clap his hands, making a sharp, slapping sound to summon a uniform attention before work resumed; it was the same sound as I had heard at a shrine, but it came now from someone who, moments later, would be helping individual actors, casually and intimately, as any European director would do.

In order to maintain an appropriate ceremony, individuality and quirks of manner are held back and a common, physical language of gesture, posture, or sound appears to take over. During the passage of some time, pressures of individual life are put on hold and each person follows a predetermined pattern of behaviour. At the same time, however, within and beneath the ceremony, the participants will continue to be themselves, alert and independent, or perhaps muddled and afraid. The inner self does not cease to exist as the outer self speaks in the familiar and comprehensible terms of ceremony. It is interplay between these two modes of being and expression – between inner and outward existences – that gives to ceremony some of its most valuable contributions to the making of theatre.

Becoming aware of the theatrical power of ceremony by spending time in a very different country from my own – in some ways, a more old-fashioned society – has changed the way I respond to the texts of Shakespeare's plays and, in particular, the way I sense the life of his characters. Such formalities may well have origins in religious rituals, but in everyday use ceremony is a common reaction to all kinds of authority. Any submission or exercise of power, or any pretence of these, can be expressed in ceremony's non-verbal language.

* * *

Actors in every production I have seen in Japan are naturally ceremonious, at least some of the time.[1] By sinking individuality under the cover of routine ceremony, they are able to make a statement with relevance outside the present moment without loss of dramatic content or inner drive. Because a ceremony takes time to make its comparatively calm effect, its visual image has an extended exposure so that it becomes a marker in a wide field that is crowded with many more fleeting impressions. A sequence of such markers may enter securely into an audience's memory-bank and, by the end of the play, these can be drawn upon to awaken a complex response that reaches outside the limits of any momentary effect or any one character's consciousness. When a ceremony is repeated in different circumstances, the earlier occasion will tend to be recalled, making a recognition of an *inward* difference part of the new experience. All this may make an audience more aware than characters in a play of significance, irony, complication, development, submission, ineffectiveness, consequence. The use of ceremony gives an extra expressiveness to performance in Japan, a valuable effect that is not so often used or seldom registers in less ceremonious countries.

These effects can be demonstrated in Nō and Kabuki, two ancient forms of theatre that retain the still more ceremonial styles of earlier ages. For example, numerous ceremonies of farewell are used successively at the end of the Kabuki play of *Shunkan*, when its hero is left alone on a remote island having sacrificed his freedom for that of his friend's wife. The scene develops from one ceremony to another, each taking its own time as in a slow dance of achievement, grief, courage, stoicism, resignation. A spectator is drawn into ever fuller knowledge of this man's experience, as if a jewel were being viewed facet by facet. Time is a vital ingredient of theatre and the time taken by ceremony introduces a kind of slow-motion which allows an audience to realise what neither direct action nor a lot of talking would be able to hold steady for their attention. Progression is also vital to good theatre and this is well served by the single-mindedness of ceremony – its simple-mindedness – because an increasingly complex or profound impression can be accumulated as it moves through its well-signalled, successive stages. Contemporary Japanese dramatists, directors, and actors seem to know this very well since they use ceremonies freely, especially at moments when feeling runs high or the extraordinary is about to take place.

When I saw Kara Juro's *Orugōru-no Haka* (*Music-box Cemetery*) in its 1992 revival by the 7th Ward Theatre Company, I found that the preparation and serving of a meal was at the heart of the play and provided the occasion for the two leading characters to establish their mutual relationship and uncertainties. To my eye, their ceremonies often seemed like childish games, but an intent and crowded audience was telling me otherwise; its attention was securely held. Even I could see that nothing was as simple as outwardly it appeared to be: these people taking part in a shared ceremony were not at all simple, nor did they have very much else in common. He was a puppet-maker who could seemingly make himself disappear and she a whore who had expected to receive her lover, the Boss. All this was expressed in the performance of commonplace domestic cere-monies in which slight variations and instinctive hesitations, or a momentary lapses, could signal significant differences and tensions.

In the action-packed *La Vie en Rose* (1992), written and directed for his Third Erotica Theatre Company by Kawamura Takeshi, ceremonies were various and numerous, often noisy and as often striking. Inspired by Dostoevski's *The Possessed* and containing crowds of characters, historical and fanciful, the production was played by a cast of (I think) twenty-four on the very small stage of a small and uncomfortable theatre. Ceremony was here a way of coping with a roller-coaster of events and many collisions of purpose in what the author called 'The Age of Confusion'. I saw a funeral with two corpses (one of which steps out of his coffin), a wedding where all the men were played by women and vice versa, a civil war with rifles, machine-guns, and poison gas in which fortunes changed rapidly. A girl reappeared in different guises – on stilts, pregnant, dressed for work, infantile, glamorous. Peter, the central character who is trying to make a verbal record of this phantasmagoria, is made to pose almost naked to be photographed in the postures of a pin-up girl with her expected expressions of allure on his face. Each element in this noisy world was presented by its appro-priate ceremony, all instantly recognisable and sufficiently brief for the hard-working actors to sustain the headlong momentum of the action.

I am not sure, in my ignorance of the language, if this play worked for its audi-ence, but I do know that I had more sensations to absorb than I could easily manage and yet seldom did I lose sight of what was afoot. If the actors had had to create individually realised performances in all the various realities the author had had in his mind, they would have been exhausted and the audience confused; and the play would have taken many more hours to perform. As it was, the produc-tion was packed close with instantly recognisable images and so able to force even an alien like me to look for connections and to question the motives and necessity for the action: in short, to think about what I saw and heard. Whereas *Music-box Cemetery* had used ceremonies to slow up stage-events, *La Vie en Rose* used them to speed up and concentrate the drama.

Sometimes simple ceremonies are used to widen the scope of a play. When Kishida Rio spoke to me of her play *Ito Jigoku*, or *Woven Hell*, she told the story of a young girl searching for her mother: she finds her in a pre-war weaving factory and here they start a long struggle with each other, at the end of which the girl kills the mother. When I heard this synopsis, I envisaged an episodic narrative play in which the mother–daughter relationship took central place, but a video of its production showed that this story was told within an elaborate staging of the continuous activity of a dozen women in routines of work that subjugated them to their male supervisors. The play was not only about the blood relationship of two individuals, but also about woman's enslavement to social, moral, and economic forces. By using almost mindless and repetitive ceremonies, the author had shown how people are tied together and kept apart by unthinking routines of living. The simple narrative thread had been presented within a vista of continuing life and drawn through a complex net of interdependence.

Seeing Suzuki Tadashi's *Waiting for Romeo* (1993) as a first or early encounter with Japanese theatre, a European or North American spectator might wonder at the complicated way in which the central character sits down to a meal, and still more at its slow and formal service, and the poised stillness of the single partaker. Yet the heart of the play is within this single figure, whose thoughts and sensations are more freely expressed by other figures who appear out of the distance to encircle the stage in other ceremonies. A line of male actors dressed in women's skirts and sitting in wheelchairs propel themselves with their feet working energetically in unison and making uniform and loud clacking noises with the bright red, high-heeled shoes they all are wearing. A non-Japanese onlooker might easily get bored as this activity goes on and on, varied chiefly by some hilarious and panicky moments when one of the automata goes astray or gets stuck against an immovable obstacle. But these non-individualised and repetitive activities are the very means by which the director-author has grounded his work in a *mélange* of the unthinking activity of everyday ceremonies. By using a mixture of repetitive actions to be found in hospitals and in popular musical entertainments, Suzuki has presented a nightmare dance of interminable, obsessive, and almost mindless fears experienced by his central character. Without such a strong physical language for their expression, such instinctive sensations could have been no more than fleeting impressions or the subject of laborious verbal statements. Meanwhile, by means of age-old ceremonies involved in serving a meal, he has held the central

Plate 4.1 The central character supported by members of the chorus in *Waiting for Romeo;* directed by Susuki Tadashi for the Suzuki Company of Toga

character still so that the audience is able to focus on what is familiar and become more aware of any variation in how the ceremonies are performed.

Shakespeare's plays are now very popular in Japan and directors make audiences feel at home in them by taking full advantage of their opportunities for using ceremonies. For the k ing's first entrance in a production of *King Lear* at the Panasonic Globe in 1991, the entire court had entered in due order and then prostrated themselves on the floor of the stage. Lear's absolute power, not mentioned in the text at this point but crucial to the drama of this scene, was everywhere apparent and impossible to ignore. Ceremony was also used to display complications which are unstated but inherent in a situation: so when the unmoving, self-contained, and outwardly respectful figures of Lear's daughters did break out of that fixed order, they drew total attention, both when speaking to their father and when hearing what their sisters said. In the original editions of this play, a simple list of characters entering is the only stage direction to aid a reader or director, but if the whole scene is staged with full respect to ceremony, each position nicely judged, all persons facing the king, each movement calculated and competitive, then instinctive glances or an inner tension can draw attention and give a sense of suppressed rivalries and fears. Within the king himself, almost unmoving as his status requires, his deepest needs can become a nontextual drama of undeniable power. Personal feelings, suggestive and incipient, rather than definitive, became apparent to the audience as they show signs of breaking

Plate 4.2 Ceremonial dance in a production of *King Lear*; performed by Banyu-Inryoku, directed by J.A. Seazer, at the Globe, Tokyo, 1991
Photograph: The Globe, Tokyo

through the outward composure of ceremony; they were more ominous than if they had been fully played out.

* * *

Experience of Japanese ceremonies and ceremonial theatre can alter the way Shakespeare's texts are read. Any group entry which includes figures of power, whether king or head of family, or even an elder with a younger brother, will be seen as an invitation for ceremonial and a consequent sharpening of attention. In Shakespeare's day all this would have been taken for granted, and so only rarely do stage directions or dialogue prompt a reader or director in what should be done. If the prince entered last, '*cum aliis*', at the start of the first court-scene in *Hamlet*, as the 'good' second Quarto specifies (I.i.0, stage direction), the focus drawn to his displaced figure would have been intense long before he spoke. When a royal person refuses his proper position he does not act alone; everyone else does not know where to place themselves, and so he brings about a general disorder and uncertainty.

Few stage directions are so helpful or bear similar signs of being authorial in origin as this in *Hamlet*, but the dialogue, if read with an eye to ceremony, will often show that Shakespeare was attentive to such matters and expected respect to be paid to them in staging. Returning again to the first ceremonially ordered scene of *King Lear*, the marked absence of speeches for Cornwall and Albany, as they move and stand in direct relationship to their wives, will bring them into focus early on, especially when Cordelia speaks pointedly of her sisters' 'husbands'. Still more searchingly, the audience will look for their responses when the king, without preparation, calls each husband by name and invests them, and not their wives, with his power as, equally, his two 'belovéd sons' (ll. 126–38). Why do they not reply, or why are they allowed no opportunity to do so? Perhaps they come forward, with or without their wives, ready to speak; and, certainly, they must kneel. What are their wives thinking as they also say nothing, and how do they relate to their husbands at this moment? In a ceremonial age these questions were bound to be asked. Ceremony has set the stage and ensures that the audience can sense undercurrents of thought and feeling in the smallest deviation from expected behaviour. It also invites the actors to mark their individual courses throughout this corporate scene.

One obvious cue for such effects is a general *exeunt*. Someone must go first: who should this be, and how will precedence be decided? In this same scene, the two princely sons-in-law will both come into focus as they take leave of their wives, without a word being spoken; and their wives will have to discover how they stay behind to be alone on stage with Cordelia and the King of France. Rules for courtly behaviour will ensure that such issues surface into the physical management of the moment and here the dialogue is also helpful. The status of the new bridegroom is defined as Lear leaves the stage calling the rejected suitor to take the place of honour at his side, with 'Come, noble Burgundy' (l. 266): in contrast, France's position is defined wholly in his physical relation, as husband, to Cordelia. Yet this is not the end of the matter, because she says nothing to him throughout the whole of this concluding episode. Only her actions and bearing will speak for her relationship to her husband: to him she *says* 'nothing', which is how she said she wanted to react to her father earlier in the scene. Silent ceremony, at this moment, can show her confidence in France as her words are concerned with her sisters and with her father who has just left the stage. It is left to the new husband to show in words the closeness of their bond and his admiration for her, with the simple, 'Come, my fair Cordelia'. The situation, that involves such a series of breakdowns in usual ceremony, is further complicated when the dialogue implies that Cordelia speaks through her tears (see ll. 267–8) and this has no effect on her sisters. When Cordelia offers a formal 'farewell', neither Goneril nor Regan replies verbally and so, once more, an expected ceremony is missing or reduced to a silent response as each sister chooses what to do. By such means, throughout the first scene of *King Lear*, individual characters are placed in self-revealing moments as expectation of ceremony is built up and broken down. When wordless improvisation has to take over from prescribed formality, the effect is similar to that of cinematic close-ups as small movements register powerfully. It also gives a more general sense that power and subservience are not securely based: this is a society under strain to maintain expected relationships, a situation in which words are not always adequate.

In more domestic circumstances, ceremony will make the Gloucesters' family relationships an equally present concern in this play. Tensions are shown in the first moments when the virile Edmund is standing behind his father, dependent but unacknowledged, and when the Earl of Kent speaks directly about him without addressing him: 'Is not this your son, my lord?' (I.i.7). How does Edmund react when all eyes turn to him and the father speaks of his son in the third person, as if he were not present? What ceremony is used as Edmund replies to Kent with: 'My services to your lordship'? Almost certainly, he should kneel, as he has not done to the father who would only have 'blushed to acknowledge him' (ll. 9–10). How is his relationship to his father expressed now? Gloucester says nothing until after Edmund again replies to Kent with 'Sir, I shall study deserving', and then he again speaks of his son in the third person: 'He hath been out nine years, and away he shall again' (ll. 31–2). The contrasts between the ceremonies used between Kent and Edmund, which are entirely regular, and those used between Edmund and his father, which are entirely irregular, would have been very noticeable and alerted the audience to Gloucester's unthinking assumption of dominance and Edmund's quick improvisation of an entirely new relationship. Unless a production or a reading recognises these disrupted and discordant ceremonies, it can misrepresent this scene: dialogue does not say it all.

Sometimes the words spoken say nothing to the purpose and ceremony is forced to take over. When the newly crowned Macbeth dismisses his court, everyone, including the newly crowned Lady Macbeth, leaves without saying a word:

> Let every man be master of his time
> Till seven at night;
> To make society the sweeter welcome,
> We will keep ourself till supper-time alone.
> While then, God be with you![2]
>
> (III.i.40–4)

Ceremony here ensures that everyone waits for the queen to leave first and everyone watches her. Why does she say nothing? Does she delay before going? Did she intend to reply? Are any of her husband's words addressed specifically to her? Can any signs of affection, mutual understanding, or uncertainty be seen between king and queen, or husband and wife? This moment is not one of those when the words of the text suggest a deep relationship between the two protagonists, but in their parting here the actors have a spot-lit opportunity for marking their differing ways through the story that they share.

In Shakespeare's comedies, ceremony is as varied as its use is constant. *Twelfth Night*, for example, offers many opportunities for contrasting effects in the two very different households of a Duke and a Countess, not least when he at last meets her and tries to behave as if 'heaven walks on earth' (V.i.91). Until then Orsino has moved only amongst young male attendants who are variously and, apparently, randomly favoured: as Valentine says to the disguised Viola, 'If the Duke continue these favours towards you, Cesario, you are like to be much advanc'd' (I.iv.1–3). In Olivia's household, funeral ceremonies are still in place at first; but two knights are taking their different pleasures in the Buttery Bar amongst servants, the steward is having noble dreams above his element, and Maria, a waiting gentlewoman, is wielding power over everyone. In both places, the fool Feste exercises his freedom from paying respect and yet can be seen to have unspoken cares and desires.

That ceremony was a major resource in the game of making Elizabethan theatre is even more obvious in the history plays with their power struggles between kings, nobles, and other persons of very different status. *Henry the Fifth* contains an account of the continuous presence of ceremony and the expository advantages a playwright gains through using ceremonies of submission. The king himself speaks it after he has disguised himself as an ordinary soldier and talked with those who are, in fact, ordinary soldiers:

> O Ceremony, show me but thy worth!
> What is thy soul of adoration?
> Art thou aught else but place, degree, and form,
> Creating awe and fear in other men?
>
> (IV.i.240–3)

Henry goes on to speak of the other side of that coin, the abuse of ceremony:

> Wherein thou art less happy being fear'd
> Than they in fearing.
> What drink'st thou oft, instead of homage sweet,
> But poison'd flattery?
>
> (IV.i.244–7)

Ceremony's message can be false and dangerous: a 'proud dream / That play'st so subtly with a king's repose' (ll. 253–4). Its effect on stage is twofold: to awaken the audience's attention to unspoken rebellion or insecurity, quite as much as to show power and fearful dependence.

Shakespeare's awareness of this seems to have grown with the years, if his characters' views of ceremony are any indication. An uneasy Brutus acknowledges its uncertainty in *Julius Caesar*:

> When love begins to sicken and decay,
> It useth an enforced ceremony.
>
> (IV.ii.20–1)

In *Lear*, a nameless attendant feels constrained to comment, his syntax betraying his unease:

> …your Highness is not entertain'd with that ceremonious affection as you were wont; there's a great abatement of kindness appears as well in the general dependants as in the Duke himself also and your daughter.
>
> (I.iv.57–61)

When an urgent servant runs in with news, Cleopatra protests:

> What, no more ceremony? See, my women!
> Against the blown rose may they stop their nose
> That kneel'd unto the buds.
>
> (*Antony and Cleopatra*, III.xiii.38–40)

Timon knows misuse as ceremony's only useful function:

> ...Ceremony was but devis'd at first
> To set a gloss on faint deeds, hollow welcomes,
> Recanting goodness, sorry ere 'tis shown...
>
> (*Timon*, I.ii.15–17)

Except in non-European societies or on the rare occasions for which old traditions are still maintained for public occasions, it is not easy for us to grasp how widespread and significant ceremony was in Shakespeare's England and in his plays. His contemporaries took it so much for granted that they did not often speak of it. In much the same way, stage directions in printed plays take so much for granted that they are inadequate guidance to what would have been shown on the stage. Lengthy and apparently tireless accounts of courtly occasions show, however, that ceremony was often used to excess. For example, Sir Dudley Carleton wrote to Mr Winwood from London in January 1604 about the marriage of Sir Philip Herbert and the Lady Susan on St John's Day at Whitehall:

> The Court was great, and for that day put on the best bravery. No ceremony was omitted of Bride-Cakes, Points, Garters, and Gloves, which have been ever since the Livery of the Court; and at night, there was sewing into the sheet, casting off the bride's left hose, with many other pretty sorceries.[3]

The monarch's arrival on a state occasion would be governed by long lists detailing who entered and in what order of precedence, who greeted the king at the first entrance, who at the second and third, what special duties each named officiant enacted, and so on. The elaborate and careful procedures could be fascinating to those who took part: each person had his or her own share of attention at a moment and in an office which signified either inherited rank or achieved merit and favour.

The long stage direction in Act IV, scene i of *Henry VIII* provides the fullest description of a ceremonial procession in Shakespeare and the dialogue that follows shows the interest two 'Gentlemen' take in small details of its arrangement:

> —— A royal train, believe me. These I know.
> Who's that that bears the sceptre?
> ——   Marquis Dorset;
> And that the Earl of Surrey, with the rod.

—   A bold brave gentleman. That should be
     The Duke of Suffolk?
—   'Tis the same – High Steward.
—   And that my Lord of Norfolk?
—   Yes.

There is no doubt who is the Queen, but the positions around her need some explanation:

—   They that bear
     The cloth of honour over her are four barons
     Of the Cinque-ports.
—   Those men are happy; and so are all are near her.
     I take it she that carries up the train
     Is that old noble lady, Duchess of Norfolk.
—   It is; and all the rest are countesses.
—   Their coronets say so. These are stars indeed,
     And sometimes falling ones.
—   No more of that.
                                          (IV.i.38–55)

And so the procession leaves '*with a great flourish of trumpets*'.

The extent to which such ceremonies could affect the imagination in Shakespeare's day is not easily illustrated from the exhaustive and occasionally enthusiastic accounts that have survived. Deeper impressions were to be given several decades later in the freer and more graphic style of prose fiction. So Margaret Cavendish describes the assembled court when the heroine of *The Contract* (1656) arrives at a ball:

> when they came to the court, all the crowds of people, as in a fright, started back, as if they were surprised with some divine object, making a lane, in which she passed through; and the keepers of the doors were struck mute, there was no resistance, all was open and free to enter. But when she came in into the presence of the lords and ladies, all the men rose up, and bowed themselves to her, as if they had given her divine worship; [excepting] only the Duke, who trembled so much, occasioned by the passion of love, that he could not stir: but the Viceroy went to her.
> Lady, said he, will you give me leave to place you?
> Your Highness, said she, will do me too much honour.
> So he called for a chair, and placed her next himself; and when she was set, she produced the same effects as a burning glass; for the beams

of all eyes were drawn together, as one point placed in her face, and by reflection she sent a burning heat, and fired every heart. But he could not keep her; . . .[4]

Such a slow-motion view of a court occasion suggests something of the power of regular ceremony and its disturbance, the polarities within which we should try to envisage Shakespeare's plays. It gives an idea of how strongly Hamlet's displacement in the first court scene might register and how the actions and behaviour implied in his talk with Ophelia as the court prepares to watch a performance of *The Murder of Gonzago* would place huge and unexpected pressures on both Ophelia and the Queen, and consequently on everyone else, including Claudius:

QUEEN: Come hither, my dear Hamlet, sit by me.
HAMLET: No, good mother; here's metal more attractive.
POLONIUS: O, ho! do you mark that?
HAMLET: Lady, shall I lie in your lap?
OPHELIA: No, my lord.

(III.ii.105–9)

Margaret Cavendish's awareness of how members of the court bear themselves also reflects on the opening words of *King Lear*, as two courtiers discuss the impressions made by the monarch's behaviour at some earlier occasion:

KENT: I thought the King had more affected the Duke of Albany than Cornwall.
GLOUCESTER: It did always seem so to us; but now, in the division of the kingdom, it appears not which of the Dukes he values most...

(I.i.1–5)

In a ceremonial world, 'appearances' are often of crucial importance; they can also be wrongly interpreted.

* * *

Would a renewed emphasis on ceremony in productions of Shakespeare's plays lead, inevitably, to museum-like reproductions, attempting to mirror a forgotten and irrecoverable society, or does the contemporary use of ceremony in Japanese theatre point towards more accessible presentations which mirror present-day living and modes of perception? These questions also have significance for readers and critics of the plays.

The very words *ceremony* and, especially, *ceremonious* and *ceremonial* speak to us of old-fashioned pomposity, pretence, or specific religious practices and beliefs. But psychologists and sociologists have given new meaning to the related word *ritual* and the usage of *ceremony* may be similarly updated. Following H.S. Sullivan's *Inter-personal Theory of Psychiatry* (1947), Erving Goffman's *Interaction Ritual* (1967) used examples from contemporary life to show how we are all liable to use similar postures, gestures, and actions, and, sometimes, forms of speech, to represent unspoken recognitions of power, dominance, fear, need, intention, and so forth. Because *ritual* was used in Shakespeare's day comparatively rarely, and then in connection with religious *rites*, I have used *ceremonies* for the unconsidered and often small actions that denote the presence of power and submission; as we have seen, this was the word Shakespeare used in entirely secular contexts.

Attention paid to ceremonies in Elizabethan and secular senses, or to rituals in Goffman's sense, need not lead to museum-like productions or readings of the plays that would fix them into a long-lost world – the reverse is true. If we look for ceremonies in contemporary life that can be used to take the place of older ones, we may find means to animate the action of the plays so that they will represent the ceremonious nature of their original enactments. More than this, the use of modern ceremonies will help us to realise the plays in action so that they reflect our own lives.

In Japan, where contemporary life is more obviously ceremonial than in Europe or North America, dramatists and directors, as we have seen, use ceremonies to reflect their own times in entirely new plays as well as in Shakespeare's. Many of these devices are not specific to this Asian culture but equally available in other technologically advanced societies. The plays and productions of Noda Hideki show this spectacularly well. This author-director-actor finds ceremonies in most aspects of life around him, and they all come together in his teasingly intellectual and highly popular productions: outward signs of power, of submission to power, or of craving for power; unconscious tricks of behaviour which express acceptance of fixed ways of life; games of hide-and-seek within a world made mechanical and frightening by the adoption of pre-made patterns of reaction. Recurrent ceremonies in Noda's plays are those associated with up-to-date processes of salesmanship, education, technical instruction, medicine, grooming and personal hygiene, military training, parties of many sorts, arrivals and departures by various forms of transport, and so on. Besides this welter of contemporary material, ancient ceremonies are also introduced from Kabuki, Nō, and Bunraku theatres, and from religious worship. Old-fashioned but still recognised emblematic figures are seen briefly and parodistically in ceremonial postures; one play has two Father Christmases, another a Lucifer, Jesus Christ, and Alice in Wonderland. Routines of performance are also taken from circuses.

In Noda's plays characters often seem to be all packaging and no substance, their actions determined by the routine and repetitive actions of submission to superior power or custom, not least to the dictates of pop-culture, mass-media advertisement, consumerism, big business, and technology. The way in which so many routine elements are fused together is highly original: these ceremonies echo each other, destroy each other, or self-destruct by increasingly frantic implementation. Contemporary ceremonies so dominate the action on stage that the characters' other responses can appear to be the ineffectual striving of dumb creatures caught in a trap or struggling helplessly in the grip of some disease. Eventually, the whole dizzying dance comes to a stop, as if by magic rather than by an individual's responsible act, or as if this world of externally imposed behaviour has burned itself out. Possibly someone has destroyed it, having seen too clearly the absurd mindlessness of the activity.

The basic actions in Noda's plays are, however, heroic enterprises: a story close to that of Wagner's *Ring Cycle*, or a family's response to the arrival of twin girls who have to be separated surgically, or the adventures of the Prisoner of Zenda and the Children's Crusade (these two in a single play), and so on. Somewhere in the huge entanglement of pre-packaged behaviour lies an aspiration struggling to achieve something or to make independent sense. Often the end comes with repeated gestures or movements associated with levitation or the flying of birds, as if the characters long to be free. Yet audiences are left to take the plays as they wish: as bright festivals of everyday clichés – fashionable, glitzy, infantile, paradoxical, funny – or as elaborate puzzles in which they may discern the forces driving a modern frenzy or seeking to transcend it.

Noda takes old and new ceremonies with equal relish and equal scepticism, and because of that his plays can seem impenetrably Japanese to foreign eyes. Besides he drives them at such a furious pace that there is little time to develop a sense of an underlying organisation, except in general and therefore abstracted terms. These elements of his dramaturgy make his work seem inimitable and insular, but to view his plays in Tokyo, with the packed and enthusiastic audience for which they were written, is to be sure that ceremonies – repetitive actions, individually mindless and yet generally meaningful – lie around everywhere in modern urban life, waiting to be used in other theatres wherever in the world mega-businesses, mass sales-techniques, bureaucratic priorities, and technical dehumanisation of effort exercise their power and enforce uniformity.

This strength of the new Japanese theatre is available anywhere, to any dramatist, director, and actor who has the wit to use it. Because our old forms of religious and class-ridden ceremony have fallen into disuse, we do not always recognise how modern ceremonies of power and submission have taken their place and how mindless activity often governs how we live and think. The use of these in the staging of Shakespeare's plays and in our appreciation of the plays as

Plate 4.3   Clear and energetic acting in *The Prisoner of Zenda;* directed and devised by
Noda Hideki
Photograph: Noda Map, Tokyo

readers offers a wide field for exploration and experimentation. None of this
would be easy but the attempt would give a clearer view of important qualities
inherent in the plays and of how Shakespeare imagined them in performance.

Some directors in Europe and the English-speaking world have staged
Shakespeare in recent years using the more ceremonious styles of performance
found in ancient Asian theatres. They go to great trouble to import foreign
behaviours, movements, costumes, and music in order to imitate the force and
sensitivity of Kabuki in Japan or Kathakali in India. Unfortunately, this practice
removes the plays from present-day reality and the instinctive reactions of
audiences. A search for new and current ceremonies in the audience's own lives
would offer a more open road to the rediscovery of that element of the plays which
uses purely physical means to concentrate attention and express relationships.
Noda has shown how much lies ready to use and how this creates productions that
speak directly to contemporary audiences in a visual language which they recognise as their own.

Repeated actions that were not in themselves meaningful were used to great
effect in Deborah Warner's production of *Richard the Second* at the National
Theatre in London (1995). In the early meeting between the Duchess of
Gloucester and John of Gaunt, in Act I, scene ii, the director had the actress
approach across the length of a long traverse stage so that each step of the elderly
woman was a separate acknowledgement of her need and his power. Peter
Holland has described the effect:

the entire scene was controlled and shaped by the slow progress of the aged and crippled Duchess of Gloucester down the theatre, leaning heavily on two sticks, while John of Gaunt stood immobile. Indeed the staging of this scene precisely enabled what was, quite simply, the most brilliant and perfect Shakespeare performance I have seen: Paola Dionisotti's Duchess, brutally hard in her vindictive grief, spitting out her words with frightening power and the utmost lucidity, confronting Graham Crowden's Gaunt, as every step of her progress and every movement of her body underlined the words with the utmost intensity.[5]

Such praise for an actress in a minor part (which is often cut from an acting script) is a tribute not only to her artistry but also to the eloquence that a director can gain by a ceremonial extension of a simple meeting.

A second reason to pay attention to the new theatre of Japan and reintroduce the ceremonial to productions of Shakespeare is that ceremony can be found in some of the newest work in theatre elsewhere. Samuel Beckett is the supreme exemplar. In the apparently casual and unthinking behaviour of Vladimir and Estragon, Pozzo and Lucky, of the women in *Happy Days* and *Rockaby*, of Hamm and Clov, and of many other characters, Beckett was showing their inward natures and the otherwise hidden implications of their more conscious efforts. By cunning repetitions and unfamiliar contexts, Beckett revealed what would have been obscured by confident verbal statements or clear-headed argument. He was not concerned to create rituals of unambiguous significance but used many small ceremonies to show the dependence, craving, isolation, courage, and other fears and resources of his characters. By these means, he could express reactions of which his characters were not fully conscious. His lead has been followed by many other dramatists who look closely at the habits of everyday life, and especially by those who are also influenced by film and its ability to focus intensely on unconsidered actions and responses. Harold Pinter and David Mamet are two of many dramatists who use current ceremonies – for example, the way coffee is served after a meal or a breakfast ordered from a nearby bar[6] – to reveal their characters' unspoken fears or desires, and their otherwise hidden intentions.

Directors and actors who make most conscious use of ceremony in Europe and North America tend to work outside established theatre companies, not basing their work on written texts but preferring to develop plays out of ordinary experiences and their own instincts; their productions are often dance-like or wordless. 'Alternative' theatre festivals are crowded with productions of this kind, but unlike their Japanese counterparts, they are not run-away successes and mount no effective challenge to established theatre. One does not have to struggle to get a ticket, as you must in Tokyo for plays by Noda.

I am not suggesting an easy correspondence between the formalities of life in

Shakespeare's day and the routines of late twentieth-century salesmanship, television, bureaucracy, education, travel, home or business life – the stuff of much contemporary theatre. Rather I would argue that both codes of behaviour have elements, involving physical actions and non-personalised forms of speech, in which timing, positioning, repetition, and small variations have a similar capacity to express relationship and, especially, the operations of power and dependency. Both give a dramatist or director opportunity to disrupt expected patterns and so reveal otherwise hidden reactions. Both enable a chosen moment to be extended and shown from varying points of view. These similarities mean that our own unconsidered ceremonies could help bring Shakespeare's plays to life on the stage in such a way that they would reflect more fully our own everyday experiences.

For readers, I would argue, the task is one of re-imagination. If we bring more of the immediate sensations of daily life to a reading of the texts by looking for currently viable ceremonies that could be relevant, we may, in our mind's eye, extend and illuminate their actions. Neither this kind of reading nor the kind of production I advocate would entail a modernising of the plays so that they reflected only repetitive and simple aspects of present experience. Rather, these are the means to realise the texts' potential in fuller accord with the imagination that was responsible for writing them.

5

PERFORMANCE

Imagination and involvement

During the morning of 15 November 1995, at Trivandrum in Kerala, towards the southernmost tip of India, I experienced a performance unlike any I have known before or since.[1] The theatre and its location, the single actor and what he was wearing, the style of his performance, the drummers, the script, perhaps the time of day, certainly the absence of many of the usual arrangements and equipment for production, my own expectations in this unfamiliar land, and many other factors all combined to make up an event that provided, without any fuss or complicated calculation, a simple and surprising conclusion, one that not only seemed correct and undeniable, but also applicable to almost everything I had previously thought about theatre and much else besides. In particular, it changed my views about Shakespeare's plays and how best they can be staged.

The nature of this actor's performance was the main factor. In retrospect, the words he spoke and the characters he portrayed – there were more than one – do not seem so important as how they were acted. In fact, the play was written in ancient Sanskrit, a language of which I know nothing and to which only students of considerable learning have any access. That the play's action was mythic, super-human, and impossible could easily be sensed and yet it was brought convincingly before me by quite unremarkable physical means if one discounts those belonging to the actor himself. I must try to explain what he did, if I am to show the consequences of this morning's experience and show how this strange event can prompt lines of enquiry for anyone to pursue.

* * *

The actor's name is Ammannur Kochukuttan Chakyar Madhu, known as Margi Madhu: *Madhu* means honey, and *Margi* is the name of the theatre of which he is a member. The third son of a Brahmin actor, Moozhikulam Kochukuttan Chakyar, he has been active in training and performance since the age of seven. At the age of twenty-nine, he has twenty-two years of experience in the extraordinarily

71

demanding acting style and the strict regimen which is known as Kutiyattam. *Kuti* means 'together' and *attam* refers to acting or dancing; 'ensemble performance' is a possible translation.

The company lives as a self-contained unit alongside the theatre in which it trains and produces its plays. Because they always perform for the gods, the theatre is situated close to a temple and is itself a place for worship. Its plan is simple: a roofed rectangle on a single level is divided into two squares, each about five metres wide, one for the stage and one for an audience. Adjoining one of the theatre's long sides are living quarters and changing rooms; here too are stores, wardrobe, laundry, and other basic facilities. The walls opposite to the rear of the stage and the company's quarters are little more than a metre high, leaving an open space up to the roof. At the rear of the stage, away from the audience, are two doorways, one at stage left for entries and the other, at the right, for exits. A third entrance to and from the stage is down-stage right. The audience enters through a gate and across a narrow open space (which was waterlogged on the day I was present, after heavy rains the night before) and then through a single entrance to the theatre itself. The audience sits on the floor to watch a play, but between them and the actors, and centrally placed, is a brass lamp on which, at the sitting audience's eye-level, three flames will be lit at the start of the prolonged rituals which precede performance. Except for musical instruments, there is no further equipment for the stage.

Descriptive texts about Kutiyattam have survived from the twelfth century (in our reckoning) and these give detailed instructions for all that has to be done: acting techniques, procedures for staging and for music and dance, regulation of performances, interpretations of the plays' stories, and more. Also extant and dating from the fourteenth or fifteenth century is a critique of Kutiyattam performances by a Brahmin scholar who believed that an original purity had been lost. In his view, too many characters had been cut from the plays, too many irrelevancies added, and the Vidushaka or fool was being allowed to play too big a part and to use the regional language rather than Sanskrit. Yet the modifications which this purist attacked were to prove their worth and have now become part of current practice. The critic had been unable to disrupt an evolutionary process that adapted performances to current interests and tastes. Today Margi Madhu inherits a tradition which has been developing constantly over the course of some two thousand years.

As usual when travelling to see theatre which is new to me, I took no notes during the performance and had no camera or recording device to take my attention. As far as I could remember when I came to make notes early the next morning, what happened on that November morning was as follows. I sat near the lamp on the floor close to the stage with an interpreter at either side to whisper explanations from time to time. They introduced the drummers and then

Margi Madhu, who was dressed in a white loin cloth with a circle of white cord worn diagonally over one shoulder, the mark of his caste. The actor then showed me how he makes an entrance, through the rear doorway to centre-stage front, his back arched hollow and head erect, feet wide apart and legs bent outward. For a short time he will take in his audience, after which he no longer sees them and ceases to be conscious of them. He acts either to another actor representing another character or, perhaps more often, towards the lamp which represents the god's presence. This means that the elaborate costumes worn by the Kutiyattam actors are designed to be seen only from the front, as it were from a god's-eye viewpoint.

Margi Madhu demonstrated the basic postures for a number of contrasted characters. He also acted the fool, to show his freer behaviour and speech. He demonstrated how an actor playing one character would impersonate other characters when required by the narrative, moving with ease from a god to a servant, from a man to a woman, with no change of costume or make-up. He spoke and chanted from the ancient Sanskrit texts. He gave examples of particular gestures of feet and hands as appropriate for various sensations of anger, lust, pride, fear, suffering, and so forth. Standing on one foot, he could raise the other high to either side, adding a further range of possible gestures to those supplied by arms and hands, backbone and head. Fingers of either hand moved at will to signal

Plate 5.1 Kutiyattam performance; Margi Madhu as Ravana in *Himakaram*
Photograph: Sangeet Natak Akademi, New Delhi, India

particular thoughts or emotions. Eyes, too, have their own vocabulary and my instructors explained that daily exercise develop their ability to open wide and to be controlled precisely as the drama requires. For performance, the whites of the eyes are reddened and their pupils brightened by applying the dried seed of the chunda, a flower which grows locally; this is said to make effects more noticeable as the drama requires.

I was shown how the Kutiyattam actor is like a dancer when impersonating his characters, body as well as voice being responsive to the drama with remarkable refinement and sensitivity. Movement is more within the body than across the stage, the actor often being stationary while assuming postures that would be impossible in life and need perfect balance to execute. The calm attention needed to achieve the extraordinary physical and mental feats required by this art meant that this demonstration, while not a performance, was an entirely serious occasion. A sense of gravity was in everything that was done – a natural gravity, weightless and unconfined – and it began to possess me too. The day was hot and humid, but in this shaded theatre, as the unhurried and complicated demonstration proceeded through a great range of dramatic situations and moods, I began to sense a cool timelessness in this art: a freedom from unwanted tension; complete concentration of mind; no sign of effort despite its great difficulty; an unstated assurance, impossible to achieve without long and specialised training.

For the last item of his demonstration, the actor became Ravana who after a victory in battle decides to abduct Sita, who is the Lord Rama's queen, and finds the path of his chariot blocked by a mountain. His charioteer can do nothing – the actor becomes the charioteer so that the audience sees his confusion and shame – and the frustrated Ravana is now driven by pride, anger, and lust. He becomes so determined that he gets down from his chariot and faces the mountain; and then he bends down to lift it out of the way. He fails; and so he draws back and tries again, every physical strength drawn from his low-bent body. Again he fails and again draws back, as if he can do nothing more. He crouches there for some time and then, slow and watchful, he again gathers strength for a supreme effort, bends still lower and seeks a firmer grip before once more applying all his might. The sinews of his back take the strain, his wide-open eyes seem to glaze over; he is alert and yet totally harnessed to the immense task. He tests his hold, shifts a little, very deliberately, and then extends all his effort. For a long time he stays there trying every means and every possible adjustment; and then slowly defeat begins to show. He sinks down, low to the ground, and stays there as if dead.

I remember thinking I had never seen anyone lie so entirely close to the ground and yet seem to touch it only with his feet. (Is that possible? I do not know, but that is how it seemed.) I also became aware of the drumming more clearly than before, for whereas Ravana was absolutely still, as if not even breathing, the drums were pounding with slow and unbroken force. From them, as if they were part of a hidden reaction and not in conflict with what I was seeing, Ravana gained strength and, slowly and deliberately, began to rise to his feet. For a moment, I became aware that nothing was out of proportion and that it seemed entirely natural for his body to rise from its deeply prostrate position to turn and face the mountain again with a steady gaze.

Slowly, now, Ravana began to look at the mountain in careful detail. He noticed each huge crag, each plateau, gully, and crevice, the trees growing out of fissures in the stone, the streams, trickling at first and then in torrents. His eyes took it all in and then he reached up and touched the topmost peak as if asserting his power over all that he had seen. Then he bent down again, felt for a grip with his hands, and again harnessed all his powers to the task of lifting the mountain. After more time than before, one side seemed to move slightly, but then dropped back. After still greater exertion, it moved again and he tried the other side as well, only to see the first dropping back so that once more it was unmovable. Nothing would move now and Ravana had to fall back, low to the ground and powerless to do more. The drums, however, were beating and lust, anger, and determination all slowly returned. Then everything happened again, each part of the mountain being taken in by his mind and its top once more within his grasp; and this time the second side also moved. But still both did not move together, so that all this gigantic power of mind and body had failed again before the immovable mass.

Yet once more he rose very slowly and turned towards the mountain, but differently this time. Ravana did not look at each part of it in turn, but stared at it until he saw it as a whole, taking it all in as one irreducible fact. I knew he had the entire mountain in view now: he bent down and, not taking his eyes away, summoned all his strength – he had done this before, but now still more firmly, and unhurried – and slowly, at the right hand first and then at the left, the mountain moved and was lifted; and then both sides were raised, just a few inches, and then a little more; and then back a little at one side. Ravana did not once take his eyes off the whole mountain and his body did not give way or buckle as it was slowly raised, higher and higher, until it was level with his chest; and then it passed his eyes and he lost sight of it. But the movement was now unstoppable and Ravana lifted the huge mass high over his head and with a new freedom swung it to the ground at his side. After a pause, he looked ahead towards Sita and slowly his body began to express pride and satisfaction, and he turned towards his chariot, mounted it and was driven away by his awed and silent servant.

That, as far as I can remember, is what happened and by the end of it I was exhausted, because *I* had lifted the mountain. So complete had been the performance, so transparent, and, I must presume, so thoroughly imagined in the actor's head and being, that I had entered into his mind and everything had become as real for me as it was for him. I did not move, but nothing distinguished our perceptions; he did the acting and I, at the same time, imagined it all with him as it happened, as my consciousness, my memories and passions, were involved, all together and in that present moment. It seemed as if it was my body, as well as my mind, that had done this gigantic deed. I cannot account for the phenomenon in any other way: I had lifted the mountain.

While I know very clearly how I felt, I am not sure that I have described accurately all that had happened. I cannot, for example, remember how much was spoken or, indeed, if anything was spoken during the entire episode: it had occurred so spontaneously, without the underlining or obvious preparation for a climax which a director would give to a production. Although no rush or imbalance was apparent in the complicated body-movements and postures, or in the movement of eyes or position of fingers, every detail had seemed fresh as if it were happening for the first time. I would say that it all had been improvised, but there was none of the quick adjustments and uncertainties that are normal in even the best theatrical improvisations. Yet the sensation of immediacy was such that watching the performance was like driving a car and being conscious of movement, the road, and other traffic, but not noticing the landscape or the act of driving. When it was over, I wondered how I had arrived where I had with such little memory of the journey; and, somehow, I had been both driver and car, since it was I who had covered the distance.

When Margi Madhu had stopped acting, he looked unremarkable; and it occurred to me that he might always seem quite ordinary except when acting. Nothing was here of the 'star actor', with that aura of self-importance which marks even the most modest of the great and renowned actors in a rehearsal room in Europe or North America. His voice, which was capable of amazing sounds when acting, in conversation was clear and unforced, but not otherwise distinguished in range or texture. He looked more patient than most actors – or most people I know – but that might have come from the land he lived in rather than as a result of his art. He seemed impersonal, even; almost uninteresting. I wanted to know how this person related to the characters he played. When playing Ravana, he answered, he was not conscious of himself, because he was being Ravana. When playing Krishna, he was conscious only as Krishna. His individual thoughts and feelings did not come into his acting, he said, but then added as an after-thought: 'Of course, the mountain Ravana sees is a mountain that I have seen; only now it is he who sees it.' I had nothing to say to this, but afterwards I wondered who was Sita and who was the Charioteer that I also had seen? And who was the Ravana whom I had become when I lifted the mountain?

* * *

Plate 5.2 Kutiyattam performance; Margi Madhu as Arjuna in *Subhadra Dhananjyan*
Photograph: Sangeet Natak Akademi, New Delhi, India

Amazement at this experience began to be joined by a great curiosity about the complicated art and compelling performance. Unexpectedly I had learned about a part of the spectrum of theatre's possibilities that I had previously not known to exist and, increasingly, I began to think that I had stumbled upon a key that would unlock some secret about Shakespeare's exceptional achievements. So I discovered as much as I could about Kutiyattam while I was in Trivandrum and, later, I read all the books and articles I could find.

The actors, I learned, are always in training, their day starting very early when it is coolest at around five in the morning. Sanskrit texts have to be studied and memorised, a huge task bearing in mind that complete plays can take months to perform. With daily prayers and rituals, the actors' lives are strictly disciplined; once, as a penance, Margi Madhu's father had given a performance that lasted for

Plate 5.3 Ammannur Kochukuttan Chakyar Madhu (Margi Madhu)
Photograph: Sangeet Natak Akademi, New Delhi, India

forty-one consecutive days. The whole company of actors, actresses, musicians, make-up artists, wardrobe attendants, teachers has settled routines for performing and for improving their skills.

Music is principally percussion. Rather than providing a support for the actors to use, by establishing the mood and shape of a scene, fixing and building certain climaxes, or driving home particular words, it more often follows the actors to add to their performance. It supplies an emotional context for the performance, so that it becomes an aural stage-setting; but this is not fixed; it responds to the smallest details of what is done on stage. It can also reflect or counterstate what the actors are expressing. It can distinguish one aspect of the drama from another and enable several to co-exist without confusion. Music is therefore dependent on the actor at all times and not the other way around, as in the operas or stage musicals of European traditions.

Small cymbals are used by an actress, sitting alongside the down-stage right entrance, and serve to mark the phrasing of dramatic action. An Edkka drum is played down-stage left, from where the drummer has the best possible view of the dramatic action. This instrument, shaped like an hourglass, is tuned with one hand and struck with a stick by the other; it has a range of nearly two octaves but the volume it produces is comparatively low. At the back of the stage are two Mizhav drums, big copper pots up to a metre high and two-thirds that in width at the greatest point. Leather is stretched across their narrow mouths on which the seated drummers play with both palms and fingers. One drum is used to keep time, the other for variations. These instruments are too powerful to accompany speech in verse or prose; they mark the entry of characters and the development of the main themes and sensations.

Perhaps the most significant fact about Kutiyattam is that both actors and musicians improvise their complicated and carefully refined art. The total performance is, therefore, both strictly controlled and essentially free. Despite their great length in enactment, the texts of the plays are short, providing only the nub of each situation from which, in movement, gesture, and speech, the actors improvise, re-imagining and elaborating the text. The musicians will then play according to what the actors have improvised, introducing their own contributions within their own set of rules. To give some idea of the degree of elaboration that can be used, D. Appukuttan Nair has written down and translated some of the Abhinaya, or amplifications of the text, which were spoken during a performance. In the text of the *Nagananda*, a prince suggests his state of mind in four lines of verse starting with the words 'Did I not brave moon-lit nights, unbearable for lovers in separation' and, in his elaboration upon it, the actor had said something like:

> Didn't I suffer nights? For separated lovers, grief intensifies at night. Suffering that grief, I managed through the night. This is not an easy task at all. How are nights? – radiant, because of the presence of the moon. How is that? After sunset, the moon rises in the west, spreads its rays everywhere and shines brightly. It looks like this: the fisherman (that is the moon), in order to attract the vanity (that is fish) of women, climbs into a boat (that is the western mountain) and spreads his net (that [is] the rays) in the pond (that is the earth) all over. How is that? The moon-fisherman sees the women happily whiling away time in the company of their husbands. When a damsel looks at her husband, she sees that there is a tinge of collyrium on his cheek. She suddenly gets up, thinking: 'Why is this? He must have kissed another one in her eye, and the collyrium must have spread into his cheek. I will not touch him now', and turns [her] back on him....[2]

Translation into twentieth-century English prose is bound to be awkward but it shows how freely the actor comments and innovates, as he amplifies a single line of his text, improvising variations and exploring one possibility after another. (This example has been cut short; he had much more to say in elaboration of this moment's thought.)

Physically, too, the actor will explore each situation. His art is more individual and independent than that of any actor who is confined by author or choreographer, or by stage-business invented and arranged beforehand. The actor on stage is personally responsible at each performance for realising the play, for extending or curtailing the time taken, for placing and defining climaxes, and for creating a fresh conception of the roles, narrative, and conflicts of the drama. He has practised many traditional means of doing this, so that the progress and embodiment of a briefly scripted play can be entirely unscripted.

According to Dr. K. Ayyappa Paniker: 'The playwright who specifies in advance what the character has to do before or during or after a piece of dialogue or monologue is not the ideal playwright for the Kutiyattam theatre.' A written text usually accounts for no more than a quarter of any performance, the actor supplying the rest: 'by the power of his imagination [he] visualizes, fantasizes, creates scenes or situations'. In this creative act, the audience is able to share: 'The greater the gift of the actor, the greater the pleasure of the spectator. The "togetherness" implied by the word Kutiyattam seems to extend from the actors to the audience as well.'[3]

Because the point of contact between audience and stage is in the minds of actor and audience, no scenic devices are necessary. When Ravana sees a mountain, that mountain is there at the centre of the dramatic experience. When he thinks of Sita, she is present and she could, if he wished to impersonate her, speak and act as well. One curious convention follows from this: when two characters are talking to each other and one of them has little to do but listen, that secondary character walks off stage to return only when there is matter that he or she will contribute. No special timing or method is involved in making such an exit; the actor simply walks off stage while the character he or she represents does not leave the on-stage situation. So long as the central character is aware of the person who is being addressed, that character is present both for the speaker and the audience.

I went back that night to see a performance with two actors and one actress, in full costume and make-up. Said to last for two-and-a-half hours, it so happened that elaboration caused the play to overrun by some thirty minutes. Again I sat just to the left of the lamp as I faced the acting area, with a handful of other people sitting on their own around the audience-space. The play showed Rama with Sita his wife while they were living alone in a forest; his father had recently died and his mother had supported her youngest son so that he now rules the kingdom. Action being limited to meetings and arguments, the chief interest of this particular play is persuasion. A younger brother, after expressing both sorrow and anger, wants to revenge the wrong that has been done; against this, Rama argues that all will work for the best since a ruler needs to spend some time alone and without power, so that he may learn about suffering and his own deepest thoughts. He also rebukes his brother for hating their mother, saying that she must always be honoured as the source of their lives and family bonds.

The nature of Rama's experience was the centre of attention, not the physical realisation of his story. On the level of actuality, there was nothing to see or hear. Rama was not dressed like a hermit with lean face and tangled hair as the narrative requires; his appearance is described in this way before his entrance and then he comes on stage in the full regalia and painted face of an all-powerful king. Similarly the forest itself was nowhere to be seen, only its effect on the minds of the three persons who have taken refuge in it. Stage-attendants brought in or removed a stool, or replenished the lamp, without the least disturbance to the drama. Words were chanted with great variety of pitch and tone, freely extending or contracting vowel-sounds and giving a steady ongoing beat when the large drums were silent. The expressive signs made by hands, feet, and eyes were as complicated and unlifelike as those of Margi Madhu in the morning's demonstration

To my ears and eyes this performance was far less accessible. Make-up and costume were unfamiliar and did nothing to increase my awareness of the performance. While emphasising eyes and mouth, the bold lines and vibrant colours of the make-up hid all other facial expression of the workings of the mind. The costume hid the actor's body in the same way, although the morning's uncostumed demonstration had shown that in this kind of performance the slightest movements and tensions could give immediately accessible expression to the character's involvement in the drama. Like the face-painting, the elaborate clothes emphasised the most expressive elements – the hands and feet – so that all other, less artificial effects were lost to view. On this night, a power failure cut off the electric lights with which the theatre had been fitted, so that the stage was lit only by the lamp at audience eye-level; the costumes being wide-skirted, this meant that the actors seemed to float in the darkness, their feet visible only when moving into the light as they were lifted for some expressive gesture. This unplanned return to earlier conditions of performance still further obscured the actors' bodies and removed the play from any sense of 'real' existence, evoking a dream-like state of being in some limitless world.

Whereas in the morning, I was affected directly by the actor's performance, here too much was new and too much hidden for that to be repeated. A sense of alienation was my strongest reaction. These plays when fully staged make no attempt to be accessible, even while enormous, life-involving pains are needed to present them. I was embarrassed that I had not experienced the play more fully and said afterwards how sorry I was that more people had not seen the performance; to that the reply was that the players should be the ones who were apologising. The ideal audience for their plays is one person sitting close to the left-hand side of the lamp; anyone else present will be a potential distraction from the intent and sensitive attention that these performances require and can satisfy. It then dawned on me that this play had been given entirely for my sake, so that I should have the opportunity to enter fully into its creation. Such magnanimity seemed to be taken for granted, as the proper procedure for the guardians of this art.

Because Margi Madhu, without ornate costume and make-up, had been alone and simply dressed with the least possible encumbrance, the morning's experience of Ravanna affected me more deeply than the evening's more complete performance and it has now become an irremovable part of my memory. Here follow some notes from my journal written over the next two weeks while I was still in India. I have not altered what I wrote then in the hope that a shifting perspective may show how my understanding slowly developed.

What parallels are there for this art? A high-wire acrobat? But difficulty and danger provide the thrills of that performance; no story is being told in time and place, with consequences and changing demands. Perhaps the Kutiyattam actor is more like a great writer, a Shakespeare: one who enters into each and every part of a fictive world, moving from one character to another with total commitment and giving no sign that he has lacked resource or lost a sense of the whole. This actor finds what may be called his 'words', both simple and unlikely, from out of his memory, and speaks them while improvising each moment of consciousness for a fictional person. The main difference is that Margi Madhu works with his actual and complete self as material, not only with words. His total act, involving mind and body, is as pure and necessary, as simple and sensuous, as a great poet's words.

This actor seems to possess nothing, for he leaves no permanent artefact or sign behind; always what he creates will melt or resolve itself into an unassuming man, waiting and ready, and seemingly without any personal needs. His art is essentially improvisational and, at the same time, carefully trained in specific skills and comprehensively knowledgeable about how to respond to demands made on it. Any challenge can be met in myriads of ways, transforming the given and expected into an unprecedented gift for the audience. Tomorrow's performance will be very like today's, calling on all the capabilities that have been accumulated in a lifetime and using them in ways that can never be predicated.

The complexity of this art is one of being, not only of saying and doing. What is done on stage is, as it were, transparent, because an audience sees through it into the actor's imaginative engagement in the drama. So it comes to share with him the character's experience and seems to take over the drama from him at each moment of creation. This transference is more than empathy: both audience and actor lose the sense of self; both, simultaneously, become the character as he or she is created in both imaginations. The audience, unused to the experience, finds itself exhausted when the performance is over.

The imaginative experience of Kutiyattam is both intimate and instinctive, distinctive and yet boundless, shared and yet separately individual, as if audience and performer were natural twins. Yet, of course, the audience is dependent on the actor: only by responding to the work of his imagination does its imagination take fire and enter into the character and the drama.

Performance is never fixed but always immanent, ready to be freshly created. It is open, so that it may be entered, enjoyed, endured, enlarged, illuminated, or ignored by its audience. Any response is possible, except an attempt to possess or define what happens. Neither performer nor audience owns anything of what happens, beyond the fact that the actor has the long-nurtured abilities which are put to use in the mutual and forever-changing enactment of the characters of the drama.

This theatre offers a drama that is experienced as if real but is, in fact, intangible. In this, it is like a contemplative or mystical religion, but it does not predicate a supernatural existence or the presence of god within the actor. Its material is entirely natural to a human being, so that performance is available to anyone who is willing to attend to its imagined fictions. This sharing of imaginative consciousness is not the 'indwelling' of a 'holy spirit' or possession by some 'other'; it is more like an intimate experience between two unself-regarding friends or lovers.

Part of the effect is due to the strangeness of what Madhu does. We, his audience, could not, mentally or physically, perform as he does. Is he like a great writer who summons up words which lie outside our reach and uses them in ways that make original music and awaken unfamiliar sensations and thoughts? This parallel may be closer than it seems at first because, as a writer's words are drawn from the same stock that we unremarkably use every day of our lives, so Madhu's actions use the same basic elements as we do: spine, limbs, nerves, muscles, blood, heart-beat, and breathing; and, also, the same wear and tear of achievement and disappointment, the same experience of growth and loss. Because these are his means, his performance, that is impossible for the untrained to imitate, is also wholly accessible to anyone who pays close and unpossessive attention.

* * *

While this archaic, unscripted, complicated, and elitist theatre is obviously far removed from Shakespeare's plays and the theatre for which they were written, an experience of Kutiyattam has changed the position from which I now view Shakespeare. I did not think so at first, but over the course of some months, after I had returned home, I began to realise that this had happened.

The freedom for the actor to be what he chooses to be and for the audience to follow him into amazing deeds and states of mind and being began to challenge earlier ideas about Shakespeare's stagecraft and the almost unchanging background of the Shakespearian theatre. In the intense focus of the Kutiyattam theatre, nothing external is needed to change from one character to another or move from one place to another wherever the drama is happening. A person who is being addressed need not be on stage. Everything is created by the imagination of the actor and formed in his consciousness and his being. In response, the audience not merely sees and hears what is happening on stage, but in its imagination moves through that into an individual experience of the play at the same time as it is being created in the mind of the actor, as if both his and their perception of the dramatic reality were one and inseparable. By doing this, the audience does not merely echo or repeat, but re-imagines the dramatic event in terms of its own individual memories and sensations, so that it seems to have achieved the experience on its own account. The actor, betraying nothing of himself, has become transparent and the play is no longer an object to look at and listen to. The question which this began to raise with regard to Shakespeare's plays is whether they allow for such interpenetration of viewer and performer.

Clearly they do not rely upon it as Kutiyattam does, because what happens on stage is changing constantly and no time is given to build up such a deep and sustained reaction. The crowded stage and pageantry, changes of costume and physical appearances, direct confrontations between a great variety of characters, and all the outward shows of the drama required by the playtext demand a lot of attention. Besides, performance imitates ordinary processes of living as if they were happening on the stage: in Shakespeare, and not in Kutiyattam, a mother may wipe the face of her son who has become 'scant of breath' and an actor's 'visage' can become 'wanned' with his 'whole function suiting / With forms to his conceit' (*Hamlet*, V.ii.286, 279; II.ii.546–50). Nevertheless, I would argue, all these important aspects of Shakespeare's stagecraft do not imply that the audience can *never* enter the mind of a character as in Kutiyattam, so that they think and feel as one. Since this is part of the spectrum of possible theatre experience, it might be called upon, instinctively, by any dramatist on some occasions

The final scenes of Shakespeare's tragedies and histories, while busy with new incidents and driven by the force of strong passions, are sometimes so very simple, verbally and visually, that they might give scope for such an exceptional transfer of consciousness. In the imagination, at these times if not at others, an audience could have direct experience of what is happening within the mind and being of a character.

Juliet's death is not to be summed up in the few rhymed and riddling lines of her last speech or in what she does in order to kill herself. At this point Shakespeare has used the simplest dramatic means – even crude ones when compared with the splendour and sensitivity of much of the dialogue elsewhere in the play – so that the inner-consciousness of the actor-as-Juliet, having reacted to all that has been said and done before this moment in this particular performance, will be something far more complicated and less describable. The dramatic reality of the play – whatever it is that holds the audience's attention – has been given life by the actor's imagination and has taken over the very being of the actor. So it is what happens in the play that outreaches the words that are said or the particular actions that are done and, at this point, the experience of Kutiyattam suggested to me, an attentive member of an audience might lose any sense of the actor and might, in the imagination, become Juliet, according to his or her own life-experiences and sensuous capabilities. The play does not depend upon this transference, as Kutiyattam does, but the comparatively simple nature of the text at this moment might make it possible.

So it is, to a greater or lesser extent, with later tragedies, which all end with some simplification of expressive means: Hamlet and Cleopatra stop in the middle of sentences; Othello reaches across to kiss the dead Desdemona after all words have been spoken; Coriolanus is silent as he '*falls*'. In each case, the dramatic reality that holds the audience's attention cannot depend on the text alone and will require further substantiation by the actor, his imaginative creativity and the audience's ability to share in that creativity.

If this hypothesis is correct, an audience has been given a task with important repercussions on its reception of the entire play. The culminating moment of Macbeth, for example, is not simply a fight that fills a spectator with horror and terror but, rather, the predicament of the character as imagined by the actor who has created the whole role and now lays it open, as it were, for the audience to make its own in varying and individually necessary ways. At this point, after Macbeth's last words have been spoken, held tight in a couplet, and just before the conclusion of the fight with Macduff or during a stand-off in the middle of it, the dramatic focus narrows inescapably on to the protagonist and Shakespeare intrudes no more words. Now an audience-member could enter into an imaginative involvement with the character and find little impediment or competition. On the other hand, the audience could switch off attention from the hero and follow only his adversary. Unless it is to be merely bloody and brutal, as Macbeth's final words would encourage it to be, on such an intangible and uncertain effect the conclusion of the tragedy will depend. It seems to me, now, that the audience is given a choice, either to become at one with Macbeth or to see him, as Malcolm subsequently does, as a 'butcher' fit for death (V.viii.69). Still later, it will have to make what it can of 'th' usurper's cursèd head' (V.viii.55), held high above the army.

This tactic of moving beyond expressive words is illustrated at the end of *King*

Lear over a longer period of time. After Lear has asked for a button to be undone, there is only:

> Thank you, sir.
> Do you see this? Look on her. Look, her lips.
> Look there, look there!
>
> (V.iii.309–11)

The Quarto text of 1608 has still less dialogue: after 'thanke you sir,' giving only 'O, o, o, o'. Neither version of the text has much that can define the king's last moments and the nature of his thoughts, little with which the actor can express or represent the character's involvement in the drama. Both texts do, however, invite an open and actively imaginative performance at this all-important moment so that, after all the words have been spoken and all actions played, the actor might become transparent and allow the audience to enter fully into the mind of King Lear and, in collusion with the actor's imagination, create the character's experience for themselves. The text does not say whether he is mad, grieved, relieved, resigned, hopeful or, at last, satisfied: in the last resort, members of the audience find what is fitting for themselves.

The speeches of other characters on stage at the end of *King Lear* mark a shift of dramatic attention to the inexpressible and imaginative. They try to speak with the dying king but then draw back:

> EDGAR: He faints. My lord, my lord!
> KENT: Break heart; I prithee break.
> EDGAR: Look up, my lord.
> KENT: Vex not his ghost. O, let him pass!
>
> (V.iii.311–13)

The play's final words refer to what has been felt like a physical pressure exerted on those who have only stood by. They imply that this audience on stage has shared imaginatively in Lear's predicament and have now emerged from an unprecedented experience:

> The weight of this sad time we must obey;
> Speak what we feel, not what we ought to say.
> The oldest hath borne most; we that are young
> Shall never see so much nor live so long.
>
> (V.iii.323–6)

After this, the characters and the actors must make their way off stage as best they can. The Folio text may represent theatre practice in adding: '*Exeunt with dead march*'; the Quarto has, more simply, '*FINIS*'. What Shakespeare expected or wanted to happen is therefore unclear, except that he has provided no Fortinbras or Horatio, no Cassio or Lodovico, no Malcolm or Macduff, no Octavius Caesar, to make a verbal judgement on what the audience has witnessed and may imaginatively have undergone at the end of the tragedy.

The comedies, of course, lack such final intensities, but here too, from time to time, the leading characters may stand still and silent so that, at these moments, the audience might enter their very minds. When interplay moves beyond wit and comic confusions, and the characters have no immediate intention or activity, the play might be apprehended, almost timelessly, at the centre of a particular character's consciousness and being. These moments are scattered throughout the later parts of the comedies. In *As You Like It*, Rosalind's disguised encounter with Orlando in the Forest of Arden can come to this brink several times if she pauses and allows pretence to fall away. Later, when Phebe commands Silvius to tell Rosalind 'what 'tis to love', Orlando's vows and Rosalind's admissions of her own experience are so simple and become increasingly so expected that the audience can travel with the two lovers or, indeed, ahead of them, until Orlando's final assertion that his love is not present brings all to a halt: a pause here can hold for a long time in performance, and during it the audience could be active in imaginative identification with either of the lovers or, possibly, with both. The significance of the moment is emphasised by Rosalind's change of tone and tactic that follows: 'Pray you, no more of this; 'tis like the howling of Irish wolves against the moon' (V.i.76–103).

In the last scene of *Twelfth Night*, amazement repeatedly brings a silence, as marked by Olivia's simple and isolated half-line, 'Most wonderful!', or by the pause before or after Sebastian's incomplete verse-line:

> VIOLA: My father had a mole upon his brow.
> SEBASTIAN: And so had mine.
>
> (V.i. 217, 234–5)

In a pause before or after his 'I'll be reveng'd on the whole pack of you' (ll. 364–5), Malvolio needs to leave the stage abruptly and the audience may go with him in imagination. If everyone else is silent for a moment, that would suit such a moment.

I used to think that all these 'simple' moments were occasions when Shakespeare had left the play to the actors who would find what they had to do in response to each performance and audience. I think now that they are occasions when an audience is invited to enter into the play and recreate it afresh in its own terms. From the actor, some astonishing way of expressing the character's reactions and clinching a performance is not required; they would intrude on the working of the audience's imagination. What the actor must do is to rely on his or her imagination to become the character and *do* very little more. In this way the character remains open for individual members of the audience to make an answering engagement for themselves.

A critic who does not recognise the potential of these outwardly very simple and often silent moments will have undervalued one of the plays' most distinctive features. The task is to recognise how they may work upon an audience: someone who has sat down in front of a single actor speaking in an unknown language and avoiding any imitation of real life and, under those conditions, has lifted a mountain, is bound to wonder whether these moments might not have a more transforming effect on the audience and its reception of a play than is marked by the words set down to be spoken. Everything that is actually on stage might go out of focus, as if in abeyance, while an individual observer, in his or her own imagination, becomes an active participator in the drama; even the actors might seem to disappear.

Of Kutiyattam, Dr Paniker writes:

> From the point of view of what the performance communicates, Kutiyattam may be thought of as the theatre of imagined reality....The actor, with the active support of the drummer, has to rouse the imagination of the spectator so that the latter can catch up with the flights of imagination of the former while presenting detail after detail of a specific passage.[4]

* * *

If we believe that this transference from the enacted drama to the audience's imagination could happen at moments of silence or textual simplicity, might it not occur at other places in Shakespeare's plays? Seldom, must surely be the answer. When his characters speak about the effect of performance, they assume otherwise: actors are 'brief chronicles' to whom the audience should pay attention; they hold a mirror 'up to nature' in which some image is to be seen (*Hamlet*, II.ii.519; III.ii.23–4). The audience's imagination has to 'amend' what is offered, not become at one with the performers' imaginations (*Midsummer Night's Dream*, V.i.210–15); its thoughts have to 'deck' the kings on stage, not identify with them (*Henry the Fifth*, Prol., 28). We may 'wonder' at the strange events that are enacted, but are not invited to make them our own (*Dream*, V.i.126–7). The whole contrivance of a play is like a dream that happens as the audience 'slumbers', not one in which they consciously participate (see *Dream*, V.i.412–18).

Nevertheless, the potential for total transference must remain: it is part of the spectrum of possibilities in an audience's response and, in other theatres, whole plays have been designed for its evocation. If it is possible when a drama draws to its close and becomes almost silent and still, perhaps it is also possible when a single character holds the stage in soliloquy or extended speech. When their words do more than pursue an argument or make a statement, or give a mental picture – the art of verbal scene-painting – but seem, rather, to transport the speaker in imagination to an off-stage reality, some members of the audience might find themselves following on their own accounts. Gertrude's account of Ophelia's death gives precise details in such a way that she seems imbued with the very movement and sound of what she saw. Macbeth seems to be actually lost in the dark, dreamlike menace of the world he depicts, and to be pursued by its phantoms. Prospero seems to be present in the gentle pastoral idyll that he evokes as he prepares to abjure his art. The more the actor draws upon his or her own active imagination at these moments, transporting the character into the other world, the more likely it will be that an audience is drawn into that other and intangible reality. This would not be achieved easily: the actor must give no sign of difficulty or provide striking actions or ways of speaking to make a particular effect. Here the imagination must be trusted and the actor be prepared to 'disappear'.

I am the more persuaded that Shakespeare sometimes sought such an effect when I find he might have used it with considerable variety of effect. The First Murderer in *Macbeth*, in tense preparation for an ambush, starts to speak his mind with a piece of 'scene-painting' which is interestingly delicate but, as a shift of consciousness, not very remarkable. Only then does he invoke the image of safety and comfort:

> The west yet glimmers with some streaks of day;
> Now spurs the lated traveller apace
> To gain the timely inn, ...
>
> (III.iii.5–7)

Description of the time and place has given way to another imagined reality. At such times, Shakespeare asks the actor for such a leap forward in imagination that the audience will almost certainly be outpaced and left behind. Examples of this are most challenging when they break through ordinary speech, as in Romeo's 'O, I am fortune's fool' (III.i.133), Othello's 'Goats and monkeys!' (IV.i.260), or Macbeth's 'She should have died hereafter' (V.v.17). Such shifts of imagination are so great and so tightly expressed that shock can prevent an audience from following at first, but they are sometimes followed by a silent exit or some very simple words, such as Macbeth's 'Tomorrow, and tomorrow, and tomorrow' (V.v.19), during which an audience might be able to catch up and begin to create the moment with the actor.

If active interplay in imagination between actor-as-character and audience-as-character is possible and can be provoked at any time in a play, the consequences would be far-reaching. Response to the rest of a performance would lack the same immediacy and personal commitment. Repeatedly the audience would lose the closer identification because so much else is present on stage, clamouring for attention and raising issues or expectations with obvious significance for a play's narrative and thematic development: the play might therefore be more difficult to comprehend as a whole and any sense of closure at its conclusion could be weakened. Theatre would become an art that beckons as well as it attempts to fulfil, offering far more than might be expected and yet leaving its audience with a sense of loss. So the play would seem to remain forever out of reach – and having written that, I realise that I have restated what I have instinctively held to be an important characteristic of Shakespeare's art. While this notion had previously seemed strange and somewhat absurd, it now presents itself as a reasonable explanation of other features of the writing and points the way towards better ways of staging the plays.

6

IMPROVISATION
Freedom and collusion

The improvisational mode of all aspects of Kutiyattam performance seemed to be an important factor in its ability to rouse the audience's imaginative activity: both actor and audience experience the play with something of the same uncertainty about what will happen next so that both make fresh discovery of it in the same instant. Could such mutual spontaneity be appropriate for plays with dialogue as complex and as subtle as Shakespeare's? Innovative and traditional imagery, sensitive and energetic syntax, new-minted words, varied allusions, and metre make so many demands upon an actor that sudden inspiration could hardly be sufficient stimulus for more than brief moments. Besides, so much happens on stage that an audience can only occasionally concentrate on the imaginative centre of an actor's performance which is where all those words must find their dramatic validity.

Nevertheless, Shakespeare's dialogue often implies that, for the speaker, new thoughts come unsummoned out of those that have just been spoken and that the task of reflecting this in performance would benefit from some element of improvisation. Examples are found in every play, for this is a hallmark of Shakespeare's writing at every stage of his career. All the speeches that have become famous out of context give an impression of spontaneity to greater or lesser extent:

> Come, night; come, Romeo; come, thou day in night;
> For thou wilt lie upon the wings of night
> Whiter than new snow on a raven's back.
> Come, gentle night; come, loving black-brow'd night,
> Give me my Romeo; and, when he shall die,
> Take him and cut him out in little stars,
> (*Romeo and Juliet*, III.ii.1–31)

Underneath the speaker's momentary commitment to each word, a further and deeper level of consciousness seems to supply an ongoing impetus for speech, the need to say something more.

Sometimes an abrupt change of attention indicates that the speaker's confidence in what has been said has broken down and another line of thought and feeling takes over as it rises from the unconscious to conscious mind. Hamlet's soliloquies are obvious examples, as in:

> Whether 'tis nobler in the mind to suffer
> The slings and arrows of outrageous fortune,
> Or to take arms against a sea of troubles,
> And by opposing end them? – To die, to sleep:
> No more; – and by a sleep to say we end
> The heart-ache and the thousand natural shocks
> That flesh is heir to. 'Tis a consummation
> Devoutly to be wish'd. – To die, to sleep;
> To sleep, perchance to dream. – Ay, there's the rub;
> For in that sleep of death what dreams may come, . . .
>
> (*Hamlet*, III.i.56–88)

Punctuation can suggest different units of thought in this speech, but not its varying speed, direction, and impetus. Modern editors differ widely on how to represent the original texts for readers or actors.

In exchanges between characters, two or more speakers must listen closely to each other's timing, phrasing, and colouring so that each reply sounds like a response to the momentary impression. Viola, talking to Orsino when pretending to be Cesario, exemplifies what she says later about a fool's need to play close attention:

> He must observe their mood on whom he jests,
> The quality of persons, and the time;
> And, like the haggard, check at every feather
> That comes before his eye. This is a practice
> As full of labour as a wise man's art;
>
> (*Twelfth Night*, III.i.59–63)

Viola also listens to her master as a hawk watches and responds to its prey. Simple replies, such as 'Say I do speak with her, my lord, what then?' or 'I think not so, my lord' (I.iv.22 and 28), must be nicely judged for each performance if they are not to give offence and yet have sufficient force to cause Orsino to veer away from his line of thought and take another tack.

Such impressions of improvised speech fall short of an insistence upon improvisation in performance. The reverse could be true: the more vivid and subtle the dialogue, the more an actor will want to be sure how to control it. While every

92

performance will have some element of improvisation, our actors like to 'make choices' before playing for an audience. This phrase, common in training manuals,[1] reflects an awareness of the many interpretations and re-tunings that a text can be given and a desire to simplify the moment of speech. Lengthy rehearsals are used to base a performance securely and strongly in a predetermined 'through-line' of interpretation, so that what an audience usually witnesses has already been tested and chosen, and more or less fixed. Such performances cannot give the same experience as being present at the creation of a drama that has never happened before, in which all participants – actors and audience – have a share in defining each moment of enactment. One of the major changes in theatre during the twentieth century in Europe and North America is the gradual increase in the length of rehearsals for Shakespeare's plays. In the 1930s, two or three weeks were given to each production at Stratford-upon-Avon, whereas today rehearsals may stretch over as many as eight.

Modern scholarship has compounded the actors' desire for preparation and pre-emptive decisions. As more is known about the subtleties and ambiguities of Shakespeare's texts, their possible reflections of everyday life in his times, and their relevance in our own, so actors will be more anxious to make a choice for each particular phrase ahead of performance, and to stick to that. They know that if they emphasise *this*, then *that* will be lost. If they take time to ensure that a particular point registers, they accept that this will modify the rhythms and thrust of a whole speech and, perhaps, the effect of an entire performance. Directors work with the actors to sift through the niceties of the text and then to decide what 'choices' are made and, consequently, how a whole scene will be shaped. By the time a production is ready for a first night, it will be held together by myriads of such choices and its actors will have come to depend on this mutual pre-arrangement in order to be confident in what they are doing and know how their performances fit together with the rest of the production. In this way, actors can be more powerful on stage and dare to be more subtle and original in their interpretations. A greater understanding of the texts has helped to turn Shakespeare's plays into carefully arranged and meaningful spectacles with opportunities for high-definition performance. A jolt is needed, like that of seeing a very different kind of theatre, to make us ask whether these procedures are not against the grain of the texts and fail to provide the performances that would best suit them.

When they were written, Shakespeare's plays would have been performed in a large repertory and seldom would one play have been repeated within a week or longer. Rehearsals of each script were few and short; stage management simple and barely adequate by modern standards. A play had to take the fortunes of each performance and so had its 'interpretation' (as we would say, but the phrase was then unknown in the theatre). By twentieth-century standards, the whole procedure seems fraught with risk and imprecision, so that we are amazed that everyone seems to have been content with the result. What a performance of Kutiyattam shows, in relation to this, is that a complicated and thoroughly demanding style of performance is no bar to improvisation: we need not presume that the procedures of Shakespeare's day were inimical to refinement or a profoundly considered performance.

In my first encounter with Kutiyattam I had sensed that everything in its elaborate contrivance was being created freely, then and there, and unpredictably. In these performances, actors accept the chances and changes of imaginative recreation; supporting music is improvised according to the actors' improvisations; even the ancient text in an otherwise dead language is recreated by an actor's instantaneous invention. Of course, many methods and set responses are ingredients of this improvised drama but, essentially, no foreknowledge can be invoked for its moment-by-moment enactment. Behind whatever outward show and whatever words are chosen is that further reach where the actors' imaginative exploration of the drama is in absolute command and open for an audience to share and recreate in its turn. Perhaps twenty or more highly individual actors in Shakespeare's theatre performed his complicated texts as if for the first time with comparable assurance. That seems improbable, but on reflection it is not such a foolish idea. The idea that one might feel at home in the highly contrived, improvised, and alien world of Kutiyattam had seemed in prospect just as unlikely and yet, in the event, that was the impression I received. I thought I could lift a mountain only after I had, so unpreparedly, done so; before that, I would have dismissed the notion as ridiculous.

* * *

At the centre of any actor's performance is a consciousness in which many strands of thought and feeling can come together, at least on occasion, with assurance, strength, and apparent simplicity. When that happens, what is done needs no argument in support and is met with an audience's instant recognition. Unfortunately, this experience is rarely offered to an audience in modern theatres within European traditions. It is experienced more often in rehearsals than in finished productions; then the actor is exploring a role and has little thought about a 'final' performance; he or she does not seek an assured effectiveness. What happens then is a matter of improvisation and collusion, not settled or predetermined but, on occasion, confident in the very moment of creation. It can live for a time on an unstoppable wave-crest of imagination that carries everything forwards. Verbal definition and suggestion, syntax and structure, imagery, metaphor, rhythm, aural texture, and the dynamics and music of speech – all these details seem as simple then, as they are necessary and cohesive. At such times, in rehearsal, the entire being of the actor, physical and mental, conscious and unconscious, can be involved and unassertively dominant: the setting and other physical circumstances of the play may then be evoked by the simplest of means as it is happening.

If performance of Shakespeare's plays could be like such a rehearsal, it would be a creative act similar to that of the dramatic poet in the act of writing and one which an audience could witness and to some extent share. Whether this mutual creativity could be sustained throughout a whole play there is no means of knowing, but for many moments its aptness and possibility can hardly be questioned.

Experiments with skilled and experienced actors could test the practicality of this kind of performance before an audience. Actors would be dressed in clothes that demonstrate status and relationships. No scenery would be used and only the fewest properties and those as unspecific as possible: some objects to sit or stand on, one rather larger than the others to serve as table, bed, or tomb, or to provide a higher level for more than one actor at a time. The larger scenes would be simply staged, relying a great deal on formal arrangements and regular cere-monies. The audience should be comparatively small, so that each member is close to the actors on an open stage, and it should be lit as the stage and actors are lit, not too brilliantly and changing only rarely when needed by practicalities of the action. The actors should be fully prepared in that they have completely mastered the technical demands of comprehending and speaking the text, but they should also be free to vary how they speak and what they do, according to how the play is coming to life and the audience responding. They should have considered various interpretations of their roles, however different from each other and contradictory in effect, and then activate whichever seems most appro-priate in interplay on the occasion of each performance. Perhaps they should also be free to repeat any lines or, even, alter what has been set down for them to speak, always subject to the cohesion of the whole performance and the actors' involvement with it at the fullest reach of his or her imagination.[2] A great many of the marvellous and affective possibilities of modern theatre productions would be lost in such performances, but they might take actors and audiences beyond their obvious and outward signs into fresh imaginative engagement with the plays.

European theatre has not always been governed by the need to develop strong and sustainable productions. Nor has the present system always been defended. Back in 1922, Harley Granville Barker, actor, dramatist, and director, argued against carefully contrived and long-running productions:

a slight objection to the whole glorious business (and the dramatist should have been the first to note this) is that it tends utterly to destroy the art of acting. This cannot prosper under such conditions of employ-ment. It may profit a little by failure, but what it cannot endure is the numbing monotony of success. So acting's place is taken by the artifice of stage effect, a mechanism guaranteed fool-proof, which makes, therefore, for the encouragement of fools both among the actors and in the audience. It may really be asserted that most young playgoers of to-day do not know what acting is.

Well-prepared and frequently repeated performances, he went on to say, are related to good acting as a reproduction is to a Rembrandt.[3]

Present-day actors can often sense what is missing in well-organised productions, although few can do much to change the conditions under which they perform. Some limited adjustments can be managed, as Judi Dench explained with regard to Peter Hall's production of *Antony and Cleopatra* at the National Theatre in London in 1987:

> Tony Hopkins [Antony] and I had established that we both like to change things, so that we would never be quite sure where the other was going to come on from. Peter Hall agreed that if we wanted we could have that freedom for the two of us. We moved the scenes in Cleopatra's court on the round stage of the Olivier [Theatre] in big circles; Peter said they should be like fish in a tank: 'Where one goes, they all go, and if it changes direction they follow.'[4]

So two actors ensured, on one occasion, that they regained a degree of freedom to improvise nightly.

One might argue that readers can respond better than actors to Shakespeare's texts because their minds are free to react to momentary suggestion. But a printed playtext does not supply enough information to ensure that a play is experienced as an imaginary performance. A reader lacks the stimulus of tangible, individual, real-life performers on a solid stage in relationship with each other as the text is enacted in real time and in conjunction with a particular audience. These are essential elements of a play which a reader must do whatever is possible to supply and then be led willingly wherever imaginary performance suggests. A patient reading of a text with a great deal of speculation about opposing and interlocked interpretations of words and actions, all of which takes its own time and raises a series of distinct visual images, is not an adequate basis for trying to discover what a playtext can achieve or the relevance of any one of its phrases.

* * *

The improvised relationship that must always exist between actors and audience is a crucial element in any performance and the most difficult of all to understand or for a reader to appreciate. A Kutiyattam actor ignores any audience other than the presence of a god; once he has made his entry he sees and hears nothing other than the drama. But that is not suitable for the public and secular art of Shakespeare's theatre. Its stage was open on three sides and its audience free to do as it liked. Actors could not ignore the spectators but needed to tame or lead them as seemed suitable for each developing performance. This audience was never the same from day to day and so an improvised reaction to its response was obligatory.

When considering Jatra theatre in Chapter 1, we saw how its audience would call out in support of the actors on the open stage, giving praise or advice, and even presenting gifts; the actors responded as members of a team to its fans or as heroes to the populace. In Asia, where audiences are not placed in artificial darkness, such interaction is not at all rare. Even in Kabuki, with its highly developed and unlifelike conventions, the star actors are greeted by name as they make their entrance in character along the hanamichi bridge from the back of the auditorium to the stage, and again when they achieve a particularly demanding feat or make a spectacular exit. In small-scale street theatres in Europe and North America, and, indeed, all round the world, audience contact with the actors is a matter of course and similarly direct and unpredictable, but what is unusual in Asia and other countries that have resisted European influences is the occurrence of the same phenomenon in their largest theatres and for extended dramas and elaborate productions. Many performances thrive according to how fully the audience participates vocally in the stage action.

Actors of Marathi theatres in and around Bombay have a strong tradition of playing directly to their audiences, even when the various characters of a play are engaged in talk with each other. They know very well how to provoke and use an audience's response. I saw the first performance of *Char Divas Premache* (*Four Days of Love*) in a crowded Bombay theatre at eleven o'clock on a Sunday morning. Four actors, two female and two male, performed a series of small plays so that they had to change rapidly from one character to another. The men were rather fat and middle aged, but adept comic performers. One of the women played all the more glamorous parts, the other a very wide range of 'characters'. No one story-line held throughout the two halves of the production, but the general theme announced in the show's title connected all the episodes, as they dealt successively with courtship, married life, inter-generation difficulties, clashes of business and family interests, and wheeling and dealing at an international conference on industrial development (which was cross-cut with a bedroom drama in which the woman was the active and aggressive partner). A final scene had a religious theme, a blind woman, and some wailful singing to a harmonium. After this, a brisk song-and-dance concluded the entertainment.

Although this 'proscenium' or picture-frame theatre sat considerably more than a thousand spectators, everyone seemed to feel included in what was happening on stage and free to respond as they wished. A good line of dialogue or a neat piece of action would at first get laughter and then applause, and sometimes both together. The actors knew how to build on this and it seemed to me – I did not know the language – that they would repeat a line several times to get still more signs of approval: certainly they did this with various pieces of stage-business which I understood very well, such as encountering physical difficulties or making mistakes, or registering double-takes and other signs of surprise. They were, frankly, pumping up the response, but they were also developing a number of bold and open performances with which the audience could go along and feel as if it were in charge of what was happening. The play was not particularly remarkable, but the audience was hugely satisfied and expressed approval openly.

Anything more different from watching a film is hard to imagine, and this may well be the reason why Marathi theatre is booming in a town where the highly productive Indian film industry is also thriving. The production I saw was enjoyed by all sorts of people, men and women, old and young, teenagers and children; and there was not an empty seat in the house. With the exception of the representatives of big business in the conference scene, the characters in the play were dressed as the audience was, only rather more smartly, and all were part of the same sort of society, only caught up in far more dramatic or comical events. The actors, with whom the audience had almost continuous contact, were not so very different either. This theatre in very many ways reflected and belonged to its audience.

As soon as the first performance was over, the production was going to travel some twenty-five kilometres for a performance at four-fifteen that same afternoon to an audience in the outskirts of Bombay. It was expected to have some two thousand performances before being withdrawn; it would be talked about and, perhaps, revisited. Another play, with the English title *Take it Easy*, was the current hit in Bombay, being played in two theatres by two companies simultaneously, and both clocking up hundreds of performances. Marathi theatre has the air of being at ease and accepted, of flourishing with and for its audience.

Aesthetically or intellectually, such productions are not demanding but, even for a visitor like me, their spirit of cooperation and pleasure-giving is infectious as it is shared between actors and audience. This experience remained in my mind and, when I next read a Shakespeare play, I found that its text asked to be played differently than I had previously imagined. One after another, short speeches *could* be said to the audience and, at times, *for* the audience. Some seemed to invite response from an audience, or its judgement about what was happening on stage. Most soliloquies and those speeches marked by modern editors with '*Aside*' can obviously be spoken like this, but now I imagined many more lines and parts of lines being acted so that they asked for the audience's attention and involvement. Through long exposure to plays written or edited in the twentieth and late nineteenth centuries, we have come to expect dialogue with regular interchange of speeches between the characters: now, I saw, that need not be. Plays can be written so that both actors and characters use the text to develop an active relationship with their audience as well.

For Shakespeare's clowns, an openness to their audiences has long been recognised as a staple of their style, a kind of performance that was inherited from more 'popular' entertainments. Now I thought I could recognise further speeches that should be spoken to audiences that were written for characters who are not usually considered to be clowns, or only partially so – in much that is said by Richard the Third, Shylock, the Nurse in *Romeo and Juliet*, Polonius, Hotspur, Falstaff, and more. Even lines for characters who are in no sense comic seemed now to have been written for speaking to an audience in much the same way. When Henry the Fourth addresses his court he could also include the theatre audience amongst his hearers. Even in private, when talking earnestly with his son, the actor-as-Henry could address many of his words to the audience, and try to sway its members to his side. Eventually, he could invite them to share his new-found confidence: 'A hundred thousand rebels die in this' (*I, Henry IV*, III.ii.160) – no personal pronoun is here to insist that this line has to be addressed to Prince Hal.

Shakespeare's handling of leading characters frequently gives scope for such a direct appeal. To whom, for example, does Macbeth address his first words, 'So foul and fair a day I have not seen' (I.iii.38)? Banquo does not acknowledge the remark. When he addresses the witches, he often speaks some lines to himself when he should, perhaps, be addressing the audience:

> ...and to be King
> Stands not within the prospect of belief,
> No more than to be Cawdor.
> (ll. 73–5)

Later comes the disjointed short sentence 'Would they had stay'd', to which Banquo again makes no response; he would not have heard it if Macbeth had spoken to the audience. Still later, as if in a progression, come lines which are so separate from the rest of the dialogue that modern editors usually mark them as asides, to no one in particular; these could be spoken to the audience:

> Glamis, and Thane of Cawdor!
> The greatest is behind.
> (ll. 116–17)

In the great mid-scene soliloquy which follows, the actor could build on an established relationship to engage directly with the audience as Macbeth grapples with his own conscience:

> This supernatural soliciting
> Cannot be ill; cannot be good. If ill,
> Why hath it given me earnest of success,
> Commencing in a truth?. . .
>
> (ll. 130ff.)

The last one-line speech in this scene – 'Till then, enough. Come, friends.' – is usually taken and marked in editions as if its first part were an '*Aside to Banquo*', yet this too could be spoken to the audience, and so mark suffering as well as resolve and political awareness. Macbeth's nature is such that his relationship with an audience can never be easy and will seldom provoke an enthusiastic response to boost a performance. If started early, however, the speaking of lines directly to the audience will increase its sense of his struggle, pain, and courage. Late in the play, his need for 'troops of friends' and for 'honour, love, obedience' (V.ii.25) could make an appeal to those who understood such feelings and so gain an insight into his terror which otherwise might outstrip their imaginations.

Few major characters are so capable of speaking to the audience as King Lear at the very end of the tragedy. The frequency and ease of such contact increases during the course of the action, until he seems to recognise no barrier between himself and anyone either in the audience or on the stage. In the play's first scene, Lear is totally bound up in what he must do with his daughters and their partners. Direct address to the audience seems to have been reserved for Cordelia so that she can gain attention for her own feelings and purposes, in this way emphasising a contrast with the closed minds of everyone else. The time for Lear to establish contact with the audience is when his family and followers begin to reject him: in Act II, scene iv, for example, with his cry for 'Vengeance!' and his brief exclamations 'plague! death! confusion!', and then his questions: 'Fiery? What quality?' (ll. 93–4). His advice to himself will be all the more affective if shared with the audience:

> No, but not yet. May be he is not well....
>   I'll forbear;
> And am fallen out with my more headier will
>   (ll. 103–11)

Once the audience is involved, as well as the characters on the stage, it will be pulled in many ways with Lear, and not least as he shares his pride and sense of justice:

> Let shame come when it will, I do not call it;
> I do not bid the thunder-bearer shoot,
> Nor tell tales of thee to high-judging Jove.
>
> (ll. 225–7)

Perhaps the very short and contrasting 'I can be patient' (l. 229) should also be played to the audience, marking for them a recourse which is not present elsewhere in the scene. If so played, the audience's feelings towards Lear will be more sensitive than those of the persons on stage who will not have heard these words. Lear's cry in the oncoming tempest could be an attempt to call witnesses for his pain and resolution:

> I have full cause of weeping; but this heart
> Shall break into a hundred thousand flaws
> Or ere I'll weep.
>
> (ll. 283–5)

An actor, who is willing and able to improvise, and is, by now, entirely open to the audience, will have to choose, at this crisis, whether he does indeed weep or remain dry-eyed – or, perhaps, I should say that his imaginative improvisation in each particular performance will show him what he must do. In the context of an experience which the king shares with the audience, his turning to the fool will be a decisive action, a prophecy that arises unexpectedly to his mind – 'O fool, I shall go mad!' The unknown horror of this possibility will seem all the more threatening on account of this narrowing of focus.

In all the main elements by which we know and judge a stage drama – in character, action, argument, diction, spectacle, music – the Marathi theatre offers nothing comparable to *King Lear*, but its openness to the audience and its audience's participation with its actors provide performances which can cause us to question how we experience Shakespeare's plays. We cannot visit Elizabethan and Jacobean theatres to join with audiences that took a more active role than in our own theatres[5] but in Bombay we can experience at first hand the improvised interplay which arises in a similar kind of performance. We will recognise that every moment in a Shakespeare production which is shared with a free audience would have to be improvised. Timing what is said and done to awaken a response, controlling, developing or in other ways reacting to that response when it does come, looking individual members of an audience in the eyes, sharing its laughter or stopping it, waiting for deep feeling to be experienced, or taunting hearers with wit or irony: all this needs the invention and judgement of a moment, and the courage and expertise to improvise. Nearer home, we may find a new interest in stand-up comedians, public speakers at disorderly meetings, musicians on stage at a pop concert, or performance artists with an appreciative audience who all show, in theatrically more limited contexts, how audience–stage reactions can add vitality and, sometimes, a sense of danger and adventure to performance.

After a visit to Jatra theatre, I saw that attendance at a Shakespeare performance might have been like going to watch football or some other sport, when spectators, by the end, feel that they have shared in the players' success or failure. When visiting Marathi theatre in Bombay and other popular theatres elsewhere in India, that comparison seemed to fall short of capturing the experience. Here the spectators were *in* the game and the actors played *with* them throughout their performance; to some extent they also played *against* the audience. They sought out, encouraged, and mastered the audience's attention; and so used it to build and direct their performances. Giving pleasure and awakening collusion were the main objects of the game: improvised action and speech were necessary to quicken and concentrate attention.

To unlock the potential of Shakespeare's texts, a new format for production is needed that will encourage openness and freedom in performance. Improvisation and its inevitable risk-taking should be encouraged so that actors live in the moment of creation rather than repeat what has been prepared and so that the audience participates in the play and influences its performance.

Should all this happen in the theatre, one consequence would be that readers and critics – for whom change can be so much easier and who have a natural appetite for it – will be encouraged to study the plays with a similar openness and sense of adventure. A recognition that the strengths of a text are not likely to be revealed to a narrow gaze or pre-programmed investigation is the first step to take; the second, that a play should awaken a competitive and self-implicating response and also, paradoxically, lead to a scrutiny of its likely effect upon others unlike oneself.

7

RESPONSE

Actors and audiences

Whatever is enacted on stage finds its fulfilment in the minds of the audience, in their perceptions and reactions. Here, in any analysis, performance should be assessed, as well as in the signs and signals given out from the stage. Travelling to unfamiliar theatres makes this abundantly clear. Many companies, such as the Jatra in India, allow audience members to talk amongst themselves, call out to the actors, move around and meet other people, or eat and drink, fall asleep, or become engrossed with their own concerns. In these theatres, attention is held and developed by more obvious and direct means than are appropriate for audiences with European standards of behaviour and sitting comfortably in darkened auditoriums where silence and no-fidgeting are expected behaviour. Elsewhere, for Nō theatre in Japan or Kutiyattam in Kerala, an audience's freedom is on a different level and, in one sense, even greater, since these performances never try to grab attention or spring surprises, or overwhelm an audience's senses with irresistible sights and sounds. These theatres encourage a willing submission and intense attention so that a few of those who watch may enter the dramatic illusion so fully that they find a quiet, deep-seated, and imaginatively active satisfaction. A major task for both critic and director is to determine what kind of audience–stage relationship between these extremes is most appropriate for each playtext and production.

A play cannot be defined solely by what is put upon on a stage because its full expression involves some form of interplay between actors and audience. This becomes very clear when a production is taken away from its own theatre and its own public; in consequence both the performance and its reception will change, however carefully actors and directors attempt to maintain their original effects. Laughs come in different places and at different speeds, and are often different in kind, so that the timing of speech and action has to be changed and sometimes the words themselves. Jokes can fall dead and others, that were not effective before, come to life. Some moments of intense silence disappear altogether because they depended on small signs that are recognised only by an audience that has

103

developed a special awareness of them. Knowledge of the actors in other plays and of other work by the author, director, and designer, besides familiarity with the theatre building itself, all contribute in the minds of audiences to what the occasion offers and what it can become.

Traffic is two-way between stage and audience. One may doubt this sitting in the dark, unmoving and silent, at the hundredth consecutive performance of a well-drilled and technically accomplished production that is at home in its own theatre and knows very well what it is doing. But travel changes that opinion. The power of an audience to influence performance becomes obvious when seeing actors confront and deal with vociferous crowd-reactions and individual protests of pleasure or disapproval, or when the actors have unlimited scope to improvise and perform in an open environment in broad daylight. The audience's more subtle influence on the actors will also register strongly when one sits amongst strangers in a strange land, as part of an audience but also an observer of it. Not knowing the language spoken, one's attention is drawn to physical language, on stage and in the auditorium, and then, even when the audience's response is outwardly restrained, a mutual sensitivity will be sensed around one, different from one's own reaction. An unspoken bond between actors and audience makes itself felt, even though neither party draws attention to it. In fact, a giving-and-receiving in both directions is fundamental to almost every theatre performance, however small its outward signs.

In a meeting with a group of theatre people from Guangxi Province in southwest China at the Theatre Academy in Shanghai, the consequences of this interplay between actors and audience were vividly brought home to me. These directors, managers, playwrights, and critics had been given time off and brought to China's most prestigious centre for theatre research for a year's study of 'theory, criticism, history, and dramaturgy'. They were a quiet, thoughtful group, eager to learn by asking me about 'Western Theatre', recent films, and the latest technical equipment. Yet this curiosity was balanced by a shared self-knowledge and soon they were also talking about the difficulties of touring in mountain villages with simple stages that had not changed much in the last few hundred years. They spoke, too, about their struggles to maintain audiences in overcrowded towns or to find good new plays. Then, gradually, they fell silent, as if absorbed in their own problems. I asked what achievements in theatre, that any of them had seen in the last few years, had confirmed their decision to work in theatre despite all the difficulties. At home, this question leads to discussion about very particular enthusiasms, such as a production by Strehler, Stein, Mnouchkine, Brook, or Lepage, a performance by a particular actress or actor, a new play by a new dramatist, the work of a highly skilled touring company, or a quite exceptional performance on a well-remembered night. Sometimes it is an entire festival which has proved decisive in maintaining a belief in theatre and a committal to it.

But here the response was very different. After some moments of silence, as if they did not understand what I had asked, one of them indicated that he would try to answer: 'It is my sense of the power – my translator thought this should perhaps be "the emotion" – that we receive from our audiences.' A pause showed others to be in agreement, and he went on: 'When I feel that power I know that I am doing what I most want to do.' A director, not an actor, was speaking, but he knew about audiences and had found confirmation for everything he struggled to do in the surge of energy that came from audience to stage during performance. He envied no other person's achievement and remembered no particular moment of his own work. He was committed to making theatre because the audiences paid the actors back with an enabling power.

All elements of theatre are affected by this interchange. As they move from rehearsal to performance, actors, designers, and directors, and everyone else involved, find that they have to make all kinds of adjustment, some drastic and many more instinctive and minuscule, but significant none the less. In European and North American theatres, a number of previews are arranged before a 'first night' to give greater opportunity for last-minute changes as the play finds its own feet, each detail settling into proper proportion and prominence. Even the play-text, fixed for rehearsals, may be changed as it is rehearsed and meets its first audiences. Only after a play has met an audience does a dramatist sense the full theatrical life of what he or she has written and knows what works and what does not, what passes expectation or fails the test of performance.

For these reasons, a literary criticism, which cares only for what words can convey to a reader, will not be sufficient to appreciate the quality of a play or the effect that it has in performance. Even a more theatrical criticism, that is intent on assessing visual images and physical activity taking place on stage, will be inadequate if it does not consider the audience's perception of performance. Between the players and the audience, and nowhere else, a dramatic text shows its true mettle and the force of its argument. The actors' performance of a text affects their audience and the audience's reception of that performance affects the players; and, because both transactions alter what a text does, a critic must try, somehow, to assess them both, however varied they may be from theatre to theatre and from day to day.

* * *

The audience–stage relationship is further complicated because what happens on stage is not, necessarily, what an audience sees or thinks that it is seeing. This becomes very clear when visiting Asian theatres or reading books about them. In the Bunraku theatre of Japan, for example, a puppet only half life-size and manipulated by three men shrouded in black can be seen to shed tears or find

105

resources of inner strength during a performance. What happens on stage is obviously manipulated and unlifelike but, in the minds of an audience, it becomes as real as the work of any flesh-and-blood actor, however skilled and experienced. At the most deeply felt part of a drama, the puppet becomes in some ways *more* real, in that every member of the audience has helped to create the illusion by letting his or her own imagination work and so give to the drama something drawn from the reality of their own individual and actual lives. Of course, this would not happen to someone who walked into a performance halfway through and saw only a few moments of it. The play's vivid and personalised 'truth' has to be built up or accumulated throughout a performance, as attention is shepherded and imagination aroused by the recitation of sensitive words and by various kinds of music and other stage devices, all of which are like nothing seen or heard in life. The sensation of an exceptional and highly refined reality which is experienced by an audience as it watches this unreal stage performance is carefully and imaginatively engineered, but it is also, in part, created by members of the audience who with their own imaginations convert the strange contrivance into something palpable, challenging, and quite as affecting as an event occurring in life itself.

The eyes and eyebrows of Bunraku puppets can be made to move and their mouths can open for speech or to show amazement, but these are crude devices which on their own would deceive no one. Nor are the playtexts naturalistic: those most frequently performed today were written in the eighteenth century and bear little relationship to present-day circumstances in Japan or anywhere else. Many, and especially those by Chikamatsu Monzaemon, are written with great refinement and their narrative shaped without regard to practicalities of time and space. All this would seem to militate against an audience's ability to feel directly and passionately about the obviously manipulated manikins, but it does not. In the minds of an audience, the strange deeds shown in the plays, which may mix violence with pathos or ingenuity with strong feeling, are made actual and affecting. So a maidservant puts the corpse of her mistress on a fallen bamboo tree and drags it off stage, the puppet's jerking movements seeming to use every possible muscle in her body. A hero, who has his hands tied behind his back, expresses feeling by a movement of his head, its effect augmented by the music, the narrator's emotional rendering of his story, and the half-seen reactions of the puppeteers; pride, submission, grief, and a determination to submit to captivity for the sake of the young son of his leader, all join together in the sustained climax of a play that is elsewhere full of more eye-catching fights and massed encounters. A child's foster mother closes her eyes and then bows her head, trembling very slightly, all crudely but carefully executed, and then, when she has become entirely still, emotion seems to fill her whole body. In the imaginations of members of an audience these are all palpable dramas to be experienced with immediate sympathy as if they had really happened.[1]

In the other direction, in an actor's response to an audience, the usual barriers between separate consciousness may also disappear, although not with such completeness because the performer faces many persons who react in different ways and all of them cannot be taken in at any single moment. But an actor does react and change before an audience, often in ways that give very little outward indication that this is happening. Theatre is not cinema, where what is done in performance is captured by the camera, and edited and given a soundtrack, and only then offered to an audience as a fixed commodity to be watched and commented upon, or to be taken for real if that is what the director intends and the audience wants. In the theatre, an actor always senses the audience, even when it is not encouraged to respond openly, and, because the audience differs in composition and mood every time the play is performed, the actor's reaction also changes; and, in consequence of that, performance will change too.

The two-way relationship between a play and each new audience at each moment of its action is necessarily complex and to some degree unpredictable and unknowable. It is also, potentially, the source of great pleasure and power which artists should foster carefully and readers and critics should try to understand and assess.

* * *

In the give-and-take between stage and auditorium, the imagination can play amazing tricks. By calling upon the instinctive involvement of both audience and performers, it can transform what is on the stage and leave the bare facts of gesture and speech far behind. What happens in any one example is far from easy to understand and knowledge of it will always be incomplete; and this is especially true when considering, as we attempt to do in this book, a theatre which no longer exists – the performances which Shakespeare had in mind as he wrote. However, an opportunity does exist to examine one very special kind of performance-and-response and to compare what we can deduce about its function in the lost Elizabethan theatre with what happens in another theatre that retains many early performance techniques, although in a very different culture. To show how an audience can respond to what is unreal on stage as if it were real, we can examine the effect of using male actors to play female roles in the English theatre of Shakespeare's day and in the Kabuki theatre of Japan both now and in the past.

Why should cross-gender casting prove successful with audiences in these two theatres at times when both were widely popular, attracting very little adverse comment except from persons who for other reasons were opponents of theatre in any form? Why did it give rise to little in the way of apology or excuse? How can plays hold a mirror up to human nature when differences of gender are obscured on the stage and all representation of heterosexual feeling between characters depends on performers who share the same sex? Here questions of performance and response come into particularly sharp focus.

Cross-gender casting was adopted for different reasons in the two traditions. In Kabuki it was a matter of necessity. This form of theatre had started at Kitano in Kyoto as the invention of a marvellous woman, famed as a singer and dancer, who was called O-Kuni. The physical attractiveness of female performers was one of the main features of Kabuki until 1629 when the government banned all appearances of women on public stages in the name of sexual morality. Theatre remained in demand none the less and so female roles were given to boys until this practice was also banned for much the same reasons. So it was that onnagata or female roles came to be played by adult men, who became highly skilful and specialised.[2] In Shakespeare's theatre, the practice of cross-gender casting is less easy to explain. Earlier practice and, perhaps, a certain amount of convenience would partly account for it, but it may also have been a question of choice, for there was no decree or regulation banning the use of actresses. Women did, indeed, perform on some occasions in non-professional shows and also in tours by foreign companies in which this was an established practice.[3] It is not altogether clear why boys and young men up to the age of twenty-two or twenty-three were cast as women in all English companies until they were shut down for the duration of the Civil War in 1640.

The later histories of the two theatres in this respect are also very different. With the Restoration in England, actresses took over the female roles and have, for the most part, continued in possession to the present day. In Japan, however, the onnagata actors have continued to perform female roles in an unbroken tradition; although audiences are now very different and theatre buildings have been modernised, the playtexts are still the same and many old acting traditions are consciously maintained. Enough has remained as it was centuries ago for the experience of seeing Kabuki to supplement historical research when we attempt to understand the effect of using all-male casts.

Many studies have been published on this topic in recent years which require a detour from Asian theatres before returning to their ancient and current practices. It has been suggested that the Elizabethans accepted boy actors because the young male body offers some resemblance to the female and might, with the corsets, farthingales, and rich adornment of that time, deceive an audience about his gender. But no such argument for female impersonation can be made for the onnagata because both pictorial records of early Kabuki and present practice show no attempt to deceive by using the adolescent male body. Men in their fifties or older still act the youngest of heroines. Make-up is distinctive and simplified, rather than reproducing that used by women in the audience. An unnatural voice is adopted with a high pitch and exaggerated modulations. The onnagata do not behave like young women in any sort of reality but present a physical presence that their audience accepts as that of a young woman: were the Elizabethan boy actors different in trying to appear and act so that they might pass as women, either off or on stage? We have few descriptions of how Elizabethan boy actors performed – that is one of the curious facts to which we will return – but prominent amongst them are some derogatory references to the inadequacy of their voices, the most famous being 'some squeaking Cleopatra' who would 'boy' the greatness of Shakespeare's queen (*Antony and Cleopatra*, V.ii.219). In this respect, at least, the boy actors could be recognised as unreal women in much the same way as onnagata actors are today.

The very use of 'boy actor' as a generic term when the performers were sometimes in their early twenties also suggests that some special 'voice' might have been used for all female parts, as in Kabuki. This would also accord with the practice of the men and boys in Jatra theatre who adopt a standard, unnaturally high pitch when acting women and maintain this tradition even when, as often today, they perform alongside actresses speaking in their own natural voices. An unreal, high-pitched voice would account for Samuel Pepys' comment in 1660 on the acting of Edward Kynaston, the last of the boy actors, who performed female roles after the Restoration when he must have been more than thirty years old: 'one Kynaston, a boy, acted the Duke's sister but made the loveliest lady that ever I saw in my life – only her voice not very good'.[4] John Downes, however, did not notice the voice when he declared this actor to be a more convincing lady on stage than any actress.[5] Perhaps one witness accepted the convention of an artificially high pitch which was by then exceptional and the other did not. In any case, their difference in this respect makes their unanimous praise for lifelikeness the more remarkable. It may be that the credibility of 'boy actors', like that of the Japanese female impersonators, was in the mind of the beholders, not in the facts of performance.

Transvestite performance is common enough today to show that appropriate casting and skill could have deceived an audience with regard to the boy actor's gender if that had been desired. An ability to represent female sexuality, however, raises other issues about which current opinion is divided. On one hand, the open stage of the Globe or Blackfriars theatre, and still more the various stages used on tour, would not have provided suitable conditions for intimate and sustained physical contact between two persons, whatever their gender and sexuality – not unless it was intended to raise laughter. With spectators in close proximity to the stage and free to move around, call out, applaud, or speak amongst themselves, simulation of actual sexual activity would scarcely have been attempted, whoever were the actors. On the other hand, the dialogue of plays performed by all-male companies in both theatres we are considering lay great emphasis on women's sexuality and many of their plots are driven by a woman's sexual passions. Something unreal must have happened on stage to represent all this and the audience must have accepted it as the real thing.

Shakespeare did not shy away from sexuality in his plays or from sensitive and intimate physical contact; in fact, he drew attention to them with a frequency that is surprising in the theatre and public culture of his times. In *Much Ado About Nothing*, for example, we hear nothing from Hero while she tells Claudio 'in his ear that she is in her heart'(II.i.283–4); the text provides other matters for the audience to attend to during most of this intimacy, but Beatrice's words bring attention back to the young girl in close physical contact with her future husband. Sometimes when sexually driven activity is required, Shakespeare's text directs an audience to observe its physical enactment: for example, when Cleopatra kisses Antony, she says nothing while the audience hears only:

> Fall not a tear, I say; one of them rates
> All that is won and lost. Give me a kiss;
> Even this repays me.
> (*Antony and Cleopatra*, III.xi.69–71)

What is the '*this*'? Something suggesting sexual potency must have been enacted when these demonstrative words are spoken and, in the silence that follows the half-line, some further action must have filled that gap of time in a way that satisfied the dramatic situation. When Shakespeare's Pandarus says of Cressida that 'she fetches her breath as short as a new ta'en sparrow', he is preparing the audience for seeing her meet with Troilus. Once she is on stage, both the young lovers are 'bereft' of all words (l. 53) and what Pandarus says encourages the audience to watch their physical and silent encounter:

> An 'twere dark, you'd close sooner. So, so; rub on, and kiss the mistress.
> How now, a kiss in fee-farm! Build there, carpenter; the air is sweet…
> (*Troilus and Cressida*, III.ii.39ff.)

For Pandarus' words to have credibility in performance, the actors of the young couple must be able to give the illusion of sexual attraction and activity.

Another current idea about cross-gender casting in European plays is that putting on the clothes and habits of another gender has the effect of simplifying stage performance and limiting the drama to the depiction of general traits rather than individual character and deep-seated feeling. Because the male actor is bound to *construct* his female performance, using observation and judgement, the result in any role, it is said, will be more *generally* truthful than that of an actress. Jan Kott has often been quoted in support of this view: 'When an actress is asked to act a woman, walk like a woman, sit like a woman, sip tea like a woman, she will at first be surprised and ask: "But *what* woman?"…Femininity can only be acted by a man.'[6] To which Alisa Solomon's reply must surely win immediate assent: 'if femininity is best performed by men, why isn't masculinity best performed by women?'[7]

In Bertold Brecht's *The Messingkauf Dialogues*, the Philosopher discusses what happened when he saw an actress playing a man. According to him, this casting had prompted an increase in the audience's understanding of gender, in generalised and critical terms:

> If a man had been playing that man he'd hardly have brought out his masculinity so forcibly; but because a woman played him…we realized that a lot of details which we usually think of as general human characteristics are typically masculine.

Here cross-gender casting is again valued for providing a thinking-man's theatre in which bipartisan reflections are stimulated by the performance. The Actor, whom Brecht imagines taking part in this dialogue, makes a rather simpler observation, but again it is general and comparative: 'I must say I've seldom seen such feminine women as at the front during the war, as played by men.' The Actress in the dialogue is quick to add: 'And you ought to see grown-ups played by children. So much of grown-up behaviour strikes one as odd and alien then.'[8] All three support the notion that cross-gender casting and other forms of 'mis-casting' make the audience's experience significantly different in a way that is more thought-provoking. It is seen here as a weapon to use on the audience's minds, alerting them to gender issues and class distinctions.

If the aim of cross-gender casting were always to construct a performance which drew attention to *general* features of the characters presented, we would expect to find a more intellectual and thoughtful audience than the popular ones that crowded to Shakespeare's plays as well as the early Kabuki. In modern Jatra performances, enthusiastic audiences respond to individual female impersonators, seeking to touch them and present them with gifts. Western parallel is the pop concert, where sexual arousal is obviously part of the attraction for many in the audience.

Against the assumption that cross-gender casting for Shakespeare's plays was intended to provoke thought about women in general, we have the evidence of our own senses and our good sense. His female characters are scarcely more or less individualised than the male, and they were written using much the same techniques. Besides, innumerable actresses have triumphed in Shakespeare's female roles by using all their physical, emotional, and sexual attributes: few of them have said they were aware of any special demands or restrictions placed upon them. Performed by women, the texts have given rise to plenty of subtle, complete, and highly individual performances in which sexuality has undoubtedly played its part. Shakespearian theatre no longer uses boys and young men in the female roles because casting according to gender has so obviously had its own rewards in the stage-life of the plays.

Another current explanation for the use of youths and young men in female roles is that the audience took pleasure in the merging and confusing of different sexualities. In *Desire and Anxiety: Circulation of Sexuality in Shakespearean Drama* (1992), Valerie Traub has argued that in *Twelfth Night* Viola becomes sexually attracted to Olivia when she is pretending to be the page Cesario and pays suit to her in Orsino's name. Moreover, looking like a male youth, which is what the actor in reality was, Viola was also able 'to elicit the similarly polymorphous desires of the audience' (p. 131). From this premise, the critic concluded that a performance of this episode is a 'theatricalization of desire' in trans-gender complexity and excitement (p. 132). The matter is complicated, of course, because Olivia was also played by a young male: so the degree of polymorphous desire would have varied, and the exact point at which any one member of the audience might sense the sexual reality under that of the fiction and be directly caught up in it. Response would have been a matter of individual choice or instinct, according to whether the deception or the actuality seemed the more attractive proposition. This line of argument suggests a collision of reactions, in which the person of the actor, the role played, and the gender indicated by dress are all active and reactive elements in a sexual and cognitive tangle. It turns a theatre with wide public appeal into a means of providing some very private satisfactions and a good deal of intellectual uncertainty.

Compared with both these explanations of European cross-gender casting and gender disguise on stage, the early accounts of Kabuki performances are in almost total contrast. For the onnagata, performance was not a matter of intelligence and skill alone: it had to have a basis in real life and also what was called a 'soul'; it should bear fruit, it was said, as well as being a flower. These are the 'Words of Ayame' as set down by Fukuoka Yagoshiro in 1727 or thereabouts, at the time of Kabuki's greatest popularity.[9] This Master always assumes that an adult male actor can have within himself the feelings of a woman and that he must nurture these and make them the source of all his art. He should also encourage their development off stage:

> if he does not live his normal life as if he was a woman, it will not be possible for him to be called a skillful *onnagata*. The more an actor is persuaded that it is the time when he appears on the stage that is the most important in his career as an *onnagata*, the more masculine he will be [and therefore the less acceptable]. It is better for him to consider his everyday life as the most important. The Master was very often heard to say this.
>
> (Item VII)

When a young man has chosen to become a player of women's roles, he has crossed a bridge which is then destroyed behind him:

Plate 7.1 An onnagata performer; Tokicho as the wife of a warrior, rehearsing at Sadler's Wells Theatre, August 1977

Photograph: Mander and Mitcheson Theatre Collection

> If one who is an *onnagata* gets the idea that if he does not do so well in his chosen career he can change to a *tachiyaku* [performer of male roles], this is an immediate indication that his art has turned to dust. A real woman must accept the fact that she cannot become a man. Can you imagine a real woman being able to turn into a man because she is unable to endure her present state? 'If an *onnagata* thinks in that way,' he used to say, 'he is ignorant of a woman's feelings.'
>
> (Item XI)

Backstage, in the green room, the actor must maintain his on-stage character:

> To [sit there] alongside a *tachiyaku* playing the lover's part, and chew away at one's food without charm and then go straight out on the stage and play a love scene with the same man, will lead to failure on both sides, for the *tachiyaku*'s heart will not in reality be ready to fall in love.
>
> (Item XXII)

If an onnagata actor is married in real life, the Master warned, he should feel like blushing if it should happen that 'people talk about his wife' (Item XXIII).

Such intimate and sustained identification with a role is comparable to 'The Method' of the Actors' Studio in New York in the decades after the Second World War. It is far from the usual assumptions about the boys and young men who played Shakespeare's heroines, or about the performances of men as a generalised 'woman' in European theatres. Elsewhere Ayame's words about originality and imagination imply the same insistent search for 'truth' and the same refusal to be content with outward manifestations of character that can be found amongst actors and actresses of almost any good theatre company today. He also warned, like a modern acting-teacher, against repeating business that is known to be successful: 'If a piece of acting comes off successfully three times in a row, the actor loses his skill' (Item XXI).

No apology is made for being a male actor playing a woman and no sense is given that performance should be an exposure of what any 'woman' is supposed to be. The male actor acts as if he were a woman and the audience is invited to perceive him as such, both in the innermost spirit, or 'soul', of his performance and in its outward manifestations. 'Soul' is, interestingly, a word which Stanislavski used often, in *Building a Character* (translated, 1949), to describe the inmost and most powerful part of an actor's performance in a role.

While the appearance and voice of an onnagata on stage were not like those of a woman in everyday life, a great deal of the preparation for performance involved the actual processes of living and the actor's persistent, imaginative attempt to think as if he were an actual woman. Behind what the audience witnessed on stage was a much more naturalistic engagement in the mind of the actor, and it was assumed that this would be perceived by other characters/actors on stage and be the means of pleasing the very varied members of an enthusiastic audience. All this reflects on the Elizabethan performances and implies that enquiry into the practice of the 'boy actor' should shift from concerns about outward appearance and actual sexuality to a consideration of the imaginative grounds of their performances and the audience's response at a comparable level.

The actual sexuality and gender of the onnagata actor were comparatively unimportant because an audience was able to sense an inner and imagined femininity and so endow the moment with a similar inner lifelikeness that outstripped the outward performance; this sexuality would be in part created by each individual spectator's imagination. The dearth of contemporary description of the performances of 'boy actors' is an argument that they received some form of acceptance as satisfactory and convincing. Could the characters played by them have been given an imaginative inner life and their audience find access to it? This could hardly be so by the same time-consuming and thorough means as in Kabuki because these young female impersonators had much shorter careers and less strict regimes of life; nor were they old enough to see very far into the minds of mature women if they had attempted do so. They might have dealt in a few stereotypes but that would not have satisfied the more popular appetite except in a broadly comic way, and could have come nowhere near the complexity and strong individuality that later actresses have revealed in the text when acting Shakespeare's roles. Searching for the means whereby such qualities of performance might have been within the reach of 'boy actors', we may find it, most plausibly, in a responsive speaking of the texts of the plays: there any actor can have direct access to a character's 'inner life' as imagined by the author. Momentarily, and occasionally for longer periods, members of an audience might sense a female character in the carefully crafted text as it excited the actor's imagination and caused the words to be spoken. If this were to happen, they might also share in the dramatic life of the play as it had been played out in Shakespeare's mind during the act of writing.

This is not to argue that Shakespeare's was a literary theatre, in which the transmission of words was all that mattered. The mere task of speaking complicated dialogue so that it can be heard in the open air by an audience of two thousand will inevitably call upon the resources of the whole body to achieve the necessary variation of breath and projection of sound. The shaping of sentences, changes of tempo and pitch, the building and placing of vocal climaxes also draw upon physical powers in execution. Complex sequences of nervous tension and relaxation are needed to give vocal force and clarity to the words and are another necessary part of performance. More than this, as an actor responds intuitively and sensuously to the images conjured up by the text and to the texture, weight, and flow of its sounds, his physical being will respond in necessarily intimate correspondence with speech and this will also add to the impression received by audience. By such means and with a thoroughly imagined and sensitive text, the sexual drive and sensations implied by the words that are spoken will inform a performance in many inevitable ways. When an audience responds to this physical component of utterance, it can accept an incomplete imitation of outward behaviour as if it were life itself – the same might be true of an intentionally falsified imitation. The reason why a theatre might choose to cast female roles with young males, whose performance was bound to be incomplete, could be that the practice had proved to be popular: their audiences enjoyed the creative act of completing the illusion of life for themselves, sharing the task with actors and dramatist, seeming to possess the drama on their own account. In the minds of the audience the illusion could work and be infinitely and variously attractive.[10]

* * *

The sustained physical commitment to speech by which an actor provides the breath and nervous tension or relaxation for making the appropriate sounds and projecting them towards the audience becomes a large part of any performance. On some occasions, Shakespeare's words make little continuous sense to an audience without this necessary accompanying effort and then the person speaking seems to be driven by unspoken desire or almost torn apart with contrary feelings. At other times, a sequence of variously affective images, or a number of hesitations followed by quick conviction and lengthening rhythms, will require the speaker to become increasingly open to new sensations so that his whole being becomes active, receptive, and attentive. The person presented on stage can appear aware, tentative, surprised, delighted, or seemingly overcome by a spontaneous inrush of sensation because of the very sounds and rhythms of speech, even though the words themselves do not directly say as much. In such ways an impression of sexuality can be imminent and infinitely varied: not limited and defined by the individual body, predilections, and real-life experience of the performer, but suggested, and so ready to be quickened and heightened in the active minds of spectators. Whether the actor is cross-dressed or not, performance can then carry conviction as the personal and sexual life of the drama quickens to its fullest life in the active minds of the audience – which is where it needs to be felt.

The end of the first scene of *All's Well That Ends Well*, where Helena is left alone after Bertram, her mistress's son and heir, has left for Paris, may be taken as an example of how the emotional and sexual content of the drama can be expressed in the physical accompaniment of speech as much as in the words themselves. Helena is easily drawn into talk with Parolles who will be travelling with Betram and soon she dares to speak, as if in soliloquy, of all the things she imagines happening at the king's court. But then she stops in mid-sentence before expressing the confusion and fears that crowd into her mind, with halting syntax, broken rhythms, and uncertain metre:

> HELENA: Now shall he —
> I know not what he shall. God send him well!
> The court's a learning-place, and he is one —
> PAROLLES: What one, i'faith?
> HELENA: That I wish well. 'Tis pity —

When she stops the second time and Parolles presses his question, Helena's reply suggests a mind in which arousal and reserve are now able to co-exist:

> PAROLLES: What's pity?
> HELENA: That wishing well had not a body in't
> Which might be felt; that we, the poorer born,
> Whose baser stars do shut us up in wishes,
> Might with effects of them follow our friends
> And show what we alone must think, which never
> Returns us thanks.
>
> (I.i.163–74)

On the page or in mere recitation, this whole passage may be analysed and shown to be a subtle presentation of a personal and social dilemma, but in a full performance they become indistinguishable parts of an affecting presentation of a young woman. At first, Helena is both assertive and hesitant, fixed on a single purpose but aroused to both gentle and turbulent sensations, thoughts speeding to extremities. Sudden stops and starts, quick intakes of breath, forceful speech and perhaps very quiet, hesitant moments are followed by more sustained rhythms towards the close and the vaguer plurals of her final thoughts. All this needs a great variety of physical engagement in uttering the words so that they make appropriate sense and that, in turn, can suggest the physicality of sexual arousal and frustration. So it is that performance goes beyond the words as found on the page and speaks directly to the senses of the audience.

A 'boy actor' playing Shakespeare's Cleopatra may not look very like a great mistress and queen, and his voice may be 'cracked within the ring' (*Hamlet*, II.ii.421–2). Yet when both his voice and physical performance are used in speaking the text, the audience's imagination can add to the facts of performance and bring Cleopatra to absolute life in their own minds – which is where the drama must find its effective life. Her sexuality need not be present on stage because it is implicit in the text and that is caught up with and, thus, expressed by the physical facts of the actor's utterance. To support this statement in a book rather than in rehearsal or performance, one can do little more than quote the text and ask readers to speak the speech aloud and so begin to hear, but not yet see, its mysterious inner power; for example:

CLEOPATRA: Courteous lord, one word.
Sir, you and I must part – but that's not it.
Sir, you and I have lov'd – but there's not it.
That you know well. Something it is I would –
O, my oblivion is a very Antony,
And I am all forgotten!
ANTONY: But that your royalty
Holds idleness your subject, I should take you
For idleness itself.
CLEOPATRA: 'Tis sweating labour
To bear such idleness so near the heart
As Cleopatra this.

(I.iii.86–95)

Two features are typical of Shakespeare's presentation of sexual passion. First, the abrupt pauses and hesitant repetitions (notably after the fourth line quoted), as the pulse of the speaker seems to quicken and sensation seems to overflow the capacity of previously spoken words. Second, the sustained sensual and active image that crowns the outburst after interruption and draws upon what the other speaker has just offered: "'Tis sweating labour....' Also typical is the way that this concluding image draws into the reception of this exceptional situation an audience's memories of an experience which is open to all humankind and associated with the pain and satisfaction of actual physical activity.

A sense of being at the limits of what can be communicated and of participating in the creative adventure of realising a text in performance is immediately attractive to audiences. It is especially so when this realisation is experienced below the surface of performance in the writer's maze of consciousness that lies behind the actual words that the actors say. There, belief may be found by everyone for him- or herself in very personal terms, according to what they are able to imagine. The onnagata actors achieved this 'soul' of performance through their disciplined absorption in the dramatic fiction of being women, on stage and off. For the female roles in the theatres of Shakespeare's day, the same grounding could not be provided, but in so far as the young actors responded, in mind and in body, to the task of speaking the texts as the drama took its course, what they said and what they became were in tune with the imaginative engagement of the dramatist in all the subtlety, sensuality, and varying strengths of those texts.

Although Shakespeare was pre-eminent in writing major female roles of compelling lifelikeness – at least until a generation later, when Webster, Middleton, and Ford followed some of his innovations – he was only one of many who wrote for the 'boy actors'. Perhaps cross-gender casting was generally acceptable in his day because all plays were then presented with bold physicality on an open stage and had the advantage of being written when the English language was growing ever more responsive and varied, and also because theatres had responded to this situation by attracting poets to be their dramatists. These talents and resources were sufficient to distinguish English theatre from others in Europe and to keep 'boy actors' in employment.

* * *

This attempt to explain how Shakespeare's female roles were performed in the light of the Kabuki's onnagata has been introduced as part of a wider enquiry into the nature of actor–audience relationships because it has a more general relevance. Two complementary practices have been identified. First, from the audience's point of view: with an appropriate text and a performance responsive to it, what is unlifelike on stage can be accepted as an experience like life, but more intense or marvellous. Second, from the actors' point of view: for this acceptance to happen, performance must be informed by an imaginative response to lived experience either by the actor or by the author of the play, or by both.

For a director responsible for staging Shakespeare's plays, the consequences of this extend to every aspect of the work in hand. Actuality on stage – full nakedness, real pain or physical exhaustion, absolute realism of setting, the accents of ordinary speech – will not be helpful because it would limit the work to be done by the audience's individual imaginations. As a corollary of this, however, the director should *inform* his or her work with an experience of everyday living, drawing on visual images, sounds, behaviour, activity, expressive means, and states of awareness that are common in the day-to-day lives of all persons on stage and in the auditorium. The task is to assist members of an audience to make good the imperfect illusion of reality on stage but not to do all that work for them. In this way, an audience becomes implicated in a performance so that it speaks directly of their own lives and the plays become up to date and immediately relevant.

A reader or critic of the plays should respond similarly. However many intellectual ideas are brought to bear on explication of the texts and whatever efforts are made to reconstruct the mind-sets of Shakespeare's England and so restore their original 'meanings', more remains to be done. The texts have to be read in relation to common experience. No idea is ever quite the same from generation to generation, as our active minds bring fresh demands or privilege certain responses, but in seeing, hearing, touching, we remain much as men and women

119

have always been. What is common between us is access to natural experiences: we all have 'eyes,…hands, organs, dimensions, senses, affections, passions; [we are] fed with the same food, hurt with the same weapons, subject to the same diseases, healed by the same means, warmed and cooled by the same winter and summer…' (*Merchant of Venice*, III.i.52ff.). The lifelikeness and force of Shakespeare's plays in the minds of audiences and readers can draw upon this common inheritance. Their ability to provoke and use such responses are one explanation of the success of Elizabethan 'boy actors' and it may also explain the plays' popularity with audiences drawn from all classes of society.

A critic should ask how a play encourages an audience to respond instinctively, with the senses and with personal memories and experience. The words of a play operate in many ways: intellectually they set other words and various ideas to work, but they also work as sounds that set actors working with their entire beings in action as well as speech. To this complex and ever-changing physical phenomenon the audience responds instinctively. It is a music and dance that calls for critical attention, just as much as statements, arguments, visual images, and stage business. That they work on the audience's consciousness, bypassing explicit verbal definitions, does not lessen their importance: quite the reverse, that only renders their effects almost unstoppable, even though inadequate performance can obstruct or obscure it. A critic who neglects these performative elements of a play has ignored a major part of their power to influence and move an audience.

8

SETTINGS

Actors and stages

I was able to learn more about India and its theatre when I spent nine weeks directing *King Lear* at the National School of Drama in New Delhi. What engaged me almost daily was an unexpected way of running rehearsals and preparing for the show's opening. I am used to relying on a stage manager, with a number of assistants, to organise rehearsals and keep me and everyone else fully informed. From a stage manager's desk, he or she will eventually give cues for actors, light and sound operators, stage crew, and front of house manager. On this desk is 'the book' with every cue marked and numbered, and usually colour-coded, and the means for electronic and audio contact with everyone concerned. A computer screen will provide complex checks and keep tally of all that happens. In the theatres of Europe and North America, the stage manager is specially trained, highly skilled, much respected, and essential to the good running of any show. He or she copes with mishaps, broken properties, miscues, fire drills, understudy rehearsals, taking the show into new theatres on tour, re-rehearsing a production should a member of the cast have to be replaced, and so on. Once a show has opened, this person is in charge of all that happens on stage and will file daily reports with the management and director of the play. It follows that he or she has much to do with the 'company feeling', the way in which many very variously gifted and motivated people work together. In New Delhi this was not the case and I soon came to realise that this was not at all remarkable, however uneasy I was made by this state of affairs.

I did have a stage manager who was able and willing to do all that was expected of him, and much more as well. But there was never a properly maintained 'book' that, in an emergency, could be understood by anyone, and the theatre, though only one year old, had neither a stage manager's desk nor the means for him to communicate directly with anyone during a performance. There was not a single assistant stage manager for a necessarily large production and a cast of twenty-four. The whole show was kept going by each and everyone doing what seemed necessary at what seemed the right time as the action took place on stage. Most of the music was played without a written score. The last weeks of technical and dress rehearsals, previews, and the official opening performance was a particularly anxious time for me without a stage manager equipped to do all that I expected of him. I had to accept that the play would be made out of whatever happened to happen, and would at any time be prone, or at least open, to disaster.

On reflection, I see that this absence of off-stage control fits well with much I already knew about Indian theatre. Folk plays, such as the Gavari of Rajasthan, are held together in performance by the leading actor who makes no attempt to hide his instructions to others, by a drummer, and by a fool-figure who makes his own contributions, interweaving with the main action wherever he wishes. So performances can last as long as convenient and take place almost anywhere, in a neighbouring village or at some new 'Folk Art Centre'. Even technically difficult forms, such as Kutiyattam or Kathakali, are improvised with everyone responding independently to the actor who is holding centre-stage. The Marathi and Jatra actors take many of their cues from the audience according to how it reacts from night to night. In Jatra, the stage assistants sit in full view behind the main stage to operate lights and microphones, not taking their eyes off the actors.

Parallels are to be found in Indian music which is mostly solo and improvisational. Attempts at ensembles or orchestras are likely to run into trouble: the instrumentalists have learned to be such individualists that seldom are more than two or three able to play together, and then only one is likely to be the main attraction and acknowledged leader.

In Indian theatre, the demarcation between leading actors and supernumeraries or attendants is very clear and by this means some order and coherence is maintained. One of the theatres I have not yet visited is called Kariyala and is found in the small towns around Shimla. I was told about this by Neerag Swod, one of the cast of *Lear*. At twenty-eight years of age he had come to Delhi after some eleven years acting with the group based in Mandi, a town of sixty thousand and also a district of Himachal Pradesh, where life depends on agriculture and, increasingly, on tourism. Twenty or more groups are to be found in the state, each playing their own variation of the same kind of theatre. Basically there are three characters only: a Sadhu (holy man) or priest; a gentleman or landowner; and a clerk (the part Neerag would usually take). The plays are all comedies about local life and are unscripted, relying on improvisation and frequent communication with the audience. They are accompanied by music, according to the musicians available, and are simply staged on the earth of village squares or on a platform the actors carry around with them. I asked how long a show would last, to be answered that they usually began in the early evening at around six and go on to about the same hour the following morning. 'With only three characters?' I asked, to which the answer was 'No, not at all.' As many as thirty or forty other characters might be introduced into the action, according to who wanted to join in. 'And this free-for-all drama keeps audience interest for all that time?', to which the answer was that the local apple wine and another drink made out of a root were available; and the leaves of a locally grown herb were used for smoking. By morning both actors and audience were sharing the play and everything else.

Listening to that account, my problems with the production of *King Lear* seemed nothing to make a fuss about. I think it was the third or fourth public performance in which all its elements seemed more or less in place and working together, so that, with just a few mishaps, everything seemed strong and eloquent, the better parts and the least satisfactory. Nothing went like clockwork, but each episode found and took its own volition and, in doing so, became changed into a performance that seemed inevitable, a strong basis for tragedy. Somehow meaning and passion had been created out of stage conditions that I would normally call chaotic: a sense of everyone else's achievement filled me with amazement and gratitude.

Only later did I realise that this concerted effort of preparation and improvisation, mixed with a kind of carelessness, had provided me with a performance that in some ways was similar to those I had conjectured taking place in Shakespeare's time. His theatre had been without stage manager or assistant stage managers, stage manager's desk or intercom. Tiremaster and book-keeper or book-holder were the two functionaries identified in surviving documents, one in charge of the many and expensive costumes, the other ready to prompt and warn actors to be ready with whatever properties were necessary for their entries. A number of 'stage-keepers' were available to assist in these tasks but they also functioned as actors in the plays. The effect of having a whole battery of cues to be followed, together with a large and varied repertory in which, as a matter of course, any play was likely to be performed at short notice for only one day at a time, must have put performances at the mercy of each moment – as had been the case with my production of *Lear*. Whereas today in the West we rehearse and re-rehearse, one play at a time, until everything is as right as it can be and able to be repeated flawlessly, in the past, for Shakespeare and his fellows, all was open to chance.

A story in Samuel Pepys' diary, concerning a company less well patronised than the King's Men, illustrates just how improvised and uncontrolled the performance of a crowded scene might be. Thomas Killigrew (1612–83) told him how he had been able to see plays when he was a boy:

> He would go to the Red Bull, and when the man cried to the boys, 'Who will go and be a devil, and he shall see the play for nothing?' then would he go in, and be a devil upon the stage, and so get to see plays.[1]

For some years I had known that the leading actors in traditional Indian theatres would improvise each performance; now I was learning what it was like for a whole production to function in a similar way. The effect was most noticeable in what are sometimes called production numbers, those episodes in which action is complicated and a large number of actors are on stage: in *Lear*, this meant the first court scene in which the three daughters are put on trial and one of them is banished, the king's return from hunting, his arrival at Gloucester's castle, the preparations for war, and the final scene of all. If the storm was created by a number of stage-keepers, so that thunder rolls round the theatre, lightning cracks in various places, wind howls, and the sound of lashing rain threatens to tear everything apart, then those central scenes would also depend on large-scale activity that was open to chance. All such scenes can be staged very effectively in Europe and North America today, with assured stage management and many technical devices, but take those props away and large, uncontrolled, and attention-grabbing effects will be pitted against the central performances. Leading actors will have to turn to improvisation and self-assertion if they are to withstand and, occasionally, subdue or lead all the people who are working in the scene with them. The dynamics of the drama will be significantly different.

I found that my understanding of the text was often changed because of the context that a necessarily improvised staging had given to the action. For example, Edgar's concluding speech:

> The weight of this sad time we must obey;
> Speak what we feel, not what we ought to say.
> The oldest hath borne most; we that are young
> Shall never see so much nor live so long.

Several aspects had always seemed strange to me. First, that he should be taking charge so quickly after Albany and then Kent had in effect left the responsibility to him, and that he had been given no speech of dedication to sovereignty or even of acceptance: compare Richmond at the end of *Richard the Third*, Malcolm at the end of *Macbeth*. (The Quarto text may acknowledge this difficulty by giving the speech to Albany, even though he has abdicated power and cannot speak of 'we that are young' as Edgar can.) Second, that he should finish by speaking of himself, for I had taken the 'we' of the penultimate line to be a newly assumed royal plural; I could not see the use of asserting this about himself. Such questions disappeared when, at Delhi, the stage was filled with sixteen younger actors, who had entered with the armies, or bringing messages or carrying the dead bodies of Regan and Goneril, all of them to some extent wearied from the long play and all used to performing as individual and improvising actors. The intense drama of Lear's drawn-out death had held them absolutely quiet and still, but the absence afterwards of anything so compelling had allowed that tension to give way. As

Albany ordered 'Bear hence the bodies' they began to move to do so, picking their way over the debris which had fallen after the battle and the trial by combat. Just as their individual responses began to be more evident, they were stopped by the speeches of Albany and Kent about the transfer of power. Briefly everything was almost still again as they wavered, not knowing how to respond, or to whom; and then they stooped to take up the bodies. It was then that Edgar spoke the play's last lines and again arrested their movements. And now, in this largely improvised staging of the scene, his words seemed to relate himself to those others who were like himself in being 'young' and had, immediately, to bear 'the weight' of those bodies from the stage. An act of identification with others completed the play, rather than one of authority and newly assumed self-consciousness.

It is easy for a director to control the ending of this play and so set an individual interpretation on it. The central figures can be so lit that they are clearly distinguished from the rest of the company on stage and the audience is directed to take notice of the different relationships of Edgar, Kent, and Albany to the dying and then dead king, and to each other. Whatever words the director chooses from the text can be given impressive statement. But in a less controlled production, a full cast of unspeaking and nameless attendants of various ranks, all silenced by the appalling event, can also take focus, and even more strongly, as instinctively they move forward together with bowed heads or averted eyes. After Edgar's last words, they each will have to respond as best they can, as they take up their burdens and, again, draw attention.

* * *

In many Asian traditional theatres – in Jatra and Kutiyattam, Bunraku and Kabuki, amongst those considered here, and also in Nō, Balinese dance dramas, Beijing Opera, and more – what happens centre-stage is supported by music, drum-beat, song, or recitation, or by a large chorus-like group of dancers or actors, or by the responses of half-hidden puppeteers. Compared with these dramas, Shakespeare's plays and many others in European traditions are remarkable for dispensing with much of this support and being content to leave a great part of the drama as the sole responsibility of the leading actors. However, an experience of other theatres will suggest that the degree of presentational support that is required by Shakespeare's texts is more extensive than would at first appear. It was probably intended to interact more strongly and constantly with what was the heart of this drama than a reading of the text or the practice of modern theatres may lead us to think.

Most of Shakespeare's plays can be staged today in a theatre of moderate size with a total cast of twenty-five; in a smaller space, with doubling and perhaps a little cutting of the text, as few as twelve can manage. Towards the end of the sixteenth century, the Chamberlain's Men had a larger company, with ten or so 'principal players'[2] supported by variable numbers of 'hired men', 'boys' and lesser actors or attendants, also known as stage- or door-keepers. There can be no doubt that considerable forces were available to interact with a play's leading actors whenever Shakespeare and his fellow actor-sharers saw the need.

Obviously in the histories he did make frequent use of them, as armies are required to march and countermarch. More than that, while they stand and wait for the main dramatic action to be carried forward by their leaders, they provide a sounding board or reflective surface that can enlarge the effect of a change of fortune or weariness after long strife, or any move to prepare for battle or surrender. Martial music was also available to extend whatever effect the dramatist required: trumpets could sound with sudden clamour, drums speak both loud and low, persistently or in sharp outbursts. Such music could give a boost to any performance: Falstaff, preparing to go off to battle, calls out instinctively, 'O, I could wish this tavern were my drum!' (*I, Henry IV*, III.iii.205), as if he knows that rousing music should be accompanying a martial exit. Perhaps he pounds on the table as if he were calling for more drink, but here improvising rough martial music.

The variety of ways in which Shakespeare used such choric and musical effects may be illustrated in *Richard the Third*. Richmond concludes his address before the Battle of Bosworth with

> Sound drums and trumpets boldly and cheerfully;
> God and Saint George! Richmond and victory!
> (V.iii.269–70)

so that here the vigorous cries of a whole army will be augmented by bold music. In contrast, Richard has two very different climaxes in his battle-speech, neither of which calls specifically for music. The first is on the sound of Richmond's drum from off stage which prompts him to call for fighting, bloodshed, and 'broken staves'; the second when he calls for action and victory:

> Advance our standards, set upon our foes;
> Our ancient word of courage, fair Saint George,
> Inspire us with the spleen of fiery dragons!
> Upon them! Victory sits on our helms.
> (V.iii.348–51)

If drums and trumpets were used here, Richard has not summoned them. The soldiers, however, will have to move off stage and how they do so will reflect or magnify whatever effect Richard makes in speaking the words that have got them underway. Perhaps they do cry out on 'fair Saint George', but if so they are given no clear cue for a concerted reaction so that the effect will be more scattered than that of their opponents. In any case, the whole episode will contrast with Richard's very precise call for military music in an earlier scene when he wishes to silence the women who confront him:

> A flourish, trumpets! Strike alarum, drums!
> Let not the heavens hear these tell-tale women
> Rail on the Lord's anointed. Strike, I say!
> (IV.iv.149–51)

These four incidents, all raising the expectation of musical support and each meaningfully varied, demonstrate the careful attention that Shakespeare gave to this way of extending and controlling dramatic interest.

In *Henry the Fifth*, he employed many sounds of warfare – soldiers' cries, cannon-shot, trumpets, and drums – to show the king putting heart into his troops before Harfleur. At the Battle of Agincourt, however, such presentational support is more muted:

> Now soldiers, march away;
> And how thou pleasest, God, dispose the day!
> (IV.iii.131–2)

Even if Shakespeare expected more music and sounds than the text insists upon here, this call for everyone to leave the stage shows a new wariness. After the battle, no stage direction specifies what should happen but, as the soldiers are ready to leave the stage, Henry calls for 'all holy rites' and the singing of '*Non nobis*' and '*Te Deum*': here the troops might all join in singing one of the ancient hymns, as if they had been given an order, or some individuals amongst them might fall to private prayers; on the other hand, the troops might very well hesitate, not knowing how to proceed after so unusual a command, and so emphasise Henry's contrasting determination to demonstrate his piety. Certainly, many soldiers are on stage so that their leaving will take time and draw attention to *how* it is effected. Possibly a silent *exeunt*, with no accompaniment, a simple but necessarily ragged response, would make greatest effect in the play's sequence of massed and regimented movements.

Once a reader of the text starts looking for use of supportive stage movements and sounds, it will yield suggestions in almost every scene. Before Agincourt, while Henry watches and prays, there may be stillness and as complete a silence as the theatre could provide but then, when the scene moves to the French camp, an unmistakable sound is heard from off stage to which the nobility immediately react: 'Hark how our steeds for present service neigh!' (IV.ii.8). A more complex chorus of off-stage sounds is suggested by the Prologue to this Act which speaks not only of 'high and boastful neighs / Piercing the night's dull ear', but also of 'busy hammers closing rivets up', 'country cocks', and clocks striking the small hours. Words may have replaced, at least for this moment, the use of the acting company to provide a sound-context for performance but, even if none of these sounds is to be heard, the aural sensibility represented in the words of the Prologue shows Shakespeare to have been well aware of a wide range of possibilities in the use of sound as support for central performances or as a contrast to them.

Shakespeare continued to use the clamorous and usually concerted chorus of war in other plays. All seven tragedies that followed *Henry the Fifth* were given its help, although by no means all their central arguments depend on winning battles. Regimented formalities, military music, and associated sound-effects enhance each play's reception and their concluding scenes are all attended by soldiers with their drums or trumpets. In *Hamlet*, for example, Fortinbras is expendable as far as the main action of the play is concerned and he has sometimes been entirely cut in production. However, the deployment of a full complement of his soldiers will ensure that the audience hears and sees more than just another character. On his first appearance only nine lines of text are spoken (and this is all that is kept of the entire Act IV, scene iv in the Folio version) and their effect would be small without his Norwegian soldiers marching '*over the stage*' and so projecting and enlarging the image of a foreign intruder who brings the possibility of war. This impression is unexpected, efficient, and perhaps rather sinister and threatening: the soldiers come to a halt, one captain is detailed for special duty, and then, on the order 'Go *softly* on', the whole stage empties noiselessly 'at ease', or even 'gently' as the Arden editor glosses *softly*. This short incident will, by these means, make a powerful impact, especially as it is in strong contrast with the hurried orders, entries, and exits, the fleering jests and sharp questions, of Hamlet's confrontation with 'the Danish king' that has immediately preceded it. By the context which his army provides for him, even more than by what he says or does, Fortinbras, a new player in the game, makes an immediate mark – the substitute scoring a goal as soon as he comes on to the field.

At the end of the last scene of *Hamlet*, Fortinbras' re-entry with the same, but now wearied, soldiers has an even greater impact as it brings military discipline to a scene of 'havoc' (V.ii.356). With his men in support, he holds the stage with undisputed authority, despite the fact that the audience has had very little preparation for this and has been told little of what he stands for. In the last words of the play, Fortinbras orders nameless soldiers to take over:

> Let four captains
> Bear Hamlet like a soldier to the stage;
> For he was likely, had he been put on,
> To have prov'd most royal; and for his passage
> The soldier's music and the rite of war
> Speak loudly for him.
> Take up the bodies. Such a sight as this
> Becomes the field, but here shows much amiss.
> Go, bid the soldiers shoot.
>
> (V.ii. 387–95)

According to the Folio stage direction, which represents either stage practice at the time of early performances or the author's second thoughts, the effect is prolonged: '*Exeunt marching, after the which a peal of ordnance are shot off.*' A drum probably marked a funeral-pace as everyone either carries or follows the bodies off stage. Then the sound of '*ordnance*' may break upon the quiet and, perhaps, momentarily stop this procession with its ear-splitting noise. By these means, the last view of Hamlet himself is prolonged: an inert corpse carried by soldiers amongst a subdued and shocked procession of persons whose minds had a moment before been

> wild, lest more mischance
> On plots and errors happen.
>
> (ll. 386–7)

This full-stage and off-stage presentational support is a potent part of the ending of this tragedy and, after all words have been spoken, it is bound to stir the audience and invite its reassessment, in its own terms, of the play's hero.

The contexts provided for the main performances are a major element in Shakespeare's plays, the effect of which a reader has to make positive efforts to hear and see. Those who stage the plays will, necessarily, take them into account, but in modern theatres of European origin one aspect of their intended effect may well be underestimated. Originally, we should remember, this choric support was largely unrehearsed and improvised. Individual reactions amongst its ranks were left to chance, except on the comparatively rare occasions when the playtext provided a few words for a common reaction or for one or two individual responses. Everything which today is subjected to long exploration and complex preparation and control was left to the moment by moment reactions of each participant. This means that while the company as a whole could give great support to the main performers, its involvement also added a great hazard in being the most unpredictable and unstable element in the carefully scripted play.

In consequence, the success or failure of any performance was far more dependent on supporting actors, musicians, and stage-technicians and attendants than the words of the text indicate. On the other hand, when all went well, a powerful and overall unison, a common judgement on events, a concerted yet instinctive reaction could emerge of its own volition and, as it were, carry the central drama on its shoulders to success. Then a sense of excited involvement would also arise amongst the audience, and spread irresistibly.

* * *

Plate 8.1 Shang Changrong in the title role of *King Qi's Dream* (based on *King Lear*)
Photograph: Shanghai Theatre Academy

Plate 8.2 Shang Changrong, actor; photographed during a break in rehearsal
Photograph: John Russell Brown

In some Asian theatres, the participation of supporting actors is more strictly controlled, as in Beijing Opera where large numbers of supporting actors and almost continuous musical support are constant features. Their plays are in every outward way far removed from life, with very elaborate costumes that call for special walks and gestures, amazing acrobatics that express excitement, large-scale and well-drilled on-stage movements of ranks of actors, and facial make-up that gives a mask-like emphasis but can, nevertheless, be variously expressive when worn by a master-actor. However, three other practices ensure an improvisational element in this well-prepared performance. First, the leading actors are highly respected and responsive artists who maintain an individual sense of performance, like a soloist playing with a great orchestra or a diva in a European opera. Second, and most significantly, the music follows the principal actors in performance and not the other way about as in European traditions of opera and musical theatre. No conductor, following a printed score, stands in front of the stage to control the performers both on stage and in an orchestra pit. Rather, the orchestra is placed at stage-level, but off to one side where only its chief percussionist faces towards the acting area. He controls the musicians, but cannot control the actors since he is unseen by them. His task is to ensure that the music takes time from the actors and supports their performance as it evolves moment by moment; he does not – and is positioned so that he could not – give time to the actors.

The third practice which ensures a strong element of improvisation is the way in which rehearsals are conducted. To watch the Shanghai Beijing Opera Company in rehearsal when its actors are without make-up and in street clothes is very like seeing a rehearsal in one of our own theatres. The reactions and behaviour of ordinary life are equally the basis from which the actors work: they slip easily out of the artificial postures and voices that will be used in performance and into familiar talk and awkward demonstrations, as if there were no barrier they cross to do so. The main difference is that no one director is in charge, but three people each with a distinct function. One of them operates in much the same way as a director in our theatres and is a comparatively recent arrival in this company. He is in charge of interpreting the script with regard to the actors' characterisations and the physical staging. The assistant director is not, as very often with us, a willing and discreet person attending on the director's personal needs. On this occasion, she was a retired actress who seemed to have the entire play by heart, both words and music, and was responsible for seeing that her practical experience of this opera was available for use in the present revival. The third person in the directorate was the technical coach who knew how to achieve each of the physical feats required of the actors and could show them what had to be done. Rehearsal would be put on hold so that all three could talk separately with members of the cast or take part in wider consultations on what seemed to be equal terms. In effect, three minds and not one were in charge and, consequently, each of the leading performers had three distinct modes of instruction to follow. In such a production, performance is like a balancing act in which the actors must satisfy all the various demands placed on them, as the accidents of each differing moment allow.

Paradoxically, theatres using very demanding techniques, which take years to learn and assimilate, are amongst those in which improvisation is most prized because it can give a sense of actuality or immediacy to a drama that is in so many respects fantastic and minutely controlled. The actor must make such unusual sounds and such complicated gestures, dependent on fine judgement as well as practised skill, that a performance cannot be achieved in exactly the same way from one occasion to another. This is analogous to a juggler's performance once he is balancing himself on seven or eight chairs or juggling with many balls. When a large number of actors are employed, they all have feats like these to do, with the additional task of adapting to each other without help from a conductor who ensures that all cues are given and taken on time.

Asian productions of European classics will sometimes include elements imitated from their own ancient theatres or from folk practices which require this high degree of specialist skill and therefore carry with them this necessary element of improvisation. Finesse and alertness give the excitement of a game that has to be won: the actors have no opponent to defeat, but a common and difficult physical feat to achieve which calls for watchfulness, inspired spontaneity,

Plate 8.3 Folk dance in Seoul
Photograph: John Russell Brown

and last-moment adjustments to cover-up any lapse that might have been made. For example, O Tae-suk's production of *Romeo and Juliet* in Seoul in 1995 used the routines of an athletic and martial folk-dance, still seen in town squares today, and so involved the young Capulets and Montagues in aggressive and communal displays of strength and energy. The young men of this Verona sprang to life as they vied with each other in demonstrating expertise, especially when one of their number took the lead in a particularly daring sequence. They often faced the audience in a show a strength before display changed into combat, with staves striking violently and advantage suddenly changing. Out of these spatially and musically presented scenes, the play's dialogue took vigorous and proud life, with a sense of danger derived from improvisation.

When expertise in performance is carried to great lengths, it is possible to break out of the pre-ordained patterning to large and disconcerting effect. In Trivandrum, the Sopanam Theatre Company (the name means 'steps leading to the holy place') directed by Kavalam Narayana Panikkar has developed its own very demanding style of acting from traditional martial arts, folk singing and narrative poetry, and the local traditional theatres of Kutiyattam and Kathakali. The result, after almost two decades, is a repertoire which includes ancient Sanskrit texts, adaptations of Western classical plays, and Panikkar's own plays on modern themes written especially for his company. *Poranadi* ('Boundaries' or

'Borders'), first staged in 1995, presents a corrupt society in an earlier India by employing music and the company's demonstrative acting style. Its action had fluency and a continuous mockery, as each cowardly character boasts of his or her own power or good sense, strutting, bowing, falling down, or quickly agreeing with whatever suits the moment. So when the Chief Minister says 'Everything is under control!', a great deal of extraordinary stage activity shows quite obviously that it is not. One low-born character, Pokkan, is different and refuses to do what he is told; expecting to be ritually killed, he gets drunk and then breaks out into a speech to the audience which ends the play. Warning them of the evils of conformity and complacency, he calls for revolutionary action. In this role Krishna Kumar, three years in the company and wooed, at that time, by film makers to leave, gave a startling performance. As his character attacks a corrupt feudal absolutism, the actor abandons the production's almost entirely comic use of the company's elaborate and well-drilled ensemble-style, but keeps its physicality and musical shaping so that his performance is simultaneously unfettered, daring and sharply defined, able to make great leaps and rapid turns in thought as in action. Something that had seemed impossible has happened as if spontaneously. Finding sudden freedom, Pokkan's anger appears raw and its power boundless. The audience must either share his passion or stand aside, as it were, unable to accept what is being said and done.

The use of ancient skills in contemporary plays shows that specialised techniques, if shared by an entire company and involving a degree of risk and improvisation, would be a way to vitalise Shakespeare's crowd-scenes. In England and North America, however, folk customs have not won wide acceptance in present times and are therefore not easily available for use in theatre; ancient theatre traditions do not even exist. Both can be imported from other cultures but then they seem artificial in the new context and this militates against alert or subtle dialogue. They also bring a sense of make-believe which obscures any attempt to reflect the concerns of their audience. Besides, when such 'ethnic' productions are attempted, even long periods of concentrated training are insufficient for actors to absorb the necessary skills so that they become second nature; without that depth of assurance their performance is not able to draw the audience into the heart of what has been made, for them, a very unfamiliar drama. A better way to achieve a concerted power is to seek out contemporary 'ceremonies' – as proposed in Chapter 3 and illustrated in the productions of Noda Hideki – and elaborate these in ways that take lessons from Asian reliance on complicated folk ceremonies and techniques.

A few small companies in Europe and the United States have shown the way: for example, Theatre de Complicite directed by Simon McBurney who worked for some years in a French circus with acrobats and clowns, and the actors of Saratoga International Theatre Institute (SITI), directed by Anne Bogart who collaborates each year in a festival with Suzuki Tadashi in Japan. Knowing the theatrical value of physically demanding ensemble performance, both these directors try to find contemporary means harness it. In Complicite's *The Three Lives of Lucie Cabrol* (1994–6), seven actors, with great dexterity and often to music, act many different persons as well as horses, goats, chickens, and parts of the scenery. The production is an amazing contrivance, like an elaborate puzzle or dance at the centre of which the story of a few individuals is clearly and sensitively exposed to the audience's view. In SITI's *The Medium* (1993–6), a small group of actors play even more characters, either appearing on television or reacting to television. Pace is often rapid, with many costume-changes and physical contortions and transformations, so that the audience is both amazed and caught up in the varying exploits. With both productions, however, constant repetition during long tours has tended to reduce the improvisational element in the work and so the directors travel with the actors to conduct re-rehearsals and add new elements in order to keep some hold on spontaneity and freshness of invention. Unfortunately, the financial and organisational difficulties of this kind of production are considerable and may well prevent a wider adoption of these techniques of training.

Highly skilled ensemble acting, even when it retains an improvisational edge, is not, however, an entirely suitable style for staging Shakespeare. For moments of concerted action, such as dances, fights, formal confrontations, displays of loyalty or subservience, or outbreaks of joy or fear amongst numbers of persons, its qualities serve very well. Yet the greater part of Shakespeare's writing has an ease and flexibility that demand acting of a kind quite contrary to regimentation and coordinated power. This is obviously so in solo moments that call for careful, sensitive, and heightened enactment of ordinary words and actions: 'Pray you undo this button'; 'She should have died hereafter'; 'My wife, my wife; I have no wife'; 'Most wonderful!'; 'My father had a mole upon his brow…And so had mine', to chose from amongst those already mentioned in this book, and there are many more of the same kind which need acting that is open, unsupported, and sensitive, as much as it is powerful.

Ensemble acting has little to offer in reaching the heart of most of the plays, the sustained presentation of two or three very independent persons in subtle and often uncertain interaction. In scenes of this sort, placed at crucial moments in the story and structure of a play, the characters are progressively revealed and the audience drawn progressively closer to the working of their very beings as they face the demands of story and situation, and of each other. They seldom join to make a united and strong impression, have no set resources to fall back on, and may have little understanding or acceptance of each other. They cannot be represented by actors who rely on the carefully nurtured expertise of a group working together under strong leadership.

This book has argued that performance of Shakespeare's plays requires actors to maintain continuous contact with the facts of ordinary lives as well as develop an ability to improvise, seek dramatic clarity, subtlety, and authority, and rely on their own resourceful imaginations. This prescription holds good for those scenes of large-scale actions or confrontations for which inventive ensemble acting would give added excitement and power: even here, concerted effects should not take over entirely from improvisation and individual actions and reactions. The authoritarian training methods used by some ensemble companies can lead to single-minded effects that are seldom suitable for Shakespeare's plays. The deployment of a large company of actors without confining their individual responses or over-organising the action seems to have been amongst the strengths of English theatre in his own day, however unlikely it may seem in ours.

Thomas Heywood, in his *Apology for Actors* of 1612, told a story which illustrates this ability to maintain an improvised impression of a real event even when many actors are involved in making a powerful effect:

> an accident happened to a company [of actors] some 12 years ago, or not
> so much; who, playing late in the night, at a place called Pe[n]ryn in
> Cornwall, certain Spaniards were landed the same night, unsuspected
> and undiscovered, with intent to take in the town, spoil, and burn it,
> when suddenly, even upon their entrance, the players (ignorant as the
> townsmen of any such attempt) presenting a battle on the stage, with
> their drum and trumpets struck up a loud alarm: which the enemy
> hearing, and fearing they were discovered, amazedly retired, made some
> few idle shot, in a bravado, and so, in a hurly-burly, fled disorderly to
> their boats. At the report of this tumult, the townsmen were immedi-
> ately armed, and pursued them to the sea, praising God for their happy
> deliverance from so great a danger. [3]

(Sig. G2r)

Part II

RETURNING

9

CRITICISM

Texts and study

Each time I returned from my travels, I became aware that I was reading Shakespeare's plays differently. The chapters in the first part of this book have set out various changes as they occurred and now they can be drawn together and questions asked about their combined effect.

I think that experiences of most far-reaching importance happened when I was either sitting or standing amongst audiences that were free to respond openly to the persons in the play and, sometimes, to the actors who were performing them. Often we were in the same light as the actors so that we could forget, at times, that there was any barrier between us and yet not be caught up in a wholly private experience, as if watching a film or sitting back in a European or North American theatre, more often than not in the dark. Along with other persons in the audience, we became involved with the action and found ourselves partisan according to our own sense of what was at stake. While free to follow our own thoughts and, if we wished, to cut ourselves off from the play, there were times when everyone seemed concentrated on one particular event or argument, or on an individual who was speaking as if for our benefit.

Even when the play's situation and action were far removed from the circumstances of the everyday, what was said and done would continually call up our personal memories and experiences so that we got caught up in the play in ways that made it seem part of our own lives and of the world in which we lived: the persons on stage became persons we knew, or had heard about or seen from a distance.

Recalling, now, the numerous occasions when I, with many others, was intent on following strange and impossibly marvellous events in a free performance on an open stage, I find myself remembering words of Shakespeare's Richard the Second:

> I live with bread like you, feel want,
> Taste grief, need friends.
>
> (III.ii.175–6)

The kings and queens, lovers and fools, wives and husbands, soldiers, scholars, politicians, servants, masters in the plays all behave as if they live by the same bread as their audience, the same day-to-day and nourishing means. They also experience emotions as we do and are open to contact with us so that we sometimes sense that they need to receive our response and endorsement. We give them our willing attention and they thrive on it; this is a very ordinary exchange, of giving and taking, but by its means the play comes alive in our minds with a force that we instinctively appreciate and accept.

When I read Shakespeare's texts now, my strongest impulse is not to grasp for the meaning of words or to delve into their messages or significance. I allow myself to be drawn into the action in my imagination, giving attention instinctively to the persons in the play, as if they were close to myself. Then I may engage with them in the action or stand back and question what is happening. Until this process has at least begun, I am not ready to pay attention to individual words in order to work out what they all imply. Stranger still, I am not yet concerned with what these various persons are talking about. When I read the text, I want to *see* what is happening, to whom, by whom, and with what intent. The words are what cause all this to happen, but I quickly go through them, look past them, as it were, to try to find out who these people are and what they are doing. Sometimes they come alive in my head in ways that have to be corrected later but, often, with a quick rush of recognition, as a sensuous and emotional experience that is special to myself.

Sometimes, it seems, that I am meant to question and feel uncertain, to want to know more and engage in very detailed speculation about the nature of the fate, history, belief, love, or ambition these people are talking about – their words provoke argument and debate – but events on stage will almost immediately pull my attention forward because these persons will not wait for me. My struggle to keep up and my surprise at a turn of events seem to be part of what the drama intended and so my uncertainties continue to be played upon for purposes I cannot guess and no person on stage will stop to define for me. These plays provoke many different responses; they do not give clear directions about what to think but seem to encourage people in an audience to stay in possession of their own minds and see everything in terms of whatever concerns they brought to the theatre with them. I have come to think that they were written so that we could all make what we want out of them in our own time and place, so long as we are prepared, always, to go on further with the play as its action draws us.

What holds each play together, and holds the attention of many different persons in a free audience, is its action or story. At certain times in the theatre, we are all caught up in the dramatic event as it occurs and now, as I read, I try to understand the nature of that central and sometimes spell-binding experience. Any perception of meaning or relevance, historical or of the present moment, has its origin and fullest life there; if it does not, it will drop away as of momentary interest only, a side-dish or condiment for the main course that stands ready on the table.

I am very aware of the variety of attention a play can provoke. We may see the actors only, and through them experience the persons in play; or the two can seem as one and, for the time being, the actor is entirely lost to mind as we encounter the person he or she enacts. We can see the persons in the play as people like ourselves and, sometimes, we may see only ourselves in them, so that we are in the play as one of its persons and even as several of them at one and the same time. On rare occasions, we see neither ourselves on stage nor the actors or the persons they play, but in our imaginations we *are* a person in the play and through that imaginary being, at the same time as the actor, we ourselves do and say whatever the fiction requires. Identifying these various kinds of reception when reading a text is by no means easy, but an attempt to do so leads to a fuller understanding of what any particular play does for an audience. At least, we may identify those places in the action where it draws most effectively on the audience's own experience and imagination and that, I have come to believe, is vital information to anyone who wishes to enjoy a play and assess what it has achieved.

As I read the texts, now, I am aware of how performance feeds on my own responses and stirs my imagination. What might happen on stage, according to calculations and deductions I can make from the text or can draw from memories of specific productions and records of earlier ones, does not have the arresting and challenging impact of what is happening as if on its own accord in the minds of an audience member, one like myself or very different from myself. More than its possible life on a stage, I want to know what a play *does* to an audience while it is being performed. When I examine a text on the page, I am scrutinising relics of what it has been, the incomplete foundations and not the building itself: highly important evidence, but inadequate in terms of height and space, purpose and use, the experience of living within the complete building. Or it is like judging animals by laboratory examination of their meat taken from a shop window or refrigerated display-case: necessary evidence for both scholarship and criticism, but with obvious limitations if we are interested in live beasts.

None of this means that the words of the text are unimportant. In some ways, I now, in due course, want to give closer attention to them than before, though not always for the same reasons. Of course, I want to know what generations of scholars and critics in the twentieth century have discovered about the probable meanings of words and their usefulness in their particular contexts. I would like to know why one word and not another has been preferred by the author and what is the force of each image or allusion. I want to understand rhetorical structures and stylistic variations. But a further question or series of questions has come to take my greatest attention when scrutinising a text: what does the play do for an audience, with an audience, to an audience? From these difficult questions still others spring: what does an audience, very varied in membership and full of independent minds, make of the play and its performance? What do the actors take from an audience? I find that I return to the text with more questions than before.

I need to know how speaking the play's words affects its physical realisation. Which passages are slow and which fast? What words have inescapable importance, like trigger points for new actions and reactions? When are large-scale group responses a necessary part of the action and how do these affect the central persons in the drama? How are entries and exits controlled by words or when is one silent person given a position of power? What unresolved conflicts of feelings or thoughts are suggested but not defined by the words spoken? What drives these persons or causes them to hold back from the ongoing action? What impression does the physical being of each person make, and how and where does this change, and why? How does the conclusion of the play supersede, sum up, or modify the various impressions each person has made during a performance? How are the events of the play shown to be like or unlike the life-experiences of an audience, and what are the effects of the disparities? What is an audience expected to give to the play, moment by moment, during a performance?

One question needs a far closer investigation of the text than I would have given previously. Ideally, I now would like to know the physical means by which any speech can be spoken. This means looking at its rhythms and pulse, its shifts of tone and weight, pitch and texture, the sensuous quality of its allusions and references, the way it echoes what has been said before, where and how it repeats itself with variations, where breath needs to be taken, and how the shaping of speech echoes the shape of the underlying thoughts and feelings, whatever meanings an actor may give to it. Then arise questions about the variations in these matters between different speakers who are on stage at the same time. When he was writing dialogue, Shakespeare's imagination was engaged in the progress of the play's action so that implicit in its every detail are indications of how he saw and considered each of the persons involved. For this reason the text deserves the closest attention and gives to an actor who is speaking its lines a direct and practical contact with Shakespeare's creative mind. In performing his roles, actors are recreating that imaginative engagement and using it, unconsciously, to shape and colour what they speak while their physical performance is instinctively moulded by the sound, suggestions, and vocal necessities of utterance. As I have already argued in this book, it may be that in a skilled actor's response to the technical difficulties of speaking Shakespeare's language he or she may offer an audience the closest and most sensitive contact with what the play becomes in performance. The actor may well be totally unconscious of what is happening in this part of a performance and an audience unaware of how it is being affected: but the physical response to the imaginative writing is always there and visible on stage; it is noticeable, too, because it provides necessary energy to the dramatic fiction and is always changing with its action.

For the critic, scholar, or reader, the performative qualities of Shakespeare's texts and an audience's response to them are not easy to identify or describe. But they demand attention and so send us off to theatres to see more productions, and to libraries and rehearsal rooms to seek further knowledge about theatre practice. At least, it was so with me, on each return from Asia where the range of theatre I had seen made me question what performances of Shakespeare's plays might be.

10

CONTROL

Directors and companies

No two theatres are alike and they would not stage Shakespeare's plays in the same way, even if they used the same director, designers, and actors. Each production is the result of many people working in close contact with one another in a particular context and bringing to a very demanding task whatever their lives have made of them at that time. In the process, to adapt the words of Shakespeare's Henry the Fifth, they will inevitably 'show the mettle of their pasture'.[1]

The power-structure of a theatre company and the culture of its members are both implicit in any performance. A director may intend a play to carry specific messages, but the organisation of the theatre and the day-to-day life of its members will be reflected in all they produce and be evident on stage, whether the director likes it or not. In some ways, this inevitable and unwilled statement communicates better, or at a deeper level, than any concept a director might impose on a production because an audience is not usually conscious of its influence.

Most experienced directors know this very well. For Peter Brook, what a theatre company brings affects the entire process of production and is to be cherished. At the end of a long series of rehearsals he told an enquirer:

> We are a small group of human beings. If our way of living and working is infused with a certain quality, this quality will be perceived by the audience, who will leave the theatre subliminally coloured by the working experience we have lived together. Perhaps that is the small contribution we can make, the only thing we have to convey to other human beings.[2]

By putting on a show, the product of a 'working experience…lived together', theatre expresses the 'form and pressure' of its life and times[3] – its cultural politics – no matter what a director might want to achieve or a censor to guard against.

Clearly the theatres of Asia represent very different cultures in their productions than European or North American ones; their employment contracts, financial administration, organisation, policies for advertisement, sales procedures, schedules, and, not least, their audiences are all quite different. On returning home, this is one of the first things a traveller concerned with the staging of Shakespeare will notice; he is bound to make comparisons and ask what working conditions would best suit the plays and how their texts could best be served by an entire theatre company.

* * *

Today companies producing Shakespeare in Europe or North America work in a variety of organisations and therefore represent different elements of contemporary culture. But a few dominant forms are everywhere present, working repeti- tively and confidently, as if there were no hope of change or regeneration. Taking a phrase from Fredric Jameson, Dennis Kennedy has identified the power of 'late monopoly capitalism' in the most admired Shakespeare productions of our times.[4] Like Coca-Cola and McDonald's hamburgers, this mode of production 'works by transcending national borders and creating attractive images of its material products designed to make their consumption inevitable'. He cited productions by Brook, Mnouchkine, Bergman, Strehler, Sturua, Ninagawa, all of which seem to thrive on this political-cultural situation and are made available for purchase around the world.

These well-financed productions share another cultural mark in that they are all the products of an accepted dictatorship. Their accomplishment depends on a supposedly benevolent but undisputable exercise of power by what Sir Peter Hall calls a 'final voice', the daily submission to an experienced 'editor' who is relatively distant from the work because never on stage and personally involved with enacting the play:

> In the early stages of rehearsal, the shape and pace of a scene must not be imposed. The actors should be free to create while their director helps to release their imaginations; and if that means going very fast or very slow, or taking enormous pauses, it must happen; everything must be allowed. But once the truth of the scene is found, the director becomes the editor.[5]

The authority of this overriding editor/director is often said to be inevitable because of the complicated technical resources which are nowadays brought to the staging of Shakespeare. If theatre is to be efficient, the argument goes, there can be no choice in this matter. Like any successful production process, it must be thoroughly organised and carefully controlled, and only one central authority can be responsible for this and so, ultimately, for everything else. Industrial firms may set up work councils and listen to unions, but these have comparatively little influence over product; and so it is in theatre. Neither committees nor representatives can argue with an authority which has control of all input and output. Maximum effectiveness will always entail some sacrifice of individual freedoms and initiatives – or so it is said.

These procedures of late capitalism operate across the whole spectrum of society and the dominant theatres are those which have been content to go along with them. Producers organise companies and hire directors to do the work. Rehearsals for each production are under the charge of a director and performances are formed by his or her decisions, as if strength were achieved only through enforced unity organised by a single authority. The pursuit of unquestioned financial success is an aim of commercial enterprises which theatres follow by trying to seduce audiences into uncritical acceptance by proclaiming the virtues of their products – as high in quality as those of the most ruthless business – and by stunningly confident presentation. In doing this, theatre remains the mirror of the age.

Cultural and political influences can be identified most easily in productions of Shakespeare when two versions of the same play are available for comparison, such as *Richard the Third* staged by the Royal National Theatre of Great Britain in 1990–1 and by the Odeon Theatre of Bucharest in 1993–4. In the English version the director, Richard Eyre, organised activities on stage as if he had inherited an old-fashioned taste for military parade: grand and formal effects were carried out with precision but not much thought for the independent and idiosyncratic creativity of the participants. Certainly the scheme of the production was grand, offering not only Shakespeare's play but also twin pictures of dictatorship in Nazi Germany and the resurgence of the extreme right wing of politics in post-war Europe, and in England more especially. The production made much the same comment on contemporary politics as Brecht's *Resistible Rise of Arturo Ui* of 1958 which had borrowed from Shakespeare's *Richard the Third*; but, in London in 1990, Richard Eyre's production kept Shakespeare's text intact while fingering it incessantly to make precise interpretative points.

The packaging was impressive. The actors appeared to order in formal white-tie evening dress, black-shirt uniforms, or serviceable everyday clothes with armbands displaying the cross of St George or the image of a boar. They employed banners and slogans, public-address systems, boardroom ceremonies. They posed for a group photo, stood around while a toy train ran across the front of the stage, and then provided a red-carpet welcome at a railway station together with a review of attendant troops. These superimposed and disciplined ceremonies were used to plug a political message into the words of the text and keep the actors in line.

Richard himself was defined by what he looked like and his manner of speaking. At first a Sandhurst-trained officer bearing the psychological and physical wounds of war and an elitist education, he then became, one after the other, a right-wing demagogue and a melodramatic actor in medieval costume who performed in front of a huge painting showing himself naked and in triumph, astride a rearing white horse. In Richard's dream before the final Battle of Bosworth, the ghosts of those he had slaughtered took on fantastic life, regardless of the stiff formality of their speeches: Clarence tried to force wine down Richard's throat, Anne danced with Richmond, the two young princes played games, and Buckingham brought on a crown of thorns. Queen Margaret, restored to youth and dressed in white, roamed the stage in gloating triumph. Here the director had pushed his actors beyond the limits of Brecht's reworking of the play, creating his own images of infantile competitiveness and hackneyed horror as signifiers of Richard's terminal state of mind and, possibly, of his motivation throughout the action. This was achieved by tight discipline on stage and in the design-rooms, workshops, and control booths.

Even the intense and compelling Richard of Ian McKellen had its effects nailed down and sometimes upstaged by what had been busily provided around him. Having wooed Elizabeth to allow him to marry her daughter, Richard's comment on her departure, 'Relenting fool, and shallow, changing woman' (IV.iv.362), had less impact than the contribution made by the watching soldiers. These henchmen were directed to break out into a loud guffaw, 'echoing with male barrack-room mockery of all women',[6] which took the audience's attention away from Richard's heartless and sardonic humour.

The means whereby the director presented the play had turned it into an unmistakable political statement about the dangers of dictatorship. But viewed as a political and cultural product, expressing the nature of the theatre that presented it, the very consistency and thorough workmanship that ensured success had a very different effect: the audience was given a production controlled by a director/dictator who had subdued individual freedom. This involved ignoring the two most obvious challenges of Shakespeare's text, both the great variety of independent engagement offered to a company of actors and the variously dynamic, egocentric, anti-establishment, witty, buffoonish, coldly cruel, self-reflective aspects of the central role that often clash with one another. The whole company on stage had been subdued and their efforts confined by the dictates of a director with a single political point to make, a view of the play that made performance narrowly effective. The brilliant and well-executed production could then settle down as part of the company's output in a small and privileged repertory and on heavily subsidised foreign tours.

The playtext had been both respected and patronised by making a great effort to emphasise one aspect of it. Some members of its audiences might have resented being led repeatedly towards the director's view of twentieth-century history, but the show was carefully promoted and sold to many more who were pleased to purchase a 'treatment' of a masterpiece that they could easily understand. Often slow and sometimes shrill, nicely judged and yet completely achieved, so carefully consistent in every effect that it seemed afraid of attempting anything uncertain, the production was praised for stage-business rather than acting, interpretation rather than passion, accomplishment rather than intellectual exploration. Critics were kept so busy noting the period of its setting and the political parallels to the present time that they had little space to consider whether the production was entertaining in any other way.

The 'working experience…lived together' by the National Theatre Company as sensed in this production could scarcely be further from that of many theatres encountered in Asia and, alerted by all these differences, a traveller returns more conscious of how far modern theatres differ in organisation from those of Shakespeare's day. Then a theatre was run by a group of actors who benefited financially from any success and bore the cost of failure. Actors dominated what was shown on stage as they performed before a lively and diverse public, sitting or standing in the same light as themselves. We have no idea how the text was 'interpreted', but we do know that *Richard the Third* was a great popular success for its author and producers. The actor playing the hero also grew in fame in the process of giving many single performances spread out over many years. There was no director/dictator, no designer, few technicians, and almost no budget for scenic effects. In contrast with this way of working, and by most other standards as well, the lifestyle made evident in the National Theatre production must be judged overwrought, repressive, and cautious. It placed Shakespeare's play in a cultural and political context which could scarcely be more different from that of the theatres where it was first staged and for which it had been written.

The production of *Richard the Third* by the Odeon Theatre of Bucharest, playing in its own Majestic Hall in the centre of town, won prizes for both its leading actor and director. The success was then exploited abroad, in the manner of 'late capitalist monopoly', and was a triumph of 'benevolent' dictatorship. Yet it differed from the National's production by still more strongly controlling most members of the cast and giving more freedom to the star performance. Twelve actors were uniformly dressed and drilled so that they were a support-team for Richard, his attentive listeners, playmates, and agents of destruction; they were as little individualised as a chorus in classical ballet, and worked as hard. In contrast, Marcel Iures as Richard had been encouraged to be extrovert, smiling, impulsive, and playful, making a great show of energy and charm. He gave the role a hyped-up dynamism which made it hard to believe that every effect was calculated and equally hard to make consistent sense of his commitment to the play's action beyond an increasingly manic, self-satisfied childishness. The other named roles achieved little individuality: the men were tough and energetic, dressed in long, heavily padded robes of uniform style and stiff with appliqué decoration; the women were strong-voiced and demonstrative, dressed in the same material but with more vibrant colours. They all had received what were essentially the same orders, so that they played along with Richard in the idiom of the production, throwing their bodies around and sharing energetic embraces, salutes, kneelings, kissings of hands and faces. On-stage laughter seemed to come whenever bidden, as victims were strangled or as Richard ordered 'Off with his head!'

In such a setting Richard's freedom had obvious limitations, as if he had been allowed free scope but in a selected and limited environment. He did not exist in any recognisable world, but within a highly contrived and theatrical fantasy. Ideas that arose in rehearsal had been developed to work efficiently and show off the leading actor in whatever he did: for example, Buckingham shared an apple with Richard who insisted on having the bigger half, and then gave Buckingham a bite out of his. The director's most striking addition to the play provided Richard with an attendant who was half-wolf and half-fool, who howled and chattered with laughter, and breathed deeply in shared commitment. In a calculated *coup de théâtre*, this attendant lost his mask at the end of the play and revealed the face of a Medusa; he or she then cradled Richard and, as he died, kissed him.

Here again was a single-minded interpretation, but applied almost exclusively to the task of placing the central character in a non-specific theatrical environment. The success of the production was that of an infectiously riotous, but circumscribed, celebration of performance. With the exception of the leading actor, the company acting under orders had subdued their individualities to the corporate discipline of the production. Little money had been spent on set or stage-effects, but great attention paid to music, choreography, and the martial arts; this gave the director an unstoppable power to seduce the audience with physical activity and histrionic display. In cultural and political terms, this Shakespeare production revealed a company committed to success, every bit as much as the National Theatre in London, but less cunning and careful, and less self-consciously solemn and restrained. The Odeon Theatre was content to create a work that made little direct reference outside the theatre, as if the real world, past or present, would be better if it were avoided. In comparison with Shakespeare's theatre this East European and late twentieth-century organisation had insisted that all the actors should have a continuously energetic presence on the stage and that all the roles except one should become well-drilled members of a team. It was the product of an operation isolated in its theatricality, an engagement in product promotion by means of well-organised and energetic group reactions and by spectacular martial arts.

Dictatorship in theatre is not always so effective. In regional companies in the United States, for example, a 'visiting' director may be put in charge of an annual Shakespeare production and yet have very limited powers. Priority must be given to the ongoing needs of a large number of patrons who have already bought their seats for the season and so the company is geared to a stable supply economy, not ready to give exceptional attention to any one production. Choice of cast will be governed by local talent and the high cost of bringing in additional actors; these will be more expensive but more acceptable if they have made a name on television or in film. Rehearsal period is likely to be no more than three or four weeks, without all the actors being available all the time. A high proportion of the company assembled to stage Shakespeare will have spent most of the previous year only occasionally acting and will be experienced chiefly in television serials, films, or new plays using modern speech and representing modern living; some may have done very little acting of any kind. Knowledge of each other and a shared attitude to Shakespeare's text are seldom found in theatre companies of North America, except at festival theatres specialising in Shakespeare, and there the actors may well be without any other significant experience.

The political and cultural consequences of these arrangements will render all but the broadest strokes of directorial invention ineffective. Productions are therefore given as much song and dance as possible, with eye-catching decoration and display, broad comedy and up-to-the-minute caricature, all devised to grab the attention of patrons seated in their pre-paid and regular seats. Actors in such a production will usually show some signs of unease in submission to what the director has required, together with a few indications of individual exertion or even defiance, but the general impression will be that everyone is putting on a 'good show' to the best of their abilities, quick to take any opportunity to please their audience and hoping that everything goes well enough. These characteristics are not essentially Shakespearian, but an index of the cultural politics of this time and place; as such, they have a pervasive and inescapable effect on performance and, consequently, on the reactions of an audience.

* * *

As the better-off theatres have either become market leaders that eliminate effective competition or tried to live secure in an established supply economy, so poorer and smaller ones have had to learn how to live at a distance from them, content with much more modest productions, reduced casts, shorter rehearsals, lower standards of performance and seldom able to stage such demanding work as a play by Shakespeare. But this does not satisfy everyone and a new generation of theatre companies has attempted alternative modes of operation. A bitter sense of dispossession, which the unmatchable success of established theatres encourage, has led to what amounts to outbreaks of civil war. Often desperate and always underfunded, militants have sometimes used violent and unexpected tactics to penetrate into what had previously been considered safe areas.

In effect, theatre reflects contemporary politics as described by Hans Magnus Enzensberger:

> Few dispute that the world market, now that it is no longer a vision of the future but a global reality, produces fewer winners and more losers as each year passes....The losers, far from regrouping under a common banner, are hard at work on their own self-destruction, and capital is retreating from the battlefields wherever possible....
>
> [In] New York as well as in Zaire, in the industrial cities as well as in the poorest countries, more and more people are being permanently excluded from the economic system.[7]

Disadvantaged theatre artists have had to search for the means to thrive outside the safe areas of the major companies. They set up business on their own, aggressively and self-importantly. Freedom and independence beckon, even if this means doing without a working wage and other hard-won workers' rights, as well as all the fruits of successful trading, such as new and powerful technical equipment, an effective propaganda machine, large subsidies, and an assured audience.

Such rebel uprisings cause little permanent damage to the large companies which remain virtually unscathed, but the emergence of small-scale, independent companies has become a part of present-day theatre which cannot be ignored. Some of the work is rushed or crippled by bad management and lack of funds, but the shows are on stage and making their own noise. The strange thing is that, while in other arts the rebellious assert their rights by working with new material and claiming ugliness, discord, or the previously unthinkable as their proper territory, in theatre the latest and most bellicose innovators turn very often to Shakespeare's plays. In their hands, the old texts, usually considered grand and sacrosanct, become unpredictable and sensational small-scale successes, contrived at minimum financial expense.

Some small companies do not look very much as if they were waging a 'civil war'. They are more like units of a cottage industry which serves a small clientele living in remote or disadvantaged areas or having a peculiar taste for performances which are individually crafted, however crude and ill-prepared. But in their own worlds, all these small theatres are starkly and boldly opposed to those which create expensive and durable productions with recognisable brand images. Even in their most painstaking work, belligerence usually shines through. These companies believe passionately that they are taking part in a necessary struggle and they perform Shakespeare as if these plays provided them with all the armament they need.

* * *

The twofold division of Shakespeare productions, the mass-market on one side and the piratical on the other, drastically simplifies a complex situation. The Budapest and London *Richard the Third*s differed significantly in the relationship developed between the show on stage and its audience. The Odeon Theatre's *Richard* was able to make contact and invite connivance in its fantasy. A reviewer from the London *Times* (13 May 1994) noted both the company discipline and the free-booting, audience-conscious hero:

> His soldiers worship him – and this production can afford to give him a bodyguard of 12 devoted swordsmen who step, turn and threaten in unison. [Marcel] Iures [as Richard] tosses a smile at the audience after putting them through their paces.

In contrast Ian McKellen's Richard was on stage for the audience to see for itself and figure out its meaning. Up there, in the carefully created world of the production, the actor made no concessions to the silent watchers in the audience. This contrast of style did not however affect the common purpose of each exercise; both companies were providers of a show that had been developed to run for a long time and impress their audiences in ways decided by a director. The small-scale, upstart, and pirate companies prefer to see themselves as sharers with their audiences, or as representatives or leaders of them, or as provocateurs and instigators sent on a mission to impress them.

The twofold distinction holds good in most of the basic choices involved in production. Market leaders are possessors and purveyors, providing their public with what they have reason to believe will sell. (No subsidy is big enough to allow any company to escape the financial restrictions of competitive commercial enterprise, and patrons no longer pay unless they are sure of their entertainment.) They manipulate the market through the media and their own self-promoting propaganda, and their skills in this grow ever more impressive. Necessarily they try to become highly distinctive on the surface, but nevertheless their products become more and more similar because they seek to satisfy much the same market-place and by much the same exploitative means. On the other side of the divide, variations are essential to existence and so each company will flaunt its difference from the rest of theatre and show that it has its own way with Shakespeare. One company uses all male actors, another all female. In others, the actors are dancer-actors, or singer-actors, mime-actors, or clowns. Some companies insist on using only contemporary costumes and fashionable manners and intonations. When money will stretch so far, a company may employ only actors who are also musicians so that their productions can be accompanied at all times by music, creating mood and sustaining forward movement and unity. Another company will maximise doubling and play *Macbeth* with a cast of three actors,

King Lear with a cast of five. Another will use only the minimum of company rehearsals, trying to 'free' their actors from prescribed movements and interpretations, and from a director's all-seeing control. Others use film clips to provide a contemporary context for the play's action. Some always perform in small, intimate spaces where there is little division between stage and auditorium. Some perform to special audiences, the old, the very young, the politically committed, or people living in particular places or social conditions. Others break up the text and play it in a different order, or use only one section of it and play that several times, each in a different way, or play it very slowly, so that the excerpt provides material for a whole evening's entertainment. All are united in trying to break through the limitations of monopoly practice, seeking their own kinds of success as if struggling to draw the very breath of life. Very few can give themselves time to develop skills and take good care of their work.

Sometimes, briefly, the dividing wall is breached. A benevolent, large-scale operator will set up a small company-within-the-company to ape the freer spirits outside its bounds and show good intentions towards innovation and young artists. This subsidiary unit will then mount workshop, studio, 'educational', 'outreach', or 'mobile' productions of Shakespeare on very tight budgets. But every enterprise of this sort remains subordinate to the dictates of its masters. Directors and actors do not stay here for long, the best being promoted into 'mainstage' productions where they will spend and earn more money, and learn the necessities of the market-place; the less good will be dropped, and often the whole 'experimental' enterprise goes with them. On the other side of the divide, small companies can be corrupted by success and restrict their own freedom by mounting productions which are designed to please the other market; these undertake long periods of touring or take up residence in a large theatre run by producers seeking the profits and stability of monopoly suppliers.

Cheek by Jowl is a British theatre company that took its name from the defiance flung at his rival by the callow Demetrius in *A Midsummer Night's Dream* (III.ii.338) and it started life in piratical vein, back in 1981:

> there's no-one who leads, no-one who follows in a Cheek by Jowl production. All participants go together in a world of the imagination.
> There's a spirit in Cheek by Jowl which is intimate but raucous, private yet public, cerebral but celebratory.... Theirs is the regeneration game, the fruition of impulses from a collective creative imagination.

So declares the Introduction to a publication celebrating the company's first ten years of life.[8] But already, in its choice of a succession of productions of Shakespeare, European classics, and adaptations of well-known novels, the company was trading on safe household names. Soon it was also balancing its books and boosting its image by holding on to productions for long tours around the world. By 1994, a production of *Measure for Measure*, after months of constant touring, settled for a further month at the Lyric Theatre, Hammersmith, close to the West End of London. The show had started as workshops in the summer of 1993, but by July of the following year the actors seemed to be enacting routines and their fully staged production played for some quarter of an hour longer than it had at first. The company's all-male version of *As You Like It*, after touring for many months in 1991, was revived in 1994–5 for a West End management as a Christmas show. For these extended engagements to be successful, the intimate, raucous, and impulsive band of actors had to become ordered enough for their product to be repeated and exploited for greatly increased consumption in the supertheatre market-place.[9] In this more established world, the company's two directors were now building their own careers and Cheek by Jowl staged ever fewer productions and kept them running for longer; its disbandment or change of image was inevitable.

Other companies staging Shakespeare, which started small, free, and valiant, have advanced right up to the gates of established citadels and then failed to continue. Some lacked the finance or skill to enter that competitive world; others found that the energies with which they had started life could not sustain work on a larger scale and for longer periods of time. Yet when the rebellious have committed themselves freely to a strong leader who works adventurously and with a loose rein, they have managed to straddle the divide long enough to give large-scale performances which remain audacious and glowing with independent life. The English Shakespeare Company, led by director Michael Bogdanov and actor Michael Pennington, managed this at least once when they finished a nation-wide tour at the Old Vic in London in 1987 and presented *Richard the Second*, *Henry the Fourth, Parts I and II*, and *Henry the Fifth* in a single day. These productions had already played in repertoire for some months and bore the marks of direct-orial decisions in every scene, but the occasion provided a quite exceptional boost with which predictability could be cast away and new invention attempted. When John Wodvine entered as Falstaff astride a barrel on a handcart, his disquisition on honour responded with effortless freedom to unscripted responses from the crowded audience which had been watching the story unfold for well over seven hours. This was not a display of secure excellence or smart efficiency, though the standard of work was comparable with that of many market leaders. Nor was it a carnival entertainment such as historians usually describe, because everything had been carefully prepared and all performers were professionals who performed every day and knew their script, their places, and their artifice. Rather it was a triumph of free thought and feeling, shared between actors and audience, that lit up the whole production. Quite exceptionally, the production was both well practised and unconstrained: intense, joyous, palpable, unprecedented, and shared openly between actors and audience.

A sufficient number of moments like this keep recurring to remind us that Shakespeare's plays in performance need not be clearly packaged and processed by directors working for the market leaders and, equally, need not have the exaggerations and obvious shortcomings of aggressive and piratical newcomers. But the politics and culture of our age are so strongly ingrained that they remain highly exceptional. We get the Shakespeare we deserve and, because theatre is a collaborative art, it will take more than a few zealots to reverse current trends. Perhaps a sufficiently financed programme of reform could succeed, but it would have to start with the organisms that create theatre, not with more new ideas about staging or more reinterpretations of individual plays: as Falstaff said of mere 'reasons', such ideas for change are 'as plentiful as blackberries' (*I, Henry IV*, II.iv.232–3) and do nothing to improve the basic situation. Reformers would have to find modern counterparts for those elements of corporate theatrical life which Shakespeare supposed would be in force for the staging of his plays and would have to draw upon the experience of working and living together in the present time.

It may seem impossible to alter the habits of our time, but theatre can be an agent for testing ideas which society as a whole will not admit. This has been proved in very recent years by theatres in Eastern Europe and is being proved again by theatres in oppressed areas of Africa, Asia, and South America. Moreover, a visit to Tokyo, for example, will soon demonstrate that theatres elsewhere can thrive in a twentieth-century, high-tech, capitalist culture using very different organisations. Knowing that the search is not hopeless and aware that other ways of running theatre are practicable, the obvious places to turn for help in finding new forms for theatre are the plays themselves and what is known about the conditions of early performances.

* * *

First of all, actors should be in charge, as a group or, to use Hamlet's word, as a 'fellowship' of players (III.ii.272). The producing company should be run by eight to ten people who have all earned their livings on the stage, and most of them should still be primarily actors. The tasks of running the company would be shared out amongst them, this arrangement being helped by the knowledge of each other – though not a total trust – that would be fostered by the common experience of acting on stage together. Individual members might be in charge of finance, repertoire, production, and public relations, but ultimate responsibility for everything would rest with the group. As they judged best they would employ administrator, accountant, technical director, or stage manager, and they might hire designers, directors, and others, but there should be no doubt that the last word, the power to hire and fire, belonged to the actors. If possible, some members would own shares in the theatre building in which they performed.

Such an arrangement worked in Shakespeare's day, but its feasibility cannot be taken for granted today. Living conditions, finance, and the theatre profession and its techniques have so changed that power has slipped away from the actors. In Europe and North America no fellowship of players has much chance of managing anything, but the idea is not necessarily a lifeless fossil of interest only to historians. Something of the kind still exists at the back of the mind of anyone who has complained about the divide between 'them' and 'us', between those who plan and those who work, those whose labour earns the money and those who control it. Somehow, this division should be removed and it could be that the small yet complex world of theatre, where on stage all life is kept within view, is one of the most hopeful sites for following such aspirations, rather than keeping to the estab-lished practices of the present time. Failure to make such an attempt only perpetuates the double breakdown of responsibility: management thinking only of efficiency and finance; operators and achievers abdicating control of their own work. Many small businesses do start as a fellowship of equals, and continue so very happily until drawn into the pattern and aspirations of larger organisations.

By the words he set down as the basis for their performances, Shakespeare developed many ways of controlling the actors' work, but he also placed an aston-ishing trust in their originality and responsibility. *Richard the Third* is an early play which would be cumbersome and repetitive without a leading actor able to hold the stage, driving the narrative forward while delighting and taunting his audi-ence. The other actors in the company have a large number of roles to play, each asking for clear definition and sufficient energy to offset that of the hero and give grist to his activity. Several of them must sustain interest when they are left alone on stage, or virtually so, in scenes crucial to the development of the drama: notably, Clarence, Margaret, Hastings, Tyrrel, the last-minute challenger, Richmond, and even the anonymous Scrivener. This pattern of demands on a company of actors was repeated with variations in other plays: *Richard the Second*, *Henry the Fifth*, *Hamlet*.

More usually Shakespeare made interplay between two or more leading actors the centre of the drama and its driving force. In the second scene of *Henry the Fourth, Part I*, Falstaff and Prince Hal are placed on stage together and left alone to animate dialogue which would be curious badinage if it were not sustained, on both sides, by a lively and deep-rooted compulsion to talk and challenge each other. Much of the interest and originality of this play stems from the individual forces at work behind the cross-talk of this opening duologue. In the first scene of *Much Ado About Nothing*, a short exchange between Benedick and Beatrice sets up the stakes for the comic and serious game which will take them to the edge of sanity and acceptable behaviour. If the actors fail in this, the scene becomes a short and tedious sparring for advantage using wise-cracks which could never by their merely verbal life grab the attention of an audience or, with repetition, be anything more than tedious to perform. At the end of *Henry the Fifth*, a similar device is used, this time in a lengthy encounter between the king, played by the company's leading actor, and Katherine, Princess of France, played originally by one of its young male actors; this duologue must have two very different sources of energy clashing with each other if it is to establish and develop the new thoughts and feelings within Henry that will carry the play to its conclusion.

The heath scenes of *King Lear* are where Shakespeare's trust in a group of actors is most in evidence. Those who represent the king, the fool, and the pretend madman, together with the sober and almost silent Kent who is locked into his disguise as Caius, have to make sense while speaking lines which on the page seem to be overladen with obscure and almost infantile jokes, together with curious and wayward phrases, repetitions, snatches of song, broken syntax, silences, and non-sequiturs. The actors must play their characters with an inner consistency underneath this great variety of wordplay and ostensible nonsense or the audience will become entirely lost and perplexed to very little purpose. Either the actors win through and are able to show the tempests in each independent mind or they have to simplify, cut large sections of the text, and concentrate on what little narrative can be extracted from an encounter of almost crazed individuals. These difficulties are compounded in that the actors cannot rely here on their strongest qualities. The leading young actor has to pretend to be a violent madman and has little opportunity for direct expression of his character's thoughts and feelings or for showing that growing strength which will allow him to challenge and defeat his brother Edmund in a sword fight. The fool has to fail when he attempts to supply grotesque comedy and so must expose his own isolation and helplessness without the help of his customary artifice. The king has to become foolish and ordinary, a frail old man who is soaking wet and disorientated by the storm, and yet he must also be angry, horrified, proud, powerful, prophetic, deranged, and dangerous – all attributes of the traditional tragic hero. Amongst these uncertainties and contradictions, the actors have to hold the play together so that it develops in a course that seems as necessary as it is unprecedented. Stage-effects efficiently marshalled for the storm can do very little to compensate for any shortcomings in the actors' performances; indeed, too great reliance on recorded sound can obliterate whatever they strive to do. In our theatres today, a director will usually make choice of a few significant sentences to be delivered in a way that forces an audience to hear them distinctly and so provide some points of certainty, some landmarks, for both actors and audience. By taking overall charge in this way, the director can gain coherence and clarity at the cost of losing that fierce and deep-seated contention which should threaten to disorientate them all.

None of these scenes, and none of the many like them, can be staged effectively to the order of any one person. Independently minded actors are needed for the wellbeing of Shakespeare's plays in the theatre, persons used to taking charge and bringing confident imagination and mutually responsible originality to each of the roles. Many other matters have to be attended to, especially control of modern technical equipment and development of acting skills, but none is so vital as this if the plays are to live on the stage and be responsive to the words of the texts. Somehow the organisation of a theatre for staging Shakespeare has to give greatest attention to imaginative and skilled acting, subordinating all other concerns.

The 'lived experience' of a company working together will always have a palpable effect on an audience. So much may readily be granted, but the consequence is more contentious because that experience must be of the right kind for the work in hand. For Shakespeare's plays it has to be strong and individually motivated, and in Shakespeare's day this was encouraged by putting experienced actors in charge. Today we use other types of organisation and none of them offers a viable equivalent. Actors employed by the larger established companies are held back by the need to please the directors and producers who are their two very different masters. Actors engaged in small pirate companies are usually without great experience and are forced to give priority to surviving and promoting themselves, rather than to maturing their talents or exploring a text so that it draws them further towards meeting its own difficult demands. Until a number of experienced and talented actors want to join in a 'fellowship' and try to make it work, no one can know whether such a group in charge of a company would improve significantly the playing of Shakespeare's plays in the present age as it did in his. As we have seen, some parts of this recipe have been tried, but not for long and not with a large and varied repertoire of plays in performance.

Many aspects of theatre work would have to be rethought if Shakespeare's plays were to be staged in accordance with the qualities of his writing and the changes involved would often have cultural and political consequences. For example, the barrier between stage and audience which has been built up in the centuries after Shakespeare's time would have to be demolished. Modern lighting and sound can be used most efficiently if the audience is placed at some remove from the stage, as if it were in another world, and the audience must be in more or less total darkness if the lighting is to have full effect. Both these aids to production have to be programmed with great care ahead of performance and operated by some person who can observe what happens on stage rather than being part of it. Some other way of using light and sound must be found so that an audience is in direct contact with performers without intervening agencies.

The form in which most modern theatres have been built, and consequently the ways in which most theatre settings are designed and manufactured, also creates a distance between stage and audience. In their seats spectators sit back comfortably to watch what is happening elsewhere, in another more amazing world which cannot be entered or fully known.

The way in which most actors live and work also implies a distance, or even a gulf, between them and their audiences. They enter the theatre by a separate entrance and live with very different routines from those of most other people. Spared the practical details of running a company and seldom meeting their audiences, they tend to inhabit the self-enclosed world of their performances, rehearsals, professional advancement, and private lives. These are amongst the factors which combine with modern technology to make theatre culturally specialised: at best, elaborately and masterfully contrived, but cut-off in what amounts to a ghetto from the minds and lives of the public which is expected to support it. Theatre works in the dark and keeps its audience in the dark: light that audience and let it come closer to the stage, and encourage the actors to know that audience, and a new situation would revolutionise every aspect of play production.

Another obvious step towards openness between actors and audience would be to avoid huge theatres in which a human being on stage appears no larger than a doll. Ideally, every member of an audience should be no more than ten metres from the stage and so able to see changes of expression in mouth and eyes, and around the eyes and in the hands, and catch the slightest movement and change of posture. They should be able to sense nervous tension and hear breathing. Large theatres have financial advantages, but some five hundred spectators can be accommodated at no great distance around three sides of a stage measuring about ten by eight metres – more if some of them are standing – and those numbers could provide sufficient income if expenses other than actors' salaries were strictly limited.

Long runs and long tours must both be rejected, even though this policy would go in the face of those current political, commercial, and cultural trends which seek to maximise returns in the shortest possible time. If plays were produced in a true repertoire, each playing for no more than one or two nights in any one week, performances would be encouraged to be open to chance and to each change of political circumstance and, as a consequence, a theatre might find itself the prized provider of irrepeatable occasions and up-to-the-minute entertainment. Actors would not be imprisoned for months or years in the same roles and texts, and the same routines of performance. Audiences would not be prepared by advance publicity and told what to expect and what to think. All this presupposes independent minds amongst actors and audience, but these might exist in greater numbers than we have come to expect if the right conditions existed – we are not all content to buy identical and mass-produced merchandise.

No matter how far away in setting or how fantastic in action their drama may be, Shakespeare's plays were written to reflect the lived experience of actors and audience. Actors should keep alive to current thoughts and feelings by performing, as a matter of course, in new plays by new writers as well as in Shakespeare's. When dressed in other than present-day clothes, as they may well be in productions of Shakespeare in order to fight with swords, travel by horse, have many servants, and so forth, actors should avoid treating them as fancy-dress; doing so encourages voices and manners far removed from those of their audience. Considerable tact and experiment are needed to represent a period way of life on stage without losing immediate contemporary relevance, but it can be done because performance, in a moment, can bring together like and unlike, not destroying difference but using it to awaken attention. Theatre need not imitate any one pattern of behaviour, because it can contain, lighten, and concentrate, and so reveal the complexities of our lives which seldom follow any single behaviour pattern.

Time alone will tell whether the culture and politics of our theatres can change. Perhaps the present generation of actors is so conditioned by the technological revolution and the effective power of the larger theatres and the corporations in charge of television and film that the future course of theatre is irrevocably fixed. Any hints of other possibilities could be merely a few weak notions surviving from the past. On the other hand, some discordant voices already testify to an unrest and may eventually gain sufficient impetus to break the present hegemony. David Mamet, dramatist and director, has sounded an alarm, blaming producers rather than directors:

> This unreasoned commercial hierarchy of actor-director-producer has drained the theater of its most powerful force: the phenomenal strength and generosity of the actor; and, as in any situation of unhappy tyranny, the oppressed must free the oppressor.[10]

The director Deborah Warner has said how necessary it is to achieve performances that are 'genuinely alive', but added that 'getting the necessary altitude for each performance is like ballooning. It simply isn't possible to achieve this seven, eight times in a row for three hours and forty-five minutes each time, as actors are sometimes asked to do.'[11]

At present, directors are leading the way. In the mid-1990s, Katie Mitchell was much in demand for productions by major national theatres in Britain, and yet she insisted on working only in small intimate theatres, with the audience close to the actors. Simon McBurney of the Theatre de Complicite is both director and actor, in a company which bases its style in skilled yet freely inventive rehearsals in which all members join. When asked to direct in the Olivier Theatre at the National in 1997, he insisted on closing its remote balcony, raising a stage in the middle of the building, and putting part of the audience on what is usually the vast stage, so that everyone was as close to the actors as possible and arranged on all sides; he then took a leading role in the production himself. These are all signs that a new style of theatre may be emerging, one in which the actors may be more dominant and more responsible.

In Asia, 'alternative' theatres – as we would say – are not rare. Performances of Kutiyattam and Theyam in Kerala, India, and, until recent times, of Nō and Kabuki in Japan, have depended not on producers, company managers or play directors, but on families of actors who have cherished and developed their art. In Kerala, some theatres are maintained as part of the ongoing life of a temple. The Jatra companies of Bengal and Orissa have a business manager to make arrangements for performances, but the most senior actor is in charge of them; he chooses the repertoire and the company, superintending every artistic activity. In Korea, companies are often run by directors who use actors who have been at the school in which they teach; their theatres have an intermittent existence, returning to life only when the director finds a new project and money can be raised. In India, director-dramatists, such K.N. Pannikar in Trivandrum, Kerala, or B.V. Karanth in Mysore, have had charge of their own companies with sufficient support from the State for continuous existence and daily training sessions with regular teachers: such theatres perform only on occasions when someone, or some village or organisation, pays for a performance and invites an audience to come for free to enjoy the show and celebrate. In Tokyo, the productions of Noda Hideki, described in Chapter 4, are based on his own experience as an actor and his active presence on stage with his company. All responsibility and decision-making are his and, from 1978 to 1992, his company produced at least one new play each year, performing it in a hired theatre for only a few consecutive months – more than sufficient to recoup all expenses. While providing no easy models to follow elsewhere, these Asian theatres show that the organisations and systems of control familiar to us are not the only possible ones. The further one looks around in other countries and the closer one studies the texts of the plays, the more urgent seems the need for radical change in how our theatres are organised for the staging of Shakespeare.

For readers who wish to respond to the printed texts of Shakespeare's plays, a search for new theatre organisations has obvious importance. Productions by the most respected and successful companies of our time do not provide appropriate sites in the mind's eye for imagining the plays in performance. Reading a play, we should feel engaged in an exploration, rather than confronted with some finished statement about a particular political or moral issue. We should be able to share and participate quite as readily as we sit back and judge. Perhaps above all, readers should not approach any of these plays expecting that they will find a guaranteed package and still less what they have been told to look for. They were written to be always changing, always ready to be performed and received in an exceptional way, and as readers we should expect to react in keeping with that mobility.

11

SCENOGRAPHY
Theatres and design

In the last decades of the twentieth century, technology changed European theatre more thoroughly than any other single influence had done before. Computer-controlled lighting, multi-channel sound, animated three-dimensional projections, and mobile, remote-controlled, and three-dimensional scenery can build up stunning effects to overwhelm the senses of an audience. Fine tuning and pre-programming have given to theatre directors and designers an absolute power: the ability to create sensational audio-visual experiences in which words and the human form need play only small parts in the whole. The 'setting', which once was hailed as a way of preventing the star actor turning every play into an opportunity for egocentric display of temperament,[1] has now become 'scenography', a word which indicates control over the entire visual presentation of a performance. The scenographer, in charge of everything the audience sees, can be the dominant partner in meetings with dramatist, director, actor, and audience.

Alongside this revolution in theatre practice, the development of film, television, journalism, and advertising has altered the way in which we respond to all phenomena and, some would say, the way we think and live our lives. We are quicker to respond to visual images than before; we have come to expect sequences of short and sharp statements; we are accustomed to having our attention switched frequently between different aspects of reality as they become instantaneously visible before us; we are used to looking, either closely or casually, at the faces of the men and women who are responsible for running the State, managing big businesses, or offering us entertainment. We can see behind designed and projected images and have learned to be aware of the artifice that has been used to make them.

Inevitably, the presentation of Shakespeare's plays in the theatre has changed and so has the way we respond as we read them. On the page, they are much the same as they have always been: editors are more knowledgeable and sometimes more conservative, but the changes they have made to texts are small compared with what goes on in theatre productions and what happens in our minds as we read. These new developments raise two large questions: do we use the new resources well when we stage the plays and has a reader's response to the texts been influenced for better or for worse?

* * *

Most of the new techniques of staging were developed for film and television, and then adapted to create mega-musicals. These huge stage shows, which match lavish spectacle with compelling music, need a great deal of money to produce and, if all goes well, bring in much more as profit. Financially, their success has been enviable and so their influence on all forms of theatre is now widespread. Although Shakespeare's plays are not natural material for this kind of production – they have too many and too complicated words, too much emphasis on conflict within their characters, too few songs and dances – the new techniques have been applied to them and changed the effect they make on audiences. To a certain extent the influence has been both ways. From the mid-nineteenth century onwards, Shakespeare's crowd scenes had given theatre directors experience of using wide stages and large-scale effects, and so, in Europe rather more than in North America, young Shakespearian directors have been recruited to stage the new spectacular musicals. Soon they were looking for opportunities to adapt their new expertise to the staging of the old plays.

For producers, as well as directors, this has been an attractive development. It offers hope of appealing to a wider audience than these 'classics' might otherwise attract. Productions of Shakespeare are likely to remain a minority taste because they cannot be promoted through videos or sound recordings of popular singers, but devices used in the new spectacular musicals can widen their appeal. Big scenes involving many actors can be made to seem even bigger and louder. Episodes of pursuit, celebration, or transformation respond very well, and so does almost any action taking place in semi-darkness, exotic places, or large open spaces. Besides, directors have found that the new technology can also be used when the drama is confined to a very few actors and the setting is not an important factor. Here subtle changes of light, sound, colour, and recorded music can provoke some highly predictable responses and hold others back; in this way the director can boost whatever effect he or she chooses to emphasise.

Lights, sound, and stage machinery can create marvels without actors having to do anything. Dennis Kennedy's description of Bob Crowley's designs for a series of history plays at Stratford-upon-Avon in the 1980s catches the wonder of 'a scenography that filled the stage with opulence' – even though the plays deal with battle, hardship, and personal crises: 'Back-lit and down-lit, often by high-powered halogen lamps, the stage pictures sometimes appeared to levitate from their solid surroundings: images literally detaching themselves from both historical and human contexts.'[2]

Sometimes the designer creates a huge mobile structure that can be lit variously as a continuous comment on the play's action. So, at the same theatre in 1990, David Fielding's set for Nicholas Hytner's production of *King Lear* was, as Bendict Nightingale described it:

> a vast turning crate whose bottom opens to reveal a stony pothole for Poor Tom, and whose inner walls are a strange shade of turquoise. That may make a suitable space for Goneril's drawing room; less so for the heath, even with a diamond-encrusted sky revolving behind it.[3]

The new scenography has greatest impact when a director uses its irresistible effects in close association with the developing action, so that costumes and stage-business work in harness with sets, light, and sound. Richard Eyre's production of *Richard the Third*, discussed in the previous chapter, used a wide and open stage appropriate for large-scale dance routines. With lights and sound busy in support, lines of soldiers, assemblies of politicians and socialites, and a procession of strangely disposed ghosts could all be manipulated as effective backgrounds to emphasise the figure of the king in whatever way the director chose. Eight years previously, the same director had used a similar stagecraft for a revival of the 1950 hit musical, *Guys and Dolls*, to resounding and very profitable effect.

Now that lighting and sound can be controlled so fluently, directors of Shakespeare's plays know that they can add small details of physical business and ensure that attention is focused upon them and will use an active group of actors on stage like a chorus in a musical. At the Royal Shakespeare Company, Katie Mitchell's 1994 production of *Henry the Sixth, Part III* had quantities of religious ceremony added with barely a hint in the text that this should be done: prayers were offered at a small illuminated shrine; the actor playing the Duke of Exeter was also a priest figure who turned up on numerous occasions to make the sign of the cross, the action being held up to allow him to do so; power figures were approached by prostration on the floor in the form of a cross; whenever possible, the characters would cross themselves and groups of them would start singing plainsong in Latin. Religion was injected into political events in these many ways and then, at the end of the play, everyone joined together in pious singing, like the chorus at the end of a musical, the lights slowly changing to a softer glow. However cruel and hopeless political life might be, all would be well, the production seemed to say, so long as one sings about heaven. Such additions are by no means new stage devices, but they are being handled now with computerised deftness and disciplined chorus-work to create impressive displays with cumulative effect: the audience has to submit to the director's view of the play, or else struggle to resist and find little in compensation. By the standards of other productions considered in this chapter, this was a low-budget, low-tech show, designed to be easily toured; yet even with these reduced means, new technology had sharpened and stabilised the director's mastery.

Almost any production today, with large budget or small, will stage a Shakespeare play like a modern musical: strong, confident, well managed, and, where possible, irresistible. The stage will be used dynamically and the production fitted out with novel visual images and impressive audio support. So much is obvious, but equally significant is a less obtrusive use of the new techniques. Speech, especially in extended soliloquy and formal address, is now frequently accompanied by music or sound and by sympathetic changes in the lighting. A single actor can be pin-pointed in bright light or high-lighted with varying intensity. A voice may be amplified or its sound modified as a director judges appropriate. A pause may precede or follow a chosen word while the actors are pre-programmed to keep still as if frozen or, perhaps, move and react with concerted effectiveness; perhaps the lights are timed to blackout on the last word or slowly increase throughout; or both lights and sound may pulsate, or one may dim as the other comes to full power – whatever the director thinks is an appropriate and reliable effect. At the end of *King Lear*, at Stratford in 1994, a narrow beam of white light appeared for the first time from behind the audience to pick out the spot downstage-right where the king was dying: he looks at it and then, leaving Cordelia where she lies dead, moves a little towards it saying, 'Look there! Look! There!' It is to the light provided by director and designer that Lear points and then collapses at some distance from his daughter whom he appears to have forgotten. In this process, an entirely new and eye-catching end has been provided to give hope to Lear and, presumably, to his audience.

In mega-musicals, the star actors who open the show, adding to its glitz and publicity value, are replaced after a decent interval with other actors who have no fame and comparatively little experience, and are very much cheaper to hire. Yet the appeal of the shows seems undiminished; they still play for years to capacity houses. This is not true of Shakespeare productions, but the new artifice has provided a useful cover-up for any shortcomings in performance. If an actor cannot bring off a climax alone, good technical support can be added so that the audience will not notice. Sound, recorded music, an alteration in the stage setting, or some well-timed stage movement, all effected with well-tested and precisely controlled pre-programming, can supply in their own scenographic way a substitute for good acting.

* * *

The stage effects that Shakespeare's plays themselves require are often compara-tively simple – other than the contributions that must come from actors. A striking example is found near the conclusion of *King Lear* when a large-scale conflict is about to take place and the blinded and suffering Duke of Gloucester is required to hold the stage entirely alone. He is brought forward by Edgar, his faithful but disguised son, and then left there. He is like one of the blind bears who were kept as special attractions in Shakespeare's day, to be tied to a stake and then whipped[4] – except that this blind man remains motionless of his own free will near the tree or shrub to which he has been led. Edgar tells him to 'pray that the right may thrive' (V.ii.2) and then leaves. All that the audience is shown of the battle is '*Alarum and retreat within*', and that will be present only in sound, if this direction is carried out off stage as the Folio text requires. While the action of the entire play hangs in the balance, waiting for the outcome of battle, the audience is shown only a worn-out old man, who can see nothing and do nothing, and does not even understand who has brought him where he is. Does Gloucester react at all as the sound of conflict rises and eventually dies away? No further words or stage-directions are provided, but the long-suffering body with sightless eyes must remain in view with no supporting character or pre-arranged stage effect to help in defining his reactions.

In present-day theatres the hunched figure of Gloucester will sit in a carefully chosen place, carefully cross-lit. Lights may dim progressively, and a vast back-cloth redden to represent the off-stage battle; perhaps carefully drilled soldiers with implements of war will cross and re-cross in front of Gloucester or behind him film clips of actual or simulated warfare will be projected in huge scale at the back of the stage. And, all this time, appropriate music and semi-realistic sound will work on the audience's minds with changing rhythm, pitch, and volume. Spectators will sit back in the dark and watch, their eyes and ears controlled completely by the play's director working with several designers and a team of highly skilled technicians. A performance at the Globe Theatre in Shakespeare's London could hardly have been more different: no light could be changed there, and the sounds of battle could not be orchestrated to be effective and meaningful; everything on stage was what it happened to be as the play was revived for that one day only. Audience members, in the same light as the stage, were free to withdraw attention, move around – many had been standing for two hours or more – or talk amongst themselves. The actor playing Gloucester had nothing to help him attract attention and not a word to say, as he sat alone with eyes shut; and he could have only the vaguest idea of how long it would be before Edgar returned. He would gain or lose attention simply because he was there, a victim of violence and of his own son's inability to tell him of his presence and his love. The audience would have looked at him or not as they chose, and would have understood for themselves, or not. Watching the performance there, if most of the audience did not seem to care or, possibly, did not even notice, one might feel very alone; Gloucester's suffering would seem to exist unregarded by his fellow human beings as well as by whatever powers could be imagined looking down upon the scene. On the other hand, among a large audience that was moved by the outrage but denied any further explication of it, a desire to lessen the suffering may well have been the dominant fact of the whole experience. Shakespeare has presented the consequences of violence so that the audience has to shoulder responsibility for its own reactions.

In some ways the handling of this incident implies a greater reliance on both actor and audience than would have been expected by audiences at early performances. The blind bear who was exhibited for public entertainment in Paris Garden, not far from the Globe Theatre, would not have been paraded on his own, but surrounded

> by five or six men standing circularly with whips, which they exercise
> upon him without any mercy, as he cannot escape because of his chain;
> he defends himself with all his force and skill, throwing down all that
> come within his reach and are not active enough to get out of it, and
> tearing the whips out of their hands, and breaking them.[5]

No one approaches to whip Gloucester and this blind victim provides no clumsy entertainment. So what might this actor do and what would this audience think?

In our own days we might expect to see a mutilated old man as he would be shown on television or film, where he would briefly fill the screen with arresting and horrific images, and then disappear before attention could flag, leaving no trace behind. That effect would have been created, not as part of an actor's continuous performance in the play, but as an image cunningly arranged by many people, just for that moment. Between them, the make-up artist, costume designer and costume fitter, the technicians in charge of setting, lights, and sound, and, most significantly, the cameramen, director, and editor would control what the audience sees and so make whatever they will out of the incident. Gloucester sitting alone on the battlefield might give rise to a few seconds or few minutes of overwhelming horror or pathos, but this could never be one part of a sustained performance by an actor who in some very real ways has been living through the whole course of the role. In Shakespeare's theatre, long before a technological revolution, an actor represented the lived experience of violence, rather than taking some part, with other people's help or hindrance, in a moment or two of sensational effect.

Shakespeare's use of stage spectacle is not always so spare in style. The stage must often be full and a scene build in effect over ten minutes or more. The resources of an entire acting company are sometimes mobilised and special properties, costumes, and music required. But even when spectacle is large scale and boldly used, the centre of attention returns repeatedly to the principal actors and the precise nature of their performances. The end of *King Lear* is an example of this. The stage is full with soldiers and their commanders, all weary after battle and after political and personal crises that have made huge emotional demands on loyalties and endurance. Drums and trumpets are available as everyone waits for the release of their aged and half-crazed king. Yet the culminating atrocity of this tragedy, Cordelia's assassination and Lear's immediate revenge upon her killer, takes place off stage and only then does the protagonist take his place for the final scene. The old man's continued physical energy is perhaps the first effect to register on the audience as Lear enters carrying his daughter's corpse, crying out in suffering, longing, and anger, and searching for a sign that Cordelia lives.

Lear asserts himself by means beyond any usual use of words, the power of his anger barely controlled in the compact grip of verse:

> Howl, howl, howl, howl! O, you are men of stones!
> Had I your tongues and eyes, I'd use them so
> That heaven's vault should crack.
>
> (V.iii.257–9)

If the audience, like Lear, notices the silence of those who stand watching, it will turn back to the speaker more aware of the isolation brought about by his suffering, and of the quick and varied ways with which he now seeks some reassurance. The central role at this time demands the actor's total absorption and commands the audience's closest scrutiny. Saying 'Never' repeatedly involves a physical struggle which leaves him in need of a deeper breath and help with undoing a button. So, for this one moment, narrative development must wait upon a very small and ordinary physical action as Lear waits for an unnamed person to do what he has asked.[6] When that is completed, he thanks the servant and, with short-phrased, repetitive questions and injunctions, emphasises his need to see, or think he sees, that Cordelia lives, and his need for others to see it too.

Shakespeare used Lear's last speeches to emphasise a series of physical actions and his concern for Cordelia's body. An audience which does not know the play may well believe that she is alive. Those of Shakespeare's contemporaries who were familiar with the story in any of the published accounts would *know* that she did indeed live and her father continued to reign: so it will watch for an eventual revival that never comes. Shakespeare gives no certain information about what Lear thinks because what he says one moment is contradicted the next. When he falls silent and the words of those on stage show only that he may, for some unstated reason, continue to struggle physically until Edgar says 'He is gone indeed', four lines later.

What King Lear thinks as he dies is not defined by words or a spectacular action on stage. The words which others speak ensure that the audience watches intently as he struggles to assert his will in a body that can bear no more and as the actor must draw on his own hidden resources to sustain the role to its end. Here in painful effort, rather than in sustained speech or eloquent words, lies the performative centre of the tragic hero's last moments.

No amount of quotation from the text is sufficient to explain the experience of violence and suffering which this tragedy provides. Nothing short of the whole progress of its action can give some sense of what is at stake at the end. The philosophical, political, and psychological issues declared in the play's dialogue are comparatively easy to grasp, and may be considered and debated at length, but to understand how Shakespeare held the mirror up to the form and pressure of his times, and so to whatever is similar in ours, attention must be paid to what is done as well as what is spoken. This requires an experience of the play as if in sustained performance, in large-scale stage effects and in very small. It also means that a critic's imagination must draw on first-hand experience of suffering and endurance in order to 'piece out' the 'imperfections' of the action (see *Henry V*, Prologue, 23) and the implications of the words.

* * *

It is hardly surprising that among all the elaborate stagecraft which is now employed in bringing Shakespeare's plays to the stage, a contrary procedure is sometimes attempted. Small playing-spaces, performances more or less free from directorial control, public rehearsals or workshops, minimal stage sets, simple lighting with no sound support have all been tried, and in various ways and special circumstances. Sometimes a lack of money is the reason for the return to non-technical theatre, but not always. Peter Brook's 1974 production of *Timon of Athens* at Les Bouffes du Nord Theatre in Paris was the result of a deliberate choice and an attempt to slough off the clichéd professionalism of other stagings. The director had reflected on the original conditions of the play's performance: 'the Elizabethan theatre was always played in the open air, in a sort of forum, a place where all the currents met'.

Consequently, as Albert Hunt and Geoffrey Reeves report in a detailed record of the occasion:

> The performance was essentially the telling of a story by a group of actors to an assembled ring of spectators. Initially, the actors consciously adopted a narrator's stance, maintaining a certain distance between themselves and their roles. The only scenic props were sack-like cushions arranged in a circle, so it looked like a carpet show.[7] When the play began the actors not performing sat on the cushions to form an inner circle of focus; they listened and watched, so there was very little separation between actor and spectator....

169

> With all the mystique stripped away, and such detached presentation of feeling, [and with] precise, economic signalling of behaviour, there was little of what traditionally might be expected: the epic grandeur of Timon's universal despair....The images were of a society in which human behaviour turned wholly on the possession or lack of money and gold.[8]

Yet even here, the instincts of a showman in the late twentieth century led Peter Brook to use powerful lights and the large spaces and great height of the building behind the main acting area to create impressive spectacles by more routine and technically accomplished means, outdistancing what the actors alone could bring to the play.

In his own fashion, Shakespeare was also a showman and used large effects. The essential difference between what his texts require and what directors bring to modern productions is that in his mind every stage effect was dependent on the actors' skill and their imaginative involvement with the play as it evolved, moment by moment, in performance. The end of *Richard the Third*, for example, must have stretched the resources of the Chamberlain's Men, backstage and on stage: the Duke of Buckingham is taken off to execution after the action is held up for a speech in which he re-evaluates his entire life; two armies encamp; a number of ghosts appear and Richard wakes from this threatening dream to find himself alone; rival armies are addressed in turn by their commanders; battle is joined and the king is seen, briefly, ready to risk everything in order to engage in single combat against Richmond; then the two commanders do fight hand-to-hand, the text giving them no words to speak; then Richard is slain and, finally, the victors fill the stage and Richmond is crowned king and makes a politically astute speech. The whole company has been mobilised and in comparatively little time the audience has had a great deal to look at, but each phase of this conclusion is dominated by the leading actors presenting themselves in sustained speech or fighting for their lives. More than this, Richard reveals himself after his dream as never before in the play, in broken speech and defiant cries; perhaps there is no trace of his characteristic humour now or of his conscious play-acting – but that will depend on the actor and his performance. Played in many different ways, Richard's 'A horse! a horse! my kingdom for a horse!' (V.iv.7 and 13) becomes a summation of each actor's interpretation of the role and, as the play's stage-history shows, a watchword for an entire production.

Throughout much of the last act of *Othello*, in contrast with those of *King Lear* and *Richard the Third*, the focus is repeatedly on the hero. He ends with a long speech in which he self-consciously sums up his life and then, suddenly at its end, discloses that it was a prelude to taking his own life. He then moves towards his dead wife and dies as he attempts to kiss her. While the central character has held focus, he addressed all the persons on stage and so, immediately after his death, the words of Lodovico can pull dramatic focus back to the silent figure of Iago whose reaction remains totally wordless. Stage-history shows how powerful and haunting the last look of Iago can be on the crowded stage, before he turns away from the 'tragic loading' of the bed which is his work (V.ii.366–7).

Shakespeare's habitual alternation between large-scale effect and a far more intense focus on the acting of particular roles is nowhere more evident than in the comedies. After the spectacular entry of Hymen at the close of *As You Like It*, for example, the god brings attention to bear on each of the pairs of lovers in turn, who will in turn react wordlessly to his words. After a song, in which all may join as at the end of a modern musical, Hymen leaves the stage and a moment or two later an entirely new person enters, Jaques de Boys, the second son of 'old Sir Rowland' of whom neither of his two brothers has ever spoken. After he has held focus to tell what has happened off stage, all seems set to come to an agreed and general conclusion, but now Jacques steps out of the assembly and soon, as Hymen has done before, he directs the focus to each pair of lovers in turn. Then he leaves, a lonely man drawing brief attention, and only then is the whole stage given over to dances in which all the other persons in the comedy will be seen as part of a general celebration.

Each play yields its own patterns of wide display and close focus. These alternations are part of its identity and an important source of that sense of active and ongoing engagement which is one of the hallmarks of all Shakespeare's writing for the stage. Tragedies, histories, and comedies all positively invite directors to use their new technical resources to set out the action with a series of impressive and often celebratory stage pictures, large in scale and expansive in reference to the world outside the theatre. Many signs in the texts suggest that the dramatist would find the new facilities for presenting lavish stage spectacles greatly to his taste, but not as they are customarily used today so that they dominate every other impression. He handled big scenes so that simple words, silence, or small-scale actions could be all-important. These crucial elements in the spectacular whole tell us that actors are intended to remain in charge and that this responsibility should not be transferred to anyone off stage giving moment-by-moment cues for technological marvels.

* * *

A task for the future is to find how to use the new techniques so that they are responsive to the actors and not the other way around, supportive of whatever they bring to the moment-by-moment realisation of their roles. This recommendation has many ramifications. The shape of many theatres, in which members of an audience sit facing the stage on only one side with many of them – perhaps the greater proportion – at considerable distance from it, is fine for watching spectacle, but not for responding to the actors' performances. A theatre for Shakespeare's plays needs to be actor-centred rather than a scenic showcase and should, if possible, be a place in which the audience can feel close to the play and aware of its own part to play in the occasion.

In staging Shakespeare's plays today, full use must be made of modern technology because that is the only way they can reflect the form and pressures of our lives, as they did for early audiences. Yet the experience given by the plays must continue to emanate from the actors' performances and respond to their leads. Readers of the plays may seem to have an easier task in adjusting their minds to this mode of performance, but that is hardly the case. Without experience of performances that are responsive to the texts in ways appropriate to them, a reader has little with which to build appropriate mental images of their active stage-life: we cannot respond to what we have not, in some manner, experienced. An inextricable part of this problem is the nature of the performances actors give in their roles, the subject of the following chapter.

12

ACTORS

Training and performance

'One cannot too often insist that the art of acting is the theatre's very flesh and blood' – the words are Harley Granville Barker's from his *Exemplary Theatre*, published in 1922. He often insisted on this, and more in sorrow than in pleasure because he found so much wrong with the actors of his day: 'Taken by and large, the present lot of English-speaking actors do not know their business.'[1] As we have seen, he argued that financially successful long runs with their limited rehearsals and repetitive performances were producing the wrong kind of actors and that a National Theatre with a repertoire of plays would do much to solve the problems. More than seventy years later, however, and also writing in England, Clive Barker voiced a similar dismay: 'I am appalled by the low standards of skill and professionalism in the two national theatres and the regional reps.' Where high skill was to be found, Barker reported that he had found 'no personality': 'the stage is peopled by actors who seemingly carry out the director's instructions to the letter, and whose faces you cannot remember fifteen minutes after the performance ends'. New experimental groups offered more to enjoy, but some of these 'appear to feel that no technique is necessary'.[2]

Against these two judgements can be cited many words of journalistic praise for actors and the theatres which are packed with audiences for some, at least, of their productions. If all actors were incompetent, it is unlikely that there would be any theatres for them to act in. Besides, many books about Shakepeare's plays in performance testify to enlightenment and pleasure received from seeing and studying the work of actors in all the styles that have been followed over the centuries since the plays were written.

A recognition that acting is the theatre's flesh and blood can do much to explain the excitement that sometimes grips an entire audience and the persistence of some of their fans and critics, but the consequences of believing this are not at all simple. 'What happens when a text is acted?' is not an easy question to answer. Other questions arise immediately. How do actors perform in our theatres today in comparison to those of the time when Shakespeare's plays were written? How *should* they act now to serve these texts well, and how *might* they act? Do we know how to define the infinite variety of actors or the subtleties of their techniques? Do all Shakespeare's plays call for the same kind of acting? Does not one play call for several different kinds of acting? Who can best act Shakespeare? Where? When? What happens when an actor rehearses a part, learns the words, 'finds the character', and performs the play with other actors and in front of an audience? How can we judge the 'very flesh and blood' with which a play's text is realised in living performance?

*   *   *

Current practices have already been questioned with reference to a range of acting styles in theatres not set up to stage Shakespeare's plays. Returning now to more familiar ground, basic issues might be raised by further consideration of surviving evidence about Elizabethan actors. But unequivocal facts are few and, in any case, we cannot create present-day actors in an old mould, as we make replicas of ancient musical instruments and play on them. Besides we must suppose that Shakespeare made demands upon his actors which none of them could fulfil: his imagination seems to have been boundless and any actor will be a slave to his or her own physical and mental limits. More progress may be made by examining references to acting and behaviour on stage in the plays themselves and then enquiring about present training and practice. Even though speculation will be involved and not hard facts, at least Shakespere's own descriptions will be part of the evidence.

A place to start is the text of *Hamlet*, a play in which the central character has definite opinions about the actors' art and a company of actors arrives on stage to perform a play within the play. We notice at once that its text has been written with exceptional energy, with new words and word usages, teeming and extended images, unusual and sometimes broken syntax, and much more. Understanding it is not always easy; speaking it demands mental quickness and subtlety from almost all the cast. When watching this tragedy and responding to its actions and dialogue, an audience is drawn to consider the inner consciousness of its leading characters, so that it becomes sensitive to their most private thoughts and feelings, and increasingly aware of what drives them. All this means that actors must give life to this text as if what their characters *think* matters, not only what they say and do.

Many speeches show that persons in this play are, at certain times, unable to understand their innermost thoughts, or unwilling to express them. Whether good or bad, instinctive reactions seem to have a force that is not always under control: 'I do not know, my lord, what I should think' (I.iii.104); 'My words fly up, my thoughts remain below' (III.iii.97); 'rank corruption, mining all within, / Infects unseen' (III.iv.148–9). From his first entry, Hamlet has 'that within which passes show' (I.ii.85), feelings that can be expressed in neither words nor behaviour. Not long before his death, he confesses 'how ill all's here about my heart' yet he gives no verbal clue to what he feels, other than that it is 'such a kind of gain-giving as would perhaps trouble a woman' (V.ii.203–8). The 'thinking' of these stage characters includes unsatisfied desires, nameless fears, shifting consciousness, and changing purposes. Thoughts enter these minds half-formed and sometimes fly 'beyond the reaches of [their] souls' (I.iv.56). The actors should perform so that an audience is aware of their characters' uncertainties and is sometimes led to consider 'curiously' what 'any show' could possibly mean (V.i.200 and III.ii.136–42).

The persons in this play interact constantly, thinking their own thoughts in a way that makes particular and different demands on the several actors involved together in a scene. They may listen, and yet not hear; they may hear, and yet move without pause to put their own gloss on what is said, botching up the speaker's words to 'fit to their own thoughts' (IV.v.10). Hamlet tells Rosencrantz and Guildenstern that for him Denmark is a prison but they do not hear what he says in the sense in which he speaks:

> HAMLET: …What have you, my good friends, deserved at the hands of
> Fortune, that she sends you to prison hither?
> GUILDENSTERN: Prison, my lord!
> HAMLET: Denmark's a prison.
> ROSENCRANTZ: Then is the world one…
>
> (II.ii.239ff.)

They continue the topic without making contact, despite Hamlet's warning that 'there is nothing either good or bad but thinking makes it so' (ll. 249–50).

As the play proceeds, these people learn to unsay what they have said earlier, as they are brought to a truer sense of their own selves or their own changeable purposes. So Claudius tells Laertes, when there is little reason to do so, that 'time qualifies the spark and fire' of love:

> And nothing is at a like goodness still;
> For goodness, growing to a pleurisy,
> Dies in his own too much. That we would do,
> We should do when we would; for this 'would' changes
> And hath abatements and delays as many
> As there are tongues, are hands, are accidents;…
>
> (IV.vii.110ff.)

For Hamlet, such changes spur both speech and action, so that he responds afresh at each moment, right up to his death:

You that look pale and tremble at this chance,
That are but mutes or audience to this act,
Had I but time, as this fell sergeant Death
Is strict in his arrest, 0, I could tell you –
But let it be. Horatio, I am dead:
Thou livest; report me and my cause aright
To the unsatisfied.

(V.ii.326–32)

An actor's task is to speak each word with the thought of the moment, whether that thought is soundly based or not, whether its expression is true or false, predetermined or unexpectedly improvised.

If actors do not show how unspoken thoughts and feelings drive certain speeches, the plotting of the play – its exposition, narrative, and action – loses much of its impetus and drawing power. Moreover, speech will become confusing and clumsily overwrought because much of Shakespeare's invention will go unused – wordplay, imagery, syntax, the shape of each thought and the fineness of its expression, and the varying support of verse and rhythm – and much of the vitality of the dialogue will be lost.

By bringing flesh and blood to the speaking of Shakespeare's texts, actors bring to the stage persons whose minds are alert, changeable, accomplished, and, on certain occasions, in contact with another person's thoughts. They will also be open to the audience's understanding as they appear to live in each unprepared-for moment. Not all the persons in the play could be called intelligent in real life, but even those who are dull, simple, or obtuse have been given speeches written with an acute intelligence so that what is stupid or unfeeling is expressed with great economy and often appears spontaneously self-revealing beyond the intention of the speaker. The talk of soldiers at the beginning of the play exemplifies this.

One of the first specialist demands that all texts of Shakespeare make upon actors is intelligence, beyond customary measure. They must be quick-witted and strongly so, able to use and reveal crucial distinctions in verbal encounter and suggest several layers of meaning. Forcefulness in argument is not enough, or vocal dexterity; these will help, but the essential requirement is a keen and well-exercised mind, a consciousness that is constantly alert. Meaning must be changeable, imminent rather than definitive, and it follows that, however skilled and well prepared an individual performance, it must often seem improvised and must, imaginatively, remain so.

* * *

At times Hamlet speaks directly about acting and, in soliloquy, is objectively descriptive:

> Is it not monstrous that this player here,
> But in a fiction, in a dream of passion,
> Could force his soul so to his own conceit
> That from her working all his visage wann'd;
> Tears in his eyes, distraction in's aspect,
> A broken voice, and his whole function suiting
> With forms to his conceit?
>
> (II.ii.544–50)

Of course, Hamlet is not a disinterested or cool observer, and he starts by thinking about his own inability to act. Moreover, the 'Tragedians of the City', that Hamlet is said to have taken such delight in, are not Shakespearian actors. But granting all this, here is a detailed account of a performance, given with such energy and discrimination that it develops beyond the comparison which was the cue for it. This soliloquy establishes that Shakespeare thought that actors could seem capable of vivid and complete physical performance.

The text of *Hamlet* calls for many eye-catching physical actions. Hamlet, himself, must appear a 'fool of nature' who is shaking 'horridly' (I.iv.54–5). The word *horrid* was more potent then than now, meaning revolting to see or hear, frightening, terrifying: in this play, Pyrrhus is said to be 'horridly trick'd / With blood of fathers, mothers, daughters, sons' (II.ii.451–2); Macbeth's 'whose horrid image doth unfix my hair' (I.iii.135) uses the word so that its original connection with hair standing on end seems to be explicitly present. Elsewhere, Hamlet must show a 'turbulent and dangerous lunacy' (III.i.4) and, a little later, must be 'blasted with ecstasy' (III.i.160). Such cues are not easy for an actor to take seriously without involving some extraordinary physical changes. Later, Hamlet must convince an audience that he could

> . . .drink hot blood,
> And do such bitter business as the day
> Would quake to look on.
>
> (Ill.ii.380–2)

Suiting action to these words, and using all the 'modesty of nature' (III.ii.20), an actor will appear as a man ready to drink blood as it flows out of new wounds and able to create as great a disturbance as an earthquake.[3]

The Tragedy of Hamlet is not unusual in these demands, nor are all such descriptions suspect as the product of a fevered imagination. Macbeth becomes a 'hell-hound' (V.viii.3) and earlier must show 'flaws and starts' and 'make...faces'; he must 'tremble' as if he were 'the baby of a girl' (III.iv.63, 67, 100–6). Othello becomes speechless and has to lie down and 'roar' (V.ii.201). Lear suffers so that thoughts and feelings tear at his mind and from his senses take 'all feeling else, / Save what beats there' (III.iv.12–14). His innermost being must struggle against tears:

> I have full cause of weeping; but this heart
> Shall break into a hundred thousand flaws
> Or ere I'll weep.
>
> (II.iv.283–5)

At his life's end, suffering is almost silently borne as he bends over the dead Cordelia to listen and look for – what is there no more – the slightest breathing through her lips; and, at this time, his whole function must suit these inward conceits as if his worn, old body were being stretched out on a torturer's 'rack' (V.iii.314–15).

At other times, when persons in these plays become speechless, physical action takes over from words: Macbeth goes to his death in a wordless fight; Othello as he kisses Desdemona, or tries to do so. When Lear and Cordelia come together in the Fourth Act, they express their feelings by kneeling or trying to do so and then touching each other as, with a kiss, she attempts to 'Repair those violent harms.' Presumably, Lear must touch Cordelia's tears before pronouncing that they are 'wet' (IV.vii.26–8, 71). None of this implies that physical performance operates only when it takes over as an alternative to speech. Only if the two have been inseparable, in tenderness or violence, in danger or calm, will a silent physical response be able to continue when words have stopped and not disturb the drama and its representation of reality.

Cues to physical performance are innumerable and incessant in the texts of the plays, showing that Shakespeare wrote with a continuous awareness of this part of an actor's task. Some actions are directly described in the dialogue. Early in *Twelfth Night* – to take examples now from the comedies – Olivia, Viola says, could only 'speak in starts distractedly', staring as if 'her eyes had lost her tongue'; Viola speaks of herself as a 'poor monster' desperate for love and of Olivia as occupied in 'thriftless sighs' (II.ii.17–37). In *Much Ado*, Claudio must leave the stage alone like a 'hurt fowl' that tries to 'creep into sedges' and Beatrice must run on 'like a lapwing...Close by the ground'; Leonato goes off stage amongst others of his family with little energy: 'Being that I flow in grief / The smallest twine may lead me' (II.i.180–1, III.i.24–5, and IV.i.249–50).

Many specific physical actions are detailed in stage directions or implied in entries and exits. The most numerous cues for action lie in the continuous and varied energy of Shakespeare's dialogue – cues which are largely hidden until an actor begins to make Shakespeare's words his or her own in the wide space of a theatre or rehearsal room. The remarkable variety of sensation implied by the words is but one part of the text's physical demands, calling for response from an actor's entire nervous system. Still more inescapable are the directions that come from the phrasing, syntax, and metre of the dialogue which sometimes require breath to be sustained over considerable periods of time without break or to be suddenly stopped; more generally, it must be continually varied and controlled. Speech in these plays is not only a collection of words that can be taken apart and analysed, but also a complex physical activity originating at the physiological centre of performance.

To appreciate these 'hidden' demands of a Shakespeare text if one has never been an actor, one should probably attend rehearsals and watch while words become part of the complete action of a human being in a role. If that does not confirm the importance of the physical component of speech, verbal references to breath and modes of thought and feeling, together with the continual change of intention, syntax, and rhythm, all argue that, in these plays, speech must go beyond ordinary measures of physical activity to achieve satisfactory performance. To some extent speech was given highly dynamic form in response to the needs of the open platform on which the plays were usually performed in Shakespeare's day, but his texts demand of actors a more varied and spirited enactment than those of most of his contemporaries – the extended periods of Marlowe, for example, or the well-judged detail of Jonson's verse dialogue.

* * *

Earlier chapters have argued that an actor's relationship to an audience is a vital element of performance on the open stage used in Shakespeare's days. His texts seldom refer to this specifically, but its importance can be inferred from the number of speeches that either must or can be spoken directly to the audience. The effect can be immense, as members of an audience feel included in the drama and their varied imaginations are set to work so that they may even take over and change what is presented to them.

One piece of evidence for this kind of response happens to have survived in the diary of Simon Forman who visited the Globe Theatre in London on 20 April 1611: 'There was to be observed, first, how Macbeth and Banquo, two noblemen of Scotland, riding through a wood, there stood before them three women, fairies or nymphs, and saluted Macbeth.'[4]

Of course, no 'wood' had been placed on the stage through which the actors could ride and in this scene no one makes even a passing verbal reference to trees; nor were any horses on stage or referred to in the text. But neither impression is foreign to the play in performance: in the last Act, there *is* a wood of sorts on stage when Birnam Wood is created by soldiers holding 'leafy screens' or '*boughs*' above their heads (V.vi.1, and stage direction); and, in Act IV, an apparition of Macbeth's adversary has '*a tree in his hand*' (IV.i.86, stage direction). Moreover, throughout the play, men are said to ride and spur their horses and the 'galloping of horse' is heard from off stage as Macbeth commits himself totally to survival, knowing that

> The flighty purpose never is o'ertook
> Unless the deed go with it.
> (IV.i.140, 145–6)

For this member of the audience, when the actors had performed the play and he had gone away and thought about the experience, its action seemed to start with two noblemen riding through a wood.

This diary entry is not hard evidence about how Elizabethan actors acted a text, but it does show that the effect of a performance could be to engage a spectator's own imagination so that he seemed to see more than the actors had performed – as it might be 'Helen's beauty in a brow of Egypt' (*Dream*, V.i.11). Shakespeare was not only imaginative in himself, but also the cause that imagination was awakened in others. In the last resort, actors are but 'ciphers to this great accompt' (*Henry the Fifth*, Prologue, 17) or, rather, they will be when they act in a way that includes members of the audience in the action by addressing them directly and responding to their responses.

* * *

What kind of actor can set about these various tasks today and serve Shakespeare well? Earlier chapters have argued that certain natural endowments are required and that some theatrical organisations and production methods are more suitable than others. But on turning back from Asian theatres, another way of tackling this question is to examine some instructions that are given to actors today and consider how well these serve the dialogue of the plays.

What is most commonly required by teachers of acting is, surely, most necessary: that physical and vocal training must ensure that actors are beyond common measure fit and agile, able to sustain long and demanding roles, both emotionally and physically, and able to speak the words of the text with sufficient clarity and projection to be heard, and with sufficient variety not to tire the hearers but, rather, to keep them alert and receptive. As well as physical and vocal fitness, a keen intelligence is necessary for acting in Shakespeare's plays, whatever the intelligence of the person portrayed. Quickness on cues, an understanding of what is being said, especially when that may not be immediately obvious, and precise pointing of sentences are all necessary if the long texts are not to seem overlong and obscure. The Chorus of *Henry the Fifth* speaks of the 'quick forge and working-house of thought' (V. Chorus, 23) and that image catches the unusual demands made by the words alone: a consciousness that is robust, burning-hot, productive, and, also, swift. To some degree, all actors and their instructors are aware of this, but in other matters, especially about how to shape a performances and use the intelligence, they differ widely.

A major influence on acting in European and North American theatres today, long since his death, is Constantin Stanislavski. The terminology which he developed at the Moscow Art Theatre is still used by actors, teachers, directors, and critics wherever his books have been available. His idea of a 'subtext' – 'that [which] makes us say the words we do in a play'[5] – has helped actors to separate different levels of intention and to distinguish inner thought and feeling from outward statement, both verbal and physical. This concept is immediately relevant to the presentation of inner consciousness that is such a major feature of Shakespeare's writing for the stage. In a more general way, Stanislavski's idealistic vision of acting as an art has given new currency to the idea that the actor provides 'the very flesh and blood of the theatre'. In Part One of *Creating a Role*, written a year or two before Granville Barker's *Exemplary Theatre*, Stanislavski had asked:

> Need one point out that while the actor is on the stage all these desires, aspirations, and actions must belong to him as the creative artist, and not to the inert paper words printed in the text of his part...? Can one live...on the stage with the feelings of others unless one has been absorbed by them body and spirit as an actor and a human being?[6]

Above all, Stanislavski – actor, director, and teacher – has encouraged generations of actors to believe that a play must live in and through them. They must attempt originality and inner truth in performance and, in doing so, see themselves alongside the greatest artists in all other art forms; in the theatre, they should yield in importance to neither playwright nor director.

Stanislavski was practical as well as inspirational, and his detailed instructions have sometimes been taken so rigorously that they developed into 'The Method' for training and performance. Actors of Shakespeare have found some procedures especially helpful: 'creating inner circumstances', distinguishing 'inner impulses and inner action', developing from 'physical actions to living image', and so on. But other instructions have proved less helpful and, potentially, dangerous. The quick thought and openness of encounter which are needed to suggest the inner consciousness of one of Shakespeare's leading roles will not be encouraged if the actor has chosen a single 'goal' for the character and holds on to it, each time he or she steps on to the stage. Yet clearly defined and boldly pursued 'goals' were recommended by Stanislavski as the means to become strong and effective. Such goals, he wrote, should change from scene to scene, but that variety must be limited because each actor should also discover an 'inner pattern' for his or her character. The task is to 'find the key to the riddle of the inner life of a character which lies hidden under the text of the play'.[7] The actor must decide upon a single 'superobjective' which is:

> the inner essence, the all-embracing goal, the objective of all objectives, the concentration of the entire score of the role, of all its major and minor units. The superobjective contains the meaning, the inner sense, of all the subordinate objectives of the play.[8]

Like reductive kinds of literary criticism which give clear definitions to 'the meaning' of a text, these instructions are bound to make a performance more intelligible, but this is at the cost of emotional and intellectual adventure. They do not encourage an actor to expose conflicts of consciousness within a character or to give a sense of moment-by-moment change in action and interaction. Instead they demand premeditated forcefulness and inner assurance. When emphasising a single superobjective, an actor may lose some of the obvious meanings of the words he or she has to speak, and much of their suggestiveness. Most seriously, following these instructions can make all intentions so settled, and so geared to an actor's own mind, that an audience has little freedom in imaginative response.

No one who has read the whole of Stanislavski's writings and followed his career throughout his long life could believe that he wished to encourage isolated and self-centred study or hard-line interpretations based on a single, 'all-embracing' subtextual choice. Yet, nevertheless, these have become the marks of the 'Method Actor' and inhibit many others, influenced less strongly, from playing Shakespeare in open encounter and with ever-varying consciousness. For example, Robert Cohen's *Acting in Shakespeare* (1991) tells student-actors that the 'choices' they make individually will define the characters they present (p. 13): 'you need to pursue a goal (a victory, an objective) for your character' (p. xiii). To follow these precepts is to depend on individual decisions and clear, inflexible intentions. There must be a 'reason' for each speech and action so that the young actor will 'understand' what he or she is about at all times. For King Lear's 'Peace, Kent! / Come not between the dragon and his wrath' (I.i.121–2), the teacher does his best to narrow the options: 'Lear seeks, through these words, to become depersonalized, mythic, and invulnerable in the court's eyes, using the power of metaphor to attempt a transformation….So, once again, try to terrify Kent and impress the court.' Actors are told to be guided by a specific reason, choice, goal, intention, 'desire for victory', or other clear and narrow motivation, so that they are able to 'seduce' and 'impress'. So, in a Stanislavski tradition, actors are taught to be definite and effective with the result that they can be inhibited from creating the open and spontaneous inner-life that Shakespeare's texts suggest.

Bertolt Brecht – playwright, play director, theatre director, and poet – is the other widely acknowledged master in the theatre of our time. His instructions are very different, emphasising service to the play and to an audience, rather than the development of individual distinction and effectiveness. He offered no 'method' for an actor but, rather, strategies for playwriting and play direction. To turn to his writings, from those of Stanislavski, is to escape from individual intensity and find an invitation to be reasonable and cool, and a reminder to be conscious of the entire play.

In some passages, Brecht seems to take up a position directly opposed to Stanislavski:

> The speeches' content was made up of contradictions, and the actor had not to make the spectator identify himself with individual sentences.... Taken as a whole it had to be the most objective possible exposition of a contradictory internal process.[9]

In 'A Short Organum for the Theatre', written in 1948, Brecht declared that 'Observation is a major part of acting.'[10] The actor must first choose a viewpoint carefully and responsibly, and then ensure that everything he or she does on stage is deliberately controlled by this choice. The alternative for an actor would be to 'become a parrot', merely mouthing the words of others.

A Brechtian performance does not seek to implicate the spectator in a stage situation but, rather, to turn the spectator into an observer who is made to face something and invited to form an opinion about it. Brecht emphasised the physical and corporal elements of performance, but not in order to focus attention on an actor or communicate an individual sensibility. Acting is *not* an isolated creative activity, but a learning process which must be 'co-ordinated so that the actor learns as the other actors are learning'.[11] Brecht advised finding a single 'gestus' – an action and gesture – which would *demonstrate* the nature of a character's involvement in a complex situation or puzzling story, and make that crystal clear.

Can Brechtian acting serve Shakespeare's plays? His instructions are probably most useful when they assert that actors must maintain the contradictions in their roles, but their main effect has been to help actors become part of a huge combined operation, a production that seeks to present a 'view of the play'. Actors are not considered the very flesh and blood of theatre. According to the 'Short Organum':

> The exposition of the story and its communication by suitable means of alienation constitute the main business of the theatre. Not everything depends on the actor, even though nothing may be done without taking him into account. The 'story' is set out, brought forward and shown by the theatre as a whole, by actors, stage designers, mask-makers, costumiers, composers and choreographers.[12]

While the director becomes the resourceful 'chronicler' of the time, the players do not 'tell all' (*Hamlet*, III.ii.138); they work for the director in order to set out or display the story of a play and the meaning that has been chosen for it.

In other ways both Stanislavski and Brecht are less appropriate for what we know about Shakespeare's plays and the theatre for which they were written. They had little to say about acting *for* and *with* an audience. Neither of them stressed the openness to an audience and willingness to improvise that these texts seem to require. Both took it for granted that actors should be rehearsed again and again, so that performances could be improved and become assured and secure before they meet with an audience – a practice which would have been impossible with the schedules of the theatres for which Shakespeare wrote. Because they foresaw well-finished productions, they did not teach that technical mastery and imaginative improvisation can give audiences opportunity to share in the moment of an actor's creation, to discover the play afresh with the actors at each performance. These are achievements which in Asia can be seen to be attainable and which the plays seem admirably fitted to support.

* * *

After Stanislavski and Brecht, who worked and wrote near the beginning and middle of the twentieth century, many other voices have been heard formulating new ways of training and performance. More emphasis is now placed on the actors' 'physical reponse' and on performances that are instinctive, complete, and true to the individuality of each actor. Training and rehearsal often take place to music so that actors have a constant spur to movement and variation, and are encouraged to work together as an 'ensemble'. Masks are frequently used to free them from habitual characteristics and limitations, and to draw out fresh responses. Interaction between actors is encouraged, as if they were improvising a dance together, allowing their impulses and sense of rhythm and shape to control what emerges from their common exploration of a theme or a piece of music. Such ensemble exercises are a powerful counteraction to the deliberately organised objectivity recommended by Brecht and the individual psychological search prescribed by followers of Stanislasvski. Working in smallish groups, these actors find confidence, both individual and corporate. When skilfully guided, their exploratory work leads to fluent performances that are especially impressive in variations of repetitive actions and speech, or when drawn towards moments of unified or unexpectedly isolated effects.

These new ensemble actors are usually released from careful study of demanding texts such as Shakespeare's. Typically, they 'devise' their own plays by 'exploring' a theme or situation together; or they take passages from a known play or novel, or from miscellaneous documentary material, and use them as a basis from which to develop a show to suit their own talents and outlooks, and the interests of their director. When they do 'work with' a text that has been written before rehearsals begin, the task will be to discover the actors' instinctive and physical responses to those words and then chose elements of whatever they find from which to develop a performance; only then will the speaking of words become part of their work and take their place in rehearsals.

Anne Bogart has directed ensemble performances for some twenty years and the playwright Eduardo Machado has described how she worked on his script, freeing his responses along with the actors':

> Anne works on a play by choreographing moves driven by the actor, which begin to fill up the stage like a moving painting. Words are super-fluous, it seems. And words to a playwright are everything. So there was a moment of panic....Actually, what the movement is doing is making the words live in a theatrical reality instead of a television reality. As the rehearsals continued I felt the most free I have ever felt as a writer. I spoke freely to the actors about what I wanted to say in the play and all of us together brought to life a moving, verbal, emotional song.[13]

Ellen Lauren has given an actor's view of the same process:

> What Anne is asking is that you build with your fellow players a physical life unrelated to the text; choreography with perhaps ten stops or moments that in and of themselves speak of a relationship. Not relation-ship as in lovers or enemies, rather a relationship to time, the surrounding architecture, physical shape.

This work, Ellen Lauren continued, allows an actor to 'begin to build a true sense of identity as an artist'.[14]

Generalisations cannot cover the great variety of the new ensembles and theatre 'groups' founded in recent decades. They acknowledge no single master. Indeed a common assumption is that the actors' task in any combination is to find their own particular form of theatre. This has been a fundamental tenet of Odin Teatret which was started in 1964 by the Italian Eugenio Barba and, since 1974, has been based in Holstebro, Denmark, and worked in many countries. As this company's recorder puts it, any production begins with 'the gathering together of a group of actors and saying, "Let's see what we can find." ' Productions arise out of periods of training and the methods for this are developed out of the needs of the investigations in hand: there is 'a continual exchange of impulses between the two'. Obviously enough, these actors have no use for Shakespeare's plays and, often, very little interest in what might interest their audiences:

> The point of departure is each individual's need to change himself or herself through the theatre. This is why all the productions also deal with Odin Teatret's own history and experiences and with the group's partic- ular conditions of existence as a unit and for its individual members....
>
> To a certain extent, the theatre becomes self-reflective, its own point of reference and its own meaning, which neither can nor must be legit- imised relative to something external.[15]

Strange though it may seem in the face of such pronouncements, many elements found in ensemble groups, even in those who reject dramatists entirely, are very fitting for Shakespeare's texts: the actors' personal commitment to playing and their spontaneity and energy; the focus in productions on the actors and their interactions, rather than on scenic devices; the use of improvisation in preparation for performance and belief in instinct and lively imagination. Training is strict and continuous so that actors often give physically virtuoso performances that would be well able to respond to Shakespeare's call for strenuous, subtle, and impassioned action. However, their physical and, sometimes, dancer-like tech- nique is seldom matched in vocal achievement or put to the task of staging a text which would lead actors out of their own range of responses and stylistic strengths.

Despite exciting performances, many of the new ensemble theatre groups would have to develop further qualities before tackling Shakespeare's plays, should they ever wish to do so. Their actors would have to rely less on self- assertion, and yet be boundlessly ambitious; to believe and delight in words in a way that encourages physicality and not inhibits it, and that can lead them into unfamiliar imaginative territory and unprecedented events; to be able to sustain long and demanding roles without the continuous collusion of other actors; and to possess a style that encompasses speed and stillness, the remarkable and the utterly and unaffectedly simple. They should be ready to play to their audience when the text calls for this and to react to the audience's response so that perfor- mance becomes a shared imaginative experience. They would also have to learn how to work on many plays at the same time so that each comes alive uniquely at each performance, rather than concentrating, as most ensembles do, on one production at a time and keeping it in rehearsal and performance for months or years at a stretch. They would have to be suspicious of purely theatrical answers to rehearsal problems and those that 'feel' good to the performers; instead of this, they should make a conscious attempt to reflect the audience's lives on stage as well their own.

This list of shortcomings in respect to Shakespeare's plays is long, but it should not blind us to one quality many of the new theatre groups are proud to possess and that is essentially Shakespearian: their acting is technically very accomplished and yet remains instinctively improvisational in rehearsal if not in performance. However, there is no company that I know that uses highly developed skills to share Shakespeare's plays with their audiences while encouraging interplay and improvisation wherever possible and responding to the concerns of each day as it comes. These procedures sound difficult to accomplish, but achieving them would be more practicable if the plays were to be staged in a manner more like that which Shakespeare would have expected as he wrote – a production process more like some to be found in Asia for performances of quite different plays.

* * *

The requirement that actors should draw on their own experiences and attempt to mirror the lives of their audience in what they achieve on the stage may strike a reader of the texts as an all but impossible task. It is, however, advice that many actors will follow in rehearsal, no matter what style of performance and production is being attempted. Indeed, an actor's 'study' for a Shakespeare role will often provide an example that students of the plays would do well to follow. For an actor preparing to present a role on the stage, the text seems to draw upon every resource of mind and body, and all that he or she knows or guesses about what it means to be alive. To cite one example, Jonathan Miller has told how Kathryn Pogson, playing Ophelia in his production of 1982:

> was constantly on the look out for characteristics she could use onstage. One afternoon, on a train journey, she saw a girl talking to herself with all the angry, knowing quality that schizophrenics have as if they alone are privy to a secret. She re-created that easy distractibility, and exaggeration of movement on stage...[and] came [to rehearsals] bearing her own discoveries and observations.

Constantly on the look out for further clues in the text, the director and actress seized upon Ophelia's brief reply to Polonius' question as to what she should think: 'I do not know, my lord, what I should think':

187

This seem[ed] to epitomize her character – she does not know what to think. Subsequently, she responds to Hamlet's similar question as to her thoughts, 'I think nothing, my lord.' All her actions are reponses to what other people think for, and of, her before they disappear and all her support is removed. There is a very touching moment in Act III scene i when Gertrude shows a strangely intimate sympathy for Ophelia, and in that split-second there is a suggestion that Ophelia could have been rescued if only that kind of affection had been available to her before.[16]

So from the words and the interactions of characters, and from the unspoken responses between characters, together with observations and experience outside the rehearsal room, the performance began to come together, tested by its ability to be sustained throughout the play and to hold attention of an audience. For a present-day actor, no matter how he or she has been trained, such a process has become second nature and this, I think, should also be instinctive while reading and studying a play, to whatever limits we are capable. The text will come alive in this way, but not so that it provides one interpretation that could hold its own against all others in argument. What was discovered for Ophelia in this production had its momentary validity and drew upon certain lines in the text of the play; another Ophelia and another occasion will uncover other ways of becoming implicated in Shakespeare's text.

The testing of what to do with any line of text that is undertaken by an actor in rehearsal and during a series of performances provides a second model for the reader-critic. Actors' accounts of their work provide countless examples of the need to be wary and to remember the whole play and the audience at each and every moment. For instance, Simon Russell Beale has told of his problems as Thersites in his first scene (*Troilus and Cressida*, II.i); he saw that:

[This] is, at its simplest, a scene of comic relief slotted between two of the most difficult debates that Shakespeare ever wrote. It is also a violent scene. I began to wonder, rather late in the run of the play, whether the sight of a huge and powerful warrior beating a smaller and apparently defenceless servant somehow restricted the audience's enjoyment of the scene. But it was important to establish that violence is a regular and expected part of Thersites's life, that it is wearying and boring as well as painful, and that far from being defenceless, Thersites has plenty of his own effective ammunition. The danger of trying to show this sense of a tired, unhappy, brutal relationship was that the beating of Thersites by Ajax tended to look a little pat, a little staged. At its best, the scene showed a neat balance of spontaneous, precise violence and dance-like predictability.[17]

A text by Shakespeare encourages an actor to consider any moment while looking before and after, and to judge what happens on stage with regard to how it is received by an audience and how he or she might respond to that. The words on the page do far more than activate speech; they are cues for mental, emotional, and physical performance; they awaken memories, ideas, and feelings so that, in the imagination and in what is said and done on stage, the actor's whole being takes on the person in the play. Any one speech affects all the actors in a scene because they are caught up in the enacted drama, interacting with each other and with the audience as the play takes its course.

A text contains much more for actors than an indication of what a succession of characters says at each moment and this should affect how a play is both played and read. A good actor can work on a single part over the course of many years, never wholly satisfied. A good critic or scholar can take the widest view of what is presented on stage so that the words of a speech are never considered in isolation as the sole clue to what a play is about and what it can achieve for both audience and reader.

FORWARD PROSPECT

In the course of this book, three issues have recurred without receiving sustained attention. Now, on looking forward, they are uppermost in my mind. All three are closely related.

The first is the subject of much current debate: how far should we try to stage Shakespeare's plays as they were originally performed? The issue is especially live at the present time because productions of Shakespeare's plays and those of some of his contemporaries are regular attractions at the reconstructed Globe Theatre that has been built close to its original site in London. At last, one can walk into a building like one of the Elizabethan theatres and stand to see a play in performance. It is exciting and makes us think afresh, in practical terms, about Shakespeare's plays and what they mean to us. At first, we may be tempted to believe that this is how Shakespeare should always be staged and that here is a way to unlock secrets in the texts. Access is easy and many writers are now engaged in assessing the experience. Each production is reviewed in major newspapers and journals.

While the very fact of the new Globe's existence will go directly to the head of anyone interested in Shakespeare, the building is only a reproduction and should be treated with caution. Seldom are all the necessary facts known to ensure a completely authentic reconstruction of anything from the past. Inevitably, a great deal that belongs to the present time will have been mixed, inextricably, into the rendering of somebody's idea of the past or of some committee's consensus about it. However much care is taken, all the prescribed materials and practised craftsmanship will not be available. In this case, some scholars argue that the new Globe on Bankside has been built some ten feet too wide in diameter, giving a total area of 8,658 square feet, rather than 7,087;[1] that means an additional 22 per cent and, consequently, changes in acoustics, the audience's lines of sight, and the scale of a human figure in relation to the stage area and its background. For a theatre, the task of reproduction extends from the building and its equipment to how it is all used, and here the new Globe has many disadvantages.

Modern fire regulations impose a maximum size of audience and forbid the unregulated thousands that would sometimes crowd into the original building. The occasion for performance is different too: in Shakespeare's day, public performances were in the afternoon so that Londoners had to take time off during their working day to see the plays – perhaps five hours or more, if travelling from the other side of the Thames, and that often in winter. In countless ways, both actors and audiences would have had very different expectations from their counterparts today: their lives were shorter and had different patterns; their education, beliefs, prejudices, loyalties, duties, habits were all different, and their pleasures and suffering. When we go to the new Globe, we do not travel backwards in time but enter a little, carefully fabricated world with the rarity, pretence, and educational advantages of an Elizabethan theme park. To stage Shakespeare's plays authentically at the new Globe, a culture which has almost entirely disappeared would have to be reconstructed along with it. To use productions there as a guide for staging a play in any other theatre would be to copy an already very imperfect copy.

Whether the Globe has been rebuilt correctly or not, the use of that theatre will confer no special authority on a production, although it will have an undoubted interest in so far as it differs markedly from generally accepted present-day practice. We may find answers to problems that are tied to theoretical notions of what Shakespeare's theatre was like, but nothing to prove whether they are right or wrong. Much more important will be what is entirely unexpected in a production because that will encourage us to think what we have not thought before and so widen the range of enquiry. For the advancement of our understanding of Shakespeare's plays or for a chance to discover how to stage them more appropriately for the present time, a restored Globe is useful in the same way as any other unfamiliar form of theatre, but probably not so useful as others because it is, in large part, dependent on what we have always thought and our theatres have got into the habit of doing.

In some ways, Asian theatres offer a better site than the new Globe for reconsideration and reform. Flourishing in their own rights as the original Globe was able to do, they have no experimental or educational agenda. The skill of their actors is often of the highest order, the result of long training and constant practice over many years. Performances are often formed directly from intact traditions and influenced by the response of audiences which have come without any further thoughts than their own interests in the play itself and which sometimes include all classes of a society. The entertainment on offer does not have to be explained to those audiences so that they behave appropriately, and the plays are not interrupted by repeated intervals when they were written to be performed continuously. The actors do not have to adapt their customary style of performance and, frequently, they need no director to tell them what to do. The playtexts may be either ancient or modern, and are sometimes both at one time.

A great range of theatres is available to enjoy elsewhere in the world and each one will be different to those we know in our own culture; they are all able to raise issues about how our response to Shakespeare might change.

The productions staged in a reproduction of Shakespeare's theatre provide no certain guidance towards a better way of staging the plays today or towards the kind of theatre that should be built to accommodate them. Anything that was done at the original Globe cannot be done, in the same way and to similar effect, in our very different times, not even in this new building that is similar in struc-ture to those for which the plays were written. Everything about a theatre changes with time and with the society it serves: old methods, even if they were available, would never be right for the present time. Whatever we can learn about what was done before, we will still have to find our own ways of staging the plays and thinking about them.

The second and related issue that has run through this book is the extent to which theatres in Europe and countries whose cultures are based in that tradition might borrow from Asian theatres. An answer, that has often been implied in this book and may now be stated more clearly, is that borrowing and direct imitation are not useful exercises, for much the same reasons as there would be no great merit in borrowing from Elizabethan theatre practice if we could know, infallibly, what that was. Any production displaced from its own cultural environment will suffer losses, changes in relevance and in effectiveness, besides those which are due to misunderstanding and the awkward processes of translation. Styles of performance are similarly non-exportable without considerable loss and damage. Actors train over whole lifetimes and their sensibilities and imaginations draw on their entire experiences in specific family, social, and geographical contexts; such processes cannot be imitated, except superficially, even if a course of special training extends over many months or a number of years.

As a study of Elizabethan theatres can bring suggestions for possible experi-ment and development, so travel can encourage new ideas and new visions in the context of one's own theatre and its culture. Whereas replication leads only to mimicry or caricature, the encounter with theatre performances of kinds never experienced before can set in motion many new lines of thought and suggest modifications of practice in terms of the theatre we thought we already knew well enough. By extending the boundaries of what we can imagine, such experiences can help us work with our own materials and processes.

I have taken nothing tangible away from my travels, no tourist trophies or cultural pillage, no special costumes for actors to wear on stage or movements and gestures for them to imitate. I see little purpose in trying to do any of this. The chief argument against such action is that, even if the ways of an Asian theatre were to be perfectly imitated in a theatre in Europe or North America, the resulting performance would not reflect the lives and concerns of its audience with that directness which is one of the most startling and enduring qualities of theatre as an art form. If the purpose of the exercise were to encourage intercultural understanding, the best result would be only an imperfect recognition of a difference imperfectly presented; much better, for this purpose, would be to make a production that uses Asian ways of working and tries to adapt them to the actors' own performance style and apply them to material that would in itself interest the theatre's audiences. Then the members of an audience might see their own selves on stage in an unfamiliar yet immediately affecting performance.

A third issue to consider, at the end of the journeys which have been the occasion for this book, is what might happen in the future to our staging and understanding of Shakespeare's plays: how will we change our ways, if at all? The obvious answer is that we are bound to change because every generation has done so. But now the changes are likely to be faster and more basic. As soon as we look at theatre in general, beyond the well-established companies that stage Shakespeare, innovation is to be found everywhere. Theatre is being forced to alter because of new methods of finance, organisation, and public relations, and because it finds itself in a very new society with new expectations. Some theatres are searching for ways to change because they realise that the alternative is death, by sudden financial failure or a slow attrition of the audiences they have previously relied on. In certain respects, change is inevitable: as noted earlier, new technology has radically altered the production resources of theatre so that it can offer many new sensations and control them with new speed and sensitivity. Moreover, all these changes are occurring at a time when theatre must redefine itself against the more easily accessible and reproducible forms of film, video, and television; it is being forced to learn how to make the very most of its unique ability to present live performers and share with an audience the moment of fresh invention and creation.

As powerful as these external reasons for change are those within the minds of people who have chosen to work in theatre. At every level of education, enrolment in theatre courses is booming around the world, which suggests that the coming generation feels a strong need to satisfy personal aspirations by making theatre and creating an imaginary world that has more attraction or more truthfulness than that in which they live. These students soon learn that to have a future in theatre they almost certainly will have to make their own opportunities to do so. There are few openings in established theatres for people who have not already proved their worth and those that are on offer hold out little hope of individual development or achievement. Educationalists often point out that job prospects are appalling in theatre and some do their best to switch their students' attention away from the creative art to 'theatre studies' and modes of performance that are found in public life. Nevertheless, the queue to join the profession grows yearly and, in this situation, alternative theatres and fringe festivals have all flourished. Countless companies start from nothing except a group of young people willing to go out and seek an audience and make its own distinctive mark; innovation is necessary for the very existence of these small pirate theatres, as well as to satisfy their need to speak for themselves.

As noticed in Chapter 10, the effect of a challenge to established ways of working has already been felt in terms of Shakespeare production, although, at present, this opposition has proved ineffective in the long run because success leads to absorption into the stronger side or the sheer hard work of being independent proves too demanding. Change is bound to be slower and more irregular in Shakespeare production than elsewhere because each new effort is unable to make a move before it reaches a scale of operation that is beyond the means of the new and mobile organisations.

That change is in the air is evident in many ways but especially in the smaller companies' relationship to their audiences. In this, they seem to be developing along some of the lines that this book has identified as current practice in well-established Asian theatres. Usually, dramatists have given the lead by challenging the assumption, so frequent in Shakespeare productions, that audiences need to be reassured by providing clear meanings and large-scale unambiguous spectacles. At least as early as the 1950s, after the premières of *Waiting for Godot* in Paris and London had set their audiences searching for meanings, dramatists have continued to prod audiences into more active responses. Plays have been written so that they surprise and wrong-foot their audiences by moving backwards or forwards in time with little or no warning; for example, Harold Pinter's *Betrayal* (1978) or Richard Nelson's *Sensibility and Sense* (1989). Others switch between reality and fantasy or dream, so that the whole stage-picture may become fractured, as in Sam Shepard's *Buried Child* (1977), Brian Friel's *Faith Healer* (1979) or Terry Johnson's *Hysteria* (1993). Some are almost wholly puzzling, with no direct clue to their meanings: Samuel Beckett continued to unsettle audiences by a succession of new demands, leaving them to make what sense they could of a play without words which lasts only thirty-five seconds (*Breath*, 1966) or one which does not say or show what is happening for the first twenty minutes and then repeats itself a second time word for word all over again, but not necessarily in the same order (*Play*, 1964); in another play, a woman's mouth is all that can be seen with absolute clarity (*Not I*, 1973). Watching many recent plays, audiences have to think for themselves, find answers for questions that have been raised and left open, or wonder why they have been involved in what has puzzled and, perhaps, not satisfied them.

The more innovatory directors, working without the restraints of a dramatist's script, have followed suit, so that their audiences will often come away arguing in terms that are largely of their own making. So, for example, a play by Richard Foreman: 'compels the audience to scan it for minute alterations. By calling attention to itself – how it works – it stimulates the audience's powers of perception.'[2]

Robert Wilson makes a point of *not* interpreting his productions for the audience, leaving that task open for them: images are presented to the public and its members are left to work out some sort of meaning for themselves. Interestingly in the present context, and against the way his plays are customarily staged, Shakespeare has been a model for Wilson:

> If you do Shakespeare in a naturalistic way, or in a psychological way, it only limits this great work. What's beautiful about Shakespeare is that you can read it one night one way, and another night read it another way, and the third night still another....I prefer a formal presentation of a text like that so that the viewer can read through the text in his own way. You as a director or designer or performer are there to help the public read through the text, but you don't interpret the text.[3]

By many different means, dramatists and some directors who work in newly formed companies have moved theatre in the direction of leaving more for audiences to contribute, almost as if they were copying Asian theatres in this respect. A review in *The Times* on 10 June 1993 reported:

> By refusing to spoon-feed the audience or pacify them with visual prettiness, *Emanuelle Enchanted* stimulates spectators into helping themselves. It makes them search for their own connections and meanings among the cryptic fragments....One can be bored or flummoxed, but that is part of Forced Entertainment's agenda...this is courageously radical, intelligent, provocative work.

Some self-professed experimental productions go further. Audience members are invited to walk around and talk, or take refreshment during a performance, or to take an active part in the dramatic event, or to consult various exhibits, monitors, or even alternative plays being performed simultaneously. Sometimes a performance is stopped and the audience asked to decide in which of several possible ways the characters should take the story. Actors may speak directly to their audience, either in character or as themselves; frequently they switch from one character to another, presenting one point of view and, immediately afterwards, its opposite. At performances of the Wooster Group in New York during the 1980s and 1990s, for instance, no one member of an audience could take in all that was on offer at any one time, on television monitors showing wholly dissimilar images, at several levels or in several compartments of the stage setting, or on moving elements of it, in simultaneous narration and enactment of different parts of the material being presented, in very different styles of performance borrowed from film and video as well as from theatrical models.

In fact, the idea of an independent audience has been around for a long time even though it is at odds with the response that well-financed and critically acclaimed productions of Shakespeare have encouraged and continue to aim for. In the 1960s, John Arden had invoked earlier forms of production when he said of his own play:

> I would have been happy had it been possible for *The Workhouse Donkey* to have lasted, say, six or seven or thirteen hours (excluding intervals), and for the audience to come and go throughout the performance.... A theatre presenting such an entertainment would, of course,...take on some of the characteristics of a fairground or amusement park.[4]

Together with Joan Littlewood and others, Arden was speaking in favour of a theatre that he could call 'vital' and, although they never achieved this, a search for such an experience still goes on, intermittently and with more or less conviction.[5]

The fact that theatre audiences were once as eager and representative as the crowds at a football game has haunted many people: Jacques Copeau, Bertolt Brecht, García Lorca, Joan Littlewood, Peter Brook, Dario Fo, Peter Schumann, Edward Bond, and John McGrath are amongst the many who have left the metropolis to perform in countryside, desert, streets or factories, in social clubs, bars, community centres, or schools, searching for a popular and lively audience for theatre. Their success has always been limited, but travel to Asia shows more clearly than anything these pioneers have achieved that this audience is still a possibility today. By studying what could never be imitated in Europe or North America, we may find clues to how we, in our own fashion, might advance towards a realisation of this goal.

Elsewhere than in Shakespeare productions by established companies, the tide is turning against many old assumptions and in directions that are accepted practice in Asia. Actors need not be imprisoned within the bounds of a stage, whether that is fashioned like a room with an absent fourth wall or as a world of its own that is carefully lit to emphasise the configuration of both actors and scenery as they have been arranged by designers and director. Necessity has led newly formed companies to perform in 'found spaces' or untheatrical environments that awaken powerful images in physical surroundings with which their audiences are already familiar. Music is being used with a new freedom, partly because a small company, with no alternative but to supply and play its own, will seize the opportunity to give a stronger and more varied dynamic to their performances; it also learns to vary the setting for a play's action by aural rather than visual means.

Change is very obvious in actor training where a wide range of new or newly revived methods is in use. Advertisements in theatre magazines offer courses based on mime, mask work, *commedia dell'arte*, tumbling and juggling, improvisation, 'theatre games', ensemble development, circus techniques, dance, 'movement', stage-combat or the 'physical language of violence', text analysis, singing and voice work, tai chi chuan, yoga, 'Alexander technique', Lee Strasburg's or 'Method' acting, stand-up comedy, performance art, and so on. Twenty years ago, the menu on offer was much shorter and very predictable.

Most of the new techniques that are being taught are concerned with what is usually called 'physical performance': young actors can be active, lively, and quickly responsive in all parts of themselves. Rather than wait for performances to develop slowly from speaking a text that provides the anchor and limits for all that they do, they are quick to use all their bodies and their wits as guided by a text or in opposition to it. In small, ill-funded companies, the results are beginning to be seen: actors themselves are the chief and, sometimes, the sole resource for a production, and so they want to maximise their input, to make the story as varied as it may be, and to grab and hold attention. These demonstrative and unruly qualities light up some hastily written new scripts, and others which stumble or drag, and they will, in time, also change how Shakespeare is presented. Again, Asian practice shows that what is being attempted in our more experimental theatres is capable of great refinement as well as popular appeal. What actors *do* on stage matters as much as what is said, when totally alive and expressive performances spring out of what the words and the story demand of them. If half the lessons that are now taught in schools are backed up with practice and appropriate talents and so prove to be effective, actors will develop a confidence similar to that found in Asian theatres and will discover it in their own ways for their own purposes.

Perhaps the most certain indication that theatre is about to undergo a great change – and Shakespearian productions with it – is that more and more influences can be identified that do not come out of current theatre practice. When asked which artists had most influenced his work, Robert Lepage, director of newly devised works as well as classic texts, went outside 'legitimate' theatre for two out of three of his heroes:

> I'd say definitely Peter Gabriel. The reason why I like Peter Gabriel is because I saw a Genesis show when I was seventeen. Rock theatre or theatrical rock is more theatrical than theatre: it was the kind of theatricality that really seduced me.…Another person would probably be Gilles Maheu in Montreal, who is a terrific director. But I'd say that the only other person would be Laurie Anderson, because she has translated information and imitation into communion and this is very different from communication. Communication can stand on stage and say 'This is what I think and this is what I'm doing the performance for'.…

communion is actually to share, it's not just to announce but to share it, to give a sensation of what you are saying: few people are concerned with this.[6]

Praise for a theatre director is the most conventional in this short catalogue and shows that Lepage still respects a director's power as much as an audience's responsiveness. It is natural for the imagination to be activated by music as well as words, but this director relishes the personal qualities of a particular musician in live performance. Theatre as 'communion' is, perhaps, the most provocative of Lepage's notions, even though it would be a staid and limited description for the interplay between actors, characters, and audiences that is found in Marathi or other popular and once-popular Asian theatres; it indicates that the invisible palisades set up around the stage are about to be dismantled in favour of a new openness and freedom in performance. It may also suggest that improvisation, which is so essential to most Asian theatres no matter how complicated their material or techniques, may be increasingly sought after amongst us: 'communion' entails a reaction at every moment to how the audience perceives and responds to a play.

* * *

Should all these changes, and more, operate upon established theatre practice, the presentation of Shakespeare's plays would be radically altered in consequence and, in turn, a reader's instinctive understanding of the texts would change because he or she would visualise and engage with them differently. As the study of Shakespeare's characters ceased to be the norm when the great star actors no longer dominated and controlled productions, so the study of themes, meanings, and political or social implications could begin to seem less interesting or less all-sufficient when interplay between stage and audience becomes more open and free. Critics and scholars, who can change so much more easily than theatre organisations and audiences, will be encouraged to engage with the texts of the plays with something like the same sense of adventure that will be found in the theatre. A recognition that the possibilities inherent in a text are not likely to be revealed to a narrow gaze or pre-programmed investigation would be a first step to take. The second priority might be to consider what a play can do for a popular audience so that the critic or reader will have to bring to its text a personal experience of day-to-day living.

   Necessarily, this approach would be limited by the critic's life-experience and ability to write about it, but amongst its ingredients must be an awareness of the physical and sensuous elements of life. At present such experiences do not figure largely in criticism and scholarship, which are dominated by intellectual, anti-quarian, or political concerns. Influenced by a more active and reactive theatre, the most valued responses would be those that are sustainable throughout the play and can be shared between many people, and not those that register sharply only at certain moments on an ideological ground-plan or some other external measure that has been supplied by the critic according to his or her own reading in related literature.

What a particular play requires of its performers and the various ways in which it engages an audience's attention will be recognised as important subjects for study. The concerns I listed on returning from Asia are immediately relevant: how are narrative and action presented; how does the text elicit and respond to enactment by actors; how and where can the play change from performance to performance; what sensations are aroused in an audience and how do these vary in effect; where will actors be most responsive to an audience and where least; how and at what moments can what happens on stage be of less power than, and be quite different from, that which take place in the imagination of individuals who are watching the play; does a spectator ever become, in the imagination, a person in the play enacting its drama; what is the progressive effect of a perfor-mance of the play in both private and public terms at the present time? Criticism must be experiential and its primary question must be: 'What does the play do to an audience?'

NOTES

INTRODUCTION

1 *Performance: A Critical Introduction* (1996), p. 189.

1 OPEN STAGES: PRESENCE AND OCCASION

1 The evidence for this and much information about the prevalent practice of travelling theatre in Shakespeare's times is to be found, conveniently, in Andrew Gurr, *The Shakespearian Playing Companies* (1996), pp. 36–54.

2 For making this visit possible and for much translating and information, I am indebted to three brothers, Byomakesh, Biswakesh, and Byotakesh Tripathy, who were my hosts and guides in Orissa in November 1992. I have given a fuller account, with special reference to Marlowe's plays as well as Shakespeare's, in 'Jatra Theatre and Elizabethan Dramaturgy', *New Theatre Quarterly*, 40 (1994), pp. 331–47.

3 In the collection of the Theatre Institute in Calcutta.

4 See John Russell Brown, 'The Worst of Shakespeare in the Theater: Cuts in the Last Scene of *King Lear*', *'Bad' Shakespeare: Revaluations of the Shakespeare Canon*, ed. Maurice Charney (1988), pp. 157–65.

5 Based on a memorandum to the author by Biswakesh Tripathy, 3 March 1993.

6 Thomas Nashe, *Strange News* (1592); *Works*, ed. R.B. McKerrow (1904), i, p. 296.

7 Quoted, with further testimonies, in E.K. Chambers, *The Elizabethan Stage* (1923), ii, pp. 308–9.

8 See *Folk Theater of India*, p. 33.

9 See *Rangvarta* (*News Bulletin of Natya Shodh Sansthan*, Calcutta), 33–4 (1988), pp. 7–12.

10 For a fuller synopsis, see *New Theatre Quarterly*, op. cit., pp. 342–3.

11 These and other reports of much the same kind are conveniently available in Gamini Salgado, *Eyewitnesses of Shakespeare: First Hand Accounts of Performance 1590–1890* (1975).

2 AUDIENCES: ON STAGE AND OFF STAGE

1 *The Theater and Its Double*, trans. Mary C. Richards (1958), p. 57.

2 *Shakespeare Negotiations: The Circulation of Social Energy in Renaissance England* (1988), p. 18.

3 See *Dream*, III.i.70–1; and *Henry the Fourth, Part I*, II.iv.378–85, *Hamlet*, II.ii.492–8 and III.ii.131–264; *Love's Labour's Lost*, V.ii.543–703.

Christopher Sly's reactions in both *The Taming of The Shrew* and *The Taming of A Shrew* are more uncertain evidence, because Sly scarcely knows where he is or what is happening; but it is relevant, in the context of this enquiry, to notice that his self-interest, as the play is performed for his benefit, outweighs any matter that properly belongs to the dramatic fiction.

3 RITUAL: ACTION AND MEANING

1 Gordon Craig, *The Art of the Theatre* (1905), p. 11, and T.S. Eliot, 'On Poetic Drama', an introduction to John Dryden, *Of Dramatik Poesie: an Essay* (ed. 1928), p. xvi.
2 See Ronald Hutton, *The Rise and Fall of Merry England: the Ritual Year 1400–1700* (1994), especially ch. 5.
3 Suzuki has written about his methods in *The Way of Acting* (trans. 1986).
4 *The Natyasastra*, XXXVI, 80, 81; trans. Manomohan Ghosh (1961; edn 1995), ii, p. 204.

4 CEREMONY: BEHAVIOUR AND RECEPTION

1 The accounts of Japanese theatre productions which follow derive mostly from visits to Tokyo, and more briefly to Kyoto and Toga, in 1991, 1992, 1993, and 1995. They are intended to be read as a visitor's response, not as fully informed accounts.
2 The verse is irregular; the text is quoted here so that a half-line suggests a pause after the first abrupt announcement.
3 *Memorials of Affairs of State...of the Right Honourable Sir Ralph Winwood*, ii (1725).
4 *The Blazing World and Other Writings*, ed. Kate Lilley (1992), p. 16.
5 'Shakespeare Performances in England, 1994–1995', *Shakespeare Survey*, 49, ed. Stanley Wells (1996), p. 265.
6 At the beginning of Act II of *The Homecoming* (1965) and early in Act I of *American Buffalo* (1976).

5 PERFORMANCE: IMAGINATION AND INVOLVEMENT

1 My theatre-going in Kerala was guided and informed by Dr K. Ayyappa Paniker. He and everyone to whom he introduced me were extraordinarily helpful in arranging for me to see the work of three companies and have discussions before and after. I am greatly indebted to them and everyone else involved.

Information about Kutiyattam can be found in a special combined issue of *Sangeet Natak*, numbers 111–14, published in 1995 by the National Academy of Music, Dance and Drama in Delhi, for which Dr Paniker was Guest Editor. Gurus, scholars, actors, musicians, translators have provided in this one volume documentation, original texts, histories, and criticisms.
2 'Abhinaya in Kutiyattam', *Sangeet Natak*, op. cit., p. 56.
3 'Introduction: The Aesthetics of Kutiyattam', op. cit., pp.8–9.
4 Op. cit., p. 8.

6 IMPROVISATION: FREEDOM AND COLLUSION

1 See Chapter 12, pp. 182–3, below.

2 The Kutiyattam practice of improvising additional text, varying what the play itself provides, offers a suggestion for a further experiment which would choose a section of Shakespeare's text and develop variations of that, changing its time and place, the characters involved and their intentions, references to off-stage reality and to political or philosophical thought, and so on. It could replay the same episode several times or present several distinct developments one beside another. Obviously no one can imitate Shakespeare's language successfully; but that need not diminish the interest of such a performance if the actors were skilled and inventive, their audience willing and able to follow closely.

3 *The Exemplary Theatre* (1922), pp. 258–9.

4 'A Career in Shakespeare', *Shakespeare: an Illustrated Stage History*, ed. Jonathan Bate and Russell Jackson (1996), p. 208.

5 In 'Shakespeare's Plays and Traditions of Playgoing', *Shakespeare and Cultural Traditions*, ed. Tetsuo Kishi, Roger Pringle, and Stanley Wells (1994), pp. 253–65, I have surveyed changes in audience handling and audience behaviour from Shakespeare's day to our own; present habits are mostly no older than the present century and the arrival of modern technology.

7 RESPONSE: ACTORS AND AUDIENCES

1 All three incidents are from different episodes of *Hirakana Seisuiki (The Battle of Genji and Heike)* in the repertoire of the National Bunraku Theatre of Japan, in Osaka, August, 1995.

2 This account is mainly indebted to Benito Ortolani, *The Japanese Theatre: From Shamanistic Ritual to Contemporary Pluralism* (1990).

3 The evidence is marshalled in *Impersonations: The Performance of Gender in Shakespeare's England* (1996) by Stephen Orgel. While advancing a different argument, this present account is greatly indebted to Professor Orgel's clear and comprehensive study.

4 *The Diary of Samuel Pepys*, ed. Robert Latham and William Matthews (1970), i, p. 224.

5 G.E. Bentley, *Profession of the Player in Shakespeare's England: 1590–1642* (1984), p. 115.

6 Jan Kott, *The Theatre of Essence* (1984), p. 124.

7 'It's never too late to switch: crossing toward power', *Crossing the Stage: Controversies on Cross-dressing*, ed. Lesley Ferris (1993), p. 145.

8 Bertolt Brecht, *The Messingkauf Dialogues*, trans. John Willett (1965), pp. 76–7.

9 Reference is made throughout to *The Actors' Analects*, ed. and trans. Charles J. Dunn and Bunzo Torigoe (Tokyo, 1969).

  The account of the onnagata in this chapter is a development of part of my paper, 'Kabuki and Shakespeare: Two Traditions', read to a Conference on Cross-Gender Casting organised and hosted by the University of Osaka in August, 1995; I am greatly indebted to the stimulus and instruction of this occasion and its participants.

10 I have argued the same case, using evidence of some Elizabethan ideas about sexuality, in 'Representing of Sexuality in Shakespeare's Plays', *New Theatre Quarterly*, 51 (1997), pp. 205–13.

8 SETTINGS: ACTORS AND STAGES

1 Quoted in G.E. Bentley, *The Jacobean and Caroline Stage*, vi (1968), p. 243.
2 See Andrew Gurr, *The Shakespearian Playing Companies* (1996), pp. 280 and 303–4.
3 Reprinted for the Shakespeare Society (1841), p. 58.

10 CONTROL: DIRECTORS AND COMPANIES

1 Cf. *Henry the Fifth*, III.i.27.
2 *Peter Brook: a Theatrical Casebook,* compiled by David Willams (1988), pp. 348–9.
3 *Hamlet*, III.ii.25–7.
4 'Shakespeare and the Global Spectator,' *Shakespeare Jahrbuch,* 131 (1995), pp. 50–64.
5 Peter Hall, *Making an Exhibition of Myself* (1993), pp. 99–100.
6 Peter Holland, 'Shakespeare Performances in England, 1990–1991', *Shakespeare Survey*, 44 (1991), p. 187; almost all the details from this production mentioned here are corroborated by this careful and perceptive review.
7 *Civil War* (1993; trans. Piers Spence, 1994), pp. 34–6.
8 Simon Reade, *Cheek by Jowl: Ten Years of Celebration* (1991), p. 11.
9 Similar stories can be told about other companies that have started out in defiance of the dominant patterns of work: the Actors Company in Britain or Seattle's Empty Space theatre in the United States during the 1970s, the quasi-independent company directed by Ian McKellen and Edward Petherbridge at the National in the 1980s, and the Bremen Shakespeare Company in the 1990s. With time and success, and because of the need to keep going and keep making money, each company became increasingly like those in opposition to which they had been founded.
10 From 'An Unhappy Family', *Writing in Restaurants* (1986); reprinted in *A Whore's Profession: Essays and Notes* (1994), pp. 130–1.
11 'Exploring Space at Play: the Making of the Theatrical Event' [an interview], *New Theatre Quarterly*, xii, 47 (1996), p.236.

11 SCENOGRAPHY: THEATRES AND DESIGN

1 See, for example, Lee Simonson, *The Stage Is Set* (1932; ed. 1963), pp. 90–1:

> The actor has ceased to dominate the modern theatre….Settings have acquired a new value because they can aid in bridging the gap between the mind of a playwright and that of his audience. The revival of scenic design as an important factor in the art of the theatre coincides exactly with the emergence of the director as a commanding and necessary figure on the modern stage.
>
> It is these directors who realized the need of changing the rôle of scenery from that of a static and perfunctory background to that of a dynamic element in projecting a play.

2 *Looking at Shakespeare: a Visual History of Twentieth-century Performance* (1993), p. 294.
3 *The Times* (London, 13 July 1990).
4 See Hentzner's *Itinerary* (1598); quoted, translated from the Latin, in Joseph Strutt, *The Sports and Pastimes of the People of England* (1801), ed. J.C. Cox (1903), p. 206.

The comparison of the Duke of Gloucester to a bear has been made explicitly earlier in the play, when he sees himself as 'tied to th' stake…[to] stand the course' of being baited by fierce dogs trained for the task (III.vii.53–7).

5 Ibid.
6 Today we would say that Lear struggles against the restriction of breath associated with a heart attack. It would seem that Shakespeare was recreating the actual circumstances he had witnessed in a death from a series of strokes.
7 When Peter Brook took his company to Africa in 1972–3 in search of totally inexperienced theatre audiences, it was his custom to lay out a carpet in a village square or other place of assembly and have his company perform on that, with no other theatrical device to support them.
8 Quoted, together with Peter Brook's preceding comment, from *Peter Brook* (1995), pp. 215, 218–19.

12 ACTORS: TRAINING AND PERFORMANCE

1 *The Exemplary Theatre* (1922)
2 'What Training – for What Theatre?', *New Theatre Quarterly*, 42 (1995), pp. 106 and 105.
3 Perhaps Hamlet only thinks he could do such things or dares himself to do them; in either case the actor has a more complex but no less demanding task.
4 Quoted in the Arden edition of *Macbeth* (1951), p. xvi.
5 Constantin Stanislavski, *Building a Character*, trans. Elizabeth Hapgood (1950), p. 113.
6 *Creating a Role*, trans. Elizabeth Hapgood (1963), p. 50.
7 Ibid., p. 42.
8 Ibid., p. 78.
9 *Brecht on Theatre*, ed. and trans. John Willett (1964), p. 54.
10 Ibid., p. 196. See, also, the table of differences between dramatic and epic theatre Brecht drew up in 1930 (Ibid., p. 37).
11 Ibid., p. 197.
12 Ibid., p. 202.
13 *Anne Bogart: Viewpoints*, ed. Michael Bigelow Dixon and Joel A. Smith (1995), p. 74.
14 Ibid., pp. 67 and 69.
15 Erik Exe Christoffersen, *The Actor's Way*, trans. Richard Fowler (1993), pp. 3, 98, 190–4.
16 Jonathan Miller, *Subsequent Performances* (1986), pp. 116–17.
17 *Players of Shakespeare 3: Further Essays in Shakespearian Performance by Players with the Royal Shakespeare Company*, ed. Russell Jackson and Robert Smallwood (1993), p. 166.

FORWARD PROSPECT

1 See R.A. Foakes, 'The Discovery of the Rose Theatre: some implications', *Shakespeare Survey*, 43 (1991), pp. 144–5.
2 Introduction by Bonnie Marranca to *Pandering to the Masses, a Misrepresentation*; *The Theatre of Images*, ed. Bonnie Marranca (1977), p. 7.
3 John Bell, 'The Language of Illusion; an Interview with Robert Wilson', *Theater Week*, January (1994).
4 Preface, *The Workhouse Donkey* (1964), p.8.

5 An account of much of this experiment can be found in Bim Mason's *Street Theatre and Other Outdoor Performance* (1992). *Engineers of the Imagination: The Welfare State Handbook*, ed. Tony Coult and Baz Kershaw (1983) is an account of one company's attempt to involve audiences actively in their work. John McGrath's *A Good Night Out* (1981) is a dramatist's defence of his search for a vital theatre.

6 Interview in *In Contact with the Gods? Directors Talk Theatre*, ed. Maria M. Delgado and Paul Heritage (1996), p. 156.

INDEX